WAR
ON THE
SAINTS

War on the Saints

on the

Saints

JESSIE PENN-LEWIS

Whitaker House

All Scripture quotations are from the *King James Version* (KJV) of the Bible.

WAR ON THE SAINTS

ISBN: 0-88368-455-1
Printed in the United States of America
Copyright © 1996 by Whitaker House

Whitaker House
30 Hunt Valley Circle
New Kensington, PA 15068

2 3 4 5 6 7 8 9 10 11 12 / 06 05 04 03 02 01 00 99 98

Contents

Chapter 1

War on the Saints

*And it was given unto him to make war
with the saints.*
—Revelation 13:7

What do you suppose is Satan's chief plan for you and me? What is the purpose for which he fights so fiercely? It is to keep us ignorant about himself and his ways, and about the evil spirits that assist him in his destructive work. And whenever the church of Jesus Christ, either through denial or apathy, remains ignorant about Satan, it unknowingly *takes sides with him.* Every believer should keep an attitude of openness to all truth and reject the false knowledge that has slain its tens of thousands, and kept the nations in the deception of the Devil.

Since the Garden of Eden, man's ignorance has been a major and essential condition that has caused him to be deceived by Satan and evil spirits. And throughout human history, ignorance on the part of the people of God concerning the powers of darkness has made it easy for the Devil to carry out his work as the Deceiver, even—or especially—among Christians.

FULFILLMENT OF PROPHECY

Today there is a special onslaught of deceiving spirits upon the church of Christ, the fulfillment of the prophecy that the Holy Spirit explicitly made known to the church through the apostle Paul: that a great deceptive attack would take place in the

11

"latter times" (1 Tim. 4:1). More than eighteen hundred years have passed since that prophecy was given, but the special manifestation of evil spirits in the deception of believers today points unmistakably to the fact that we are at the close of the age.

It was revealed to Paul that the peril to the church during the latter times was to come especially from the *supernatural realm*, from which Satan would send forth an army of "teaching spirits," to deceive all who would be open to teachings by spiritual revelation, drawing them unknowingly away from full allegiance to God. We are warned that it is not worldliness that is the great danger to believers in the end times. It is spiritual deception, for those who are open to the work of the Holy Spirit and spiritual revelation.

Yet, in the face of this clear prediction of danger in the end times, we find that the church is almost entirely ignorant of the work and activities of this army of evil spirits. Most believers too readily accept everything "supernatural" as coming from God. Supernatural experiences are received without question or discernment, because all such experiences are thought to be divine.

The majority of even the most spiritual people do not carry out a full and continuing war upon this army of wicked spirits. Many Christians shy away from the subject and from the call to war against evil forces, saying that, if Christ is preached, it is not necessary to give prominence to the existence of the Devil or to enter into direct conflict with him and his hosts.

ARE YOU PREPARED FOR THE ONSLAUGHT?

Yet large numbers of the children of God are becoming prey to the Enemy due to their lack of knowledge. Through the silence of teachers on this vital truth, the church of Christ is moving toward the peril of the closing days of the age unprepared to meet the onslaught of the Enemy. Because of this, and in view of the clearly given prophetic warnings in the Scriptures, the already evident influx of the evil hosts of Satan among the children of God, and the many signs that we are actually in the "latter times" referred to by the apostle, all believers must gain knowledge about the powers of darkness. This knowledge will enable them to endure the "fiery trial" (1 Pet. 4:12) of these days without being ensnared by the Enemy.

Without this knowledge, it is quite possible for a believer who thinks he is fighting for truth and is defending God and His works to actually be fighting for, defending, and protecting evil spirits and their works, because if he thinks something is divine, he will protect and stand for it. It is possible for a Christian, through ignorance, to stand against God, to attack the very truth of God, and to defend the Devil!

Knowledge of the powers of darkness may be gained by an understanding of the Scriptures combined with personal experience. The Bible gives us much insight into satanic powers. But those who have gained an understanding of these evil forces through personal experience—interpreted by the Holy Spirit and shown to be in line with the truth of the Word of God—will benefit the most. Scripture, apart from experience, does not enable the believer to know, and realize, the actual existence of the Devil and his hosts of evil and the way they deceive and mislead people. The believer may have a direct witness in his spirit to the truth of the Bible; however, through experience he receives a personal witness to the inspiration of Scripture and to its testimony concerning the existence of supernatural beings and their works.

WE CONTINUALLY FACE THE ENEMY'S DECEPTION

It is crucial to understand that being deceived by the Evil One does not end when a person becomes a Christian and receives the regenerating life of God. Satan's ability to blind our minds is only frustrated as much as his deceptive lies are driven away by the light of truth. Even though a believer's heart is renewed and his will has turned to God, the deeply ingrained tendency toward self-deception and the presence, in some measure, of the blinding power of the Deceiver on his mind, still manifest themselves in many forms, as the following statements from Scripture show:

1. A person is deceived if he is a "hearer," and not a "doer," of the Word of God (James 1:23).
2. He is deceived if he says he has no sin (1 John 1:8).
3. He is deceived when he thinks he is "something" when he is "nothing" (Gal. 6:3).
4. He is deceived when he thinks he is wise with the wisdom of this world (1 Cor. 3:18).
5. He is deceived by seeming to be religious, when an unbridled tongue reveals his true condition (James 1:26).
6. He is deceived if he thinks he will sow and not reap what he sows (Gal. 6:7).
7. He is deceived if he thinks the unrighteous will inherit the kingdom of God (1 Cor. 6:9).
8. He is deceived if he thinks that contact with sin will not have its effect on him (1 Cor. 15:33).

Deceived. How the word repels us, and how involuntarily every human being resents it when it is applied to himself. We do not realize that this very resentment is the work of the Deceiver for the purpose of keeping the deceived ones from knowing the truth and being set free from deception.

If men can be so easily deceived by the deception arising from their own fallen nature, how eagerly will the forces of Satan seek to bring about even more deception. How cunningly will they work to keep men in bondage to the old creation, out of which will spring numerous forms of self-deception, enabling the evil spirits to more readily carry on their deceiving work. Their methods of deception are both old and new, adapted to suit the nature, state, and circumstances of their "victim." Instigated by hatred, malice, and bitter ill will toward mankind and all goodness, the emissaries of Satan do not fail to execute their plans with a perseverance worthy of imitation by Christians who are working for godly goals!

BE ALERT FOR SUBTLE DECEPTION

The Arch-deceiver is not only the deceiver of the entire unregenerate world, but also of the children of God, with this vital difference: in the deception he seeks to practice upon Christians, he changes his tactics and works with subtle, penetrating strategies and in tricks of error and guile concerning the things of God. (See Matthew 24:24; 2 Corinthians 11:3, 13–15.)

Deception is the chief weapon that the Prince of Darkness relies on to keep the world in his power—deception planned to beguile men at every stage of life: (1) deception of the unregenerate who are already deceived by sin; (2) deception suited to the "carnal" Christian; and (3) deception matched to the mature or "spiritual" believer, who has moved out of the preceding stages into a realm where he is now open to more subtle tricks.

Once the deception that holds a person in an unregenerate condition or in the stage of the carnal Christian life is removed and he emerges into the heavenly places described by Paul in Ephesians, he will find himself amid the most intense workings of the deceptions of the Enemy, where the deceiving spirits are actively attacking those who are united to the risen Lord.

The work of the Deceiver among the most mature and effective believers is especially disclosed in Ephesians 6:10–18, where the veil is pulled away from the satanic powers, revealing their war upon the church of God and the individual believer's armor and weapons for conquering the Foe. From this passage we learn the crucial truth that when the believer is in his highest experience of union with the Lord, and in the "high places" of the spiritual maturity of the church, he will fight the sharpest and closest battle with the Deceiver and his hosts.

WARNINGS ABOUT THE LAST DAYS

Therefore, as the church gets closer to the end time, and is being matured for translation by the inworking power of the Holy Spirit, the full force of the Deceiver and his hosts of lying spirits will be directed upon the body of Christ. A glimpse into the onslaught of deceiving spirits is given in the gospel of Matthew, where the Lord uses the word *deceived* in describing some of the particular characteristics of the "latter days." He said: "Take heed that no man deceive you. For many shall come in my name, saying, I am Christ; and shall deceive many" (Matt. 24:4–5); "Many false prophets shall rise, and shall deceive many (Matt. 24:11); "There shall arise false Christs, and false prophets, and shall show great signs and wonders; insomuch that, if it were possible, they shall deceive the very elect" (Matt. 24:24).

A SPECIAL FORM OF DECEPTION FOR CHRISTIANS

It is important to remember that this special form of deception against Christians is described in connection with spiritual, and not worldly, things. This incidentally shows that the people of God, at the end time, will be expecting the coming of the Lord. They will therefore be extremely aware of all movements from the supernatural world to such a degree that deceiving spirits will be able to take advantage of this, and will anticipate the Lord's appearing by "false Christs" and false "signs and wonders," or by mixing their counterfeits with the true manifestations of the Spirit of God.

In the above passages from Matthew, the Lord says that men will be deceived concerning: (1) Christ and His Parousia, or coming, (2) prophecy or teaching from the spiritual world through inspired messengers, and (3) the giving of proofs that the "teachings" are truly of God, by "signs" and "wonders" so godlike and therefore so exact a counterfeit of the working of God as to be practically indistinguishable from His true working by those described as His elect. Therefore, God's elect—if they are to be able to discern the false from the true—will need to possess some other test than judging by appearances to determine whether or not a "sign" is from God.

The apostle Paul's words to Timothy (see 1 Timothy 4), containing the special prophecy given to him by the Holy Spirit for the church of Christ in the last days, exactly coincide with the words of the Lord recorded by Matthew. The two letters of Paul to Timothy are the last epistles that he wrote before his departure to be with Christ. Both were written in prison. Paul's prison was to him what Patmos was to John, when John was shown things to come "in the Spirit" (Rev. 1:10).

Paul was giving his last directions to Timothy for administering the church of God up to the end of her time on earth. Yet he was not giving these rules to guide only to Timothy. He was giving them to all God's servants in dealing with God's household. In the midst of all these detailed instructions, his keen prophetic vision looks on to the "latter times," and, by express command of the Spirit of God, he depicts in a few brief sentences the peril of the church in those times. This warning was given to Paul in the same way that the Spirit of God gave the Old Testament prophets some significant prophecy, only to be fully understood after the events had come to pass. Paul wrote,

Now the Spirit speaketh expressly, that in the latter times some shall depart from the faith, giving heed to seducing spirits, and doctrines of devils; speaking lies in hypocrisy; having their conscience seared with a hot iron.   *(1 Tim. 4:1–2)*

Paul's prophetic statement appears to be all that is foretold in specific words about the church and its history at the close of the age. The Lord spoke in general terms about the dangers that would encompass his people at the end time, and Paul wrote to the Thessalonians more fully about the apostasy and the wicked deceptions of the lawless one in the last days. Yet, the passage in Timothy is the only one that specifically shows the special cause of the peril to the church in its closing days on earth, and how the wicked spirits of Satan will break in upon her members and, by deception, beguile some away from their purity of faith in Christ.

In the brief message given to Paul, the Holy Spirit describes the character and work of evil spirits, recognizing their existence and their efforts directed toward believers to deceive them and to draw them away from the path of simple faith in Christ and all that is included in the "faith which was once delivered unto the saints" (Jude 1:3). The character of the spirits—rather than the men they sometimes use in their work of deception—is described in 1 Timothy 4:1-3.

The grave danger to the church at the close of the age is therefore from supernatural beings who are hypocrites, who pretend to be what they are not, who give teachings that appear to bring about greater holiness by producing ascetic severity to the flesh, but who themselves are wicked and unclean and bring the foulness of their own presence to those they deceive. For where they deceive they gain a foothold; and while the deceived believer thinks he is more holy and more sanctified and more delivered from the desires of the flesh, these hypocritical spirits defile him by their presence, and, under the pretense of sanctity, hold their ground and hide their activities.

The spiritual danger involves every child of God, and no believer can dare say he is exempt from peril. The prophecy of the Holy Spirit declares that (1) "some shall depart from the faith" (1 Tim. 4:1); (2) the fall will result from giving heed to deceiving spirits, not through obvious evil but by hidden workings, for the essence of deception is that the operation is looked upon as sincere and pure; (3) the nature of the deception will be in doctrines of demons, i.e., the deception will be in a doctrinal sphere; (4) the doctrines will be delivered with hypocrisy, that is, spoken as if true; and (5) two instances of the effect of these evil spirit doctrines will be the forbidding of marriage and abstaining from meats, both, Paul wrote, "which God hath created" (1 Tim. 4:3). Therefore, their teaching will be marked by opposition to God, even in His work as Creator.

TYPES OF SATANIC FORCES

There is a vast realm of doctrinal deception by deceiving spirits that is penetrating and interpenetrating evangelical Christianity, and by which evil spirits, in more or less degree, influence the lives of Christians and bring them under their power. Even mature Christians, who battle "spiritual wickedness in high places" (Eph. 6:12), are affected. These satanic forces described in the above-quoted verse are shown to be divided into (1) principalities—force and dominion dealing with nations and governments; (2) powers—having authority and power of action in all the spheres open to them; (3) world rulers—governing the darkness and blindness of the world at large; and (4) wicked spirits in heavenly places—forces being directed in and upon the church of Jesus Christ, in "wiles" (Eph. 6:11), "fiery darts" (Eph. 6:16), onslaughts, and every conceivable deception through doctrines that they are capable of planning.

ALL BELIEVERS ARE IN DANGER

The danger to the household of God is therefore not only for a few, but for all believers, for obviously none can "depart from the faith" (1 Tim. 4:1) except those who are actually in the faith to begin with. The peril is from an army of teaching spirits poured forth by Satan upon all who are open to teachings from the spiritual world, and who, in their ignorance of danger, are unable to detect the wiles of the Enemy.

The peril comes from supernatural spirits who (1) are persons, or beings (Mark 1:25), (2) have intelligent power of planning (Matt. 12:44–45), and (3) use strategy (Eph. 6:11). The deception comes to those who "give heed" (1 Tim. 4:1) to them.

To reemphasize, the peril is supernatural. And those who are in danger are the spiritual children of God, who are not often deceived by the world or the flesh, but who are open to all they can learn of spiritual things and who have a sincere longing to be more spiritual and more advanced in the knowledge of God.

Deception by doctrines does not concern the world as much as the church. Evil spirits would not urge spiritual Christians into open sin such as murder, drinking, gambling, etc., but would plan deception in the form of teaching and doctrines.

Yet, believers do not realize that deception from teaching and doctrines allows evil spirits to oppress a deceived person as much as through sin.

HOW EVIL SPIRITS DECEIVE

How the evil spirits get men to receive their teachings may be summed up in three specific ways.

First, evil spirits give their doctrines or teachings as spiritual revelations to Christians who are unaccustomed to the spiritual realm and who accept anything supernatural as coming from God, simply because it *is* supernatural. This form of teaching is given directly to a person in sudden "flashes" of insight on a particular Scripture, "revelations" by visions of Christ, or streams of Scripture texts apparently given by the Holy Spirit.

Secondly, evil spirits mix their teachings with the person's own reasoning, so that he thinks he has come to his own conclusions. The teachings of the deceiving spirits in this form appear so natural that they seem to come from the person himself, as if they were the product of his own mind and reasoning. The spirits counterfeit the working of the human brain and inject thoughts and suggestions into the mind, for they can directly communicate with the mind, apart from gaining possession of the mind or body. Those who are deceived in this way are ignorant that the deceiving spirits have incited them to reason without sufficient data, or on a wrong premise, and that, therefore, they have come to false conclusions. The teaching spirit has achieved his purpose by putting a lie in the person's mind through false reasoning.

Thirdly, evil spirits use the indirect means of deceived human teachers who are presumed to be conveying undiluted divine truth, and who are implicitly believed because of their godly life and character. Christians say, "He is a good man and a holy man, and I believe him." They presume that the life of the man is a sufficient guarantee for his teaching, instead of judging his teaching by the Scriptures, apart from his personal character. This erroneous practice has its foundation in the widespread idea that everything Satan and his evil spirits do is obvious evil, yet the truth is that they work under cover of light (2 Cor. 11:14). If they can get a good man to accept some idea from them and pass it on as truth, he is a better instrument for deceptive purposes than a bad man who would not be believed.

FALSE VERSUS DECEIVED TEACHERS

There is a difference between false teachers and deceived ones. There are many who are deceived among the most devoted teachers today because they do not recognize that an army of teaching spirits has come forth from the abyss to deceive the people of God. Teaching spirits will make a special effort to deceive those who have to transmit doctrine, and will seek to mingle their own teachings with truth in order to get them accepted.

Every believer must test all teachers for himself—by the Word of God and by their attitude to the atoning Cross of Christ and other fundamental truths of the Gospel. We must not be misled into testing teaching by the character of the teacher. Good men can be deceived, and Satan needs good men to float his lies under the guise of truth.

The apostle Paul described how teaching spirits teach. He said they speak lies in hypocrisy (1 Tim. 4:2). That is, they speak lies as if they were truth. And the effect of their working sears the conscience. For example, if a believer accepts the teachings of evil spirits as divine because they come to him supernaturally, and he obeys and follows those teachings, his conscience is idle so that it practically becomes dulled and passive—or seared—and he does things under the influence of supernatural "revelation" that an actively-awakened conscience would sharply rebuke and condemn.

These believers give heed to evil spirits, first by listening to them and then by obeying them. They are deceived by accepting such things as wrong thoughts about God's presence and about divine love, and they unknowingly give themselves up to the power of lying spirits. Working in the line of teaching, deceiving spirits will insert their lies spoken in hypocrisy and deceive believers about sin, themselves, and all other truths connected with the spiritual life.

THE ENEMY USES SCRIPTURE TO DECEIVE

Scripture is generally used as the basis of these teachings and is skillfully woven together like a spider's web, so that believers are caught in the snare. Single texts are wrenched from their context and place in the perspective of truth; sentences are taken from their correlative sentences; or, texts are carefully picked out from over a wide field and netted together so that they appear to give a full revelation of the mind of God—but the intervening passages, giving historical setting, actions, and circumstances connected with the speaking of the words, and other elements that give insight on each separate text, are skillfully dropped out.

In this way, a wide net is made for the unwary or untaught in the principles of Scripture exegesis, and many a life is sidetracked and troubled by this false use of the Word of God. Because the experience of ordinary Christians in regard to the Devil is limited to knowing him as a tempter or as an accuser, they have no conception of the depths of his wickedness and of the wickedness of evil spirits, and are under the impression that evil spirits will not quote Scripture, whereas they will quote the whole Book if they can deceive just one soul!

The teachings that deceiving spirits are now promoting are many. They are often thought to be found only in false religions, but the teaching spirits who suggest their doctrines or religious ideas to the minds of men are ceaselessly at work in every nation, seeking to play upon people's religious instincts and to substitute lies for truth.

THE BIBLE IS THE ONLY TRUE TEST OF TRUTH

All truth comes from God, and all that is contrary to truth comes from Satan. Therefore, truth alone dispels the deceptive doctrines of the teaching spirits of Satan—the truth of God, not merely views of truth—truth concerning all the principles and laws of the God of Truth. "Doctrines of demons" simply consist of that which a man thinks and believes as the outcome of suggestions made to his mind by deceiving spirits. All thoughts and beliefs belong to one of two realms—the realm of truth or the realm of falsehood—each having its source in God or Satan.

Even the thoughts that apparently originate in a man's own mind come from one of these two sources, for the mind itself is either darkened by Satan (2 Cor. 4:4), and therefore fertile soil for his teachings, or renewed by God (Eph. 4:23), purified from the veil of Satan and made open to the reception and transmission of truth. Since thought or belief originates either from the God of Truth or the Father of Lies (see John 8:44), there is only one basic principle for testing the source of all doctrines or thoughts and beliefs held by believers or unbelievers: the test of the Word of God—the only channel of revealed truth in the world.

All teachings originating from deceiving spirits

1. weaken the authority of the Scriptures
2. distort the teaching in the Scriptures
3. add the thoughts of men to the Scriptures
4. put the Scriptures entirely aside

The ultimate purpose is to hide, distort, misuse, or put aside the revelation of God concerning the Cross of Calvary, where Satan was overthrown by the God-man, and where freedom was obtained for all his captives. The test of all thoughts and beliefs is therefore their harmony with the written Scriptures as a whole—in their full body of truth—and their attitude to the Cross and sin.

Some doctrines of demons, tested by these two primary principles, are Christian Science, spiritualism, and New Theology. All do not acknowledge sin, the Savior, or the Cross. Islam, Confucianism, and Buddhism also do not acknowledge the Savior or the Cross. They are "moral" religions, with man as his own savior. And while demon worshippers have no knowledge of a Savior or of His Calvary sacrifice, they do have true knowledge of evil powers, which they try to appease because they have seen evidence of their existence.

"SIGNS AND WONDERS" ARE NOT PROOF

In the church, countless thoughts and beliefs that are opposed to the truth of God are injected into the minds of Christians by teaching spirits. This renders them ineffective in the warfare with sin and Satan, and subject to the power of evil spirits—even though they are saved for eternity through their faith in Christ (see 1 Peter 1:3–5) and accept the authority of the Scriptures and know the power of the Cross.

All thoughts and beliefs should therefore be tested by the truth of God revealed in the Scripture, not merely by certain Scripture texts or portions of the Word, but by the principles of truth revealed in the Word. Satan will endorse his teachings by "signs and wonders" (Matt. 24:24; Mark 13:22; 2 Thess. 2:9; Rev. 13:13). Therefore, "power," "signs," and "fire...from heaven" are no proof that a teaching is of God. Nor is a teacher's "beautiful life" to be the infallible test, for Satan's ministers can be "ministers of righteousness" (2 Cor. 11:13–15).

SUPERNATURAL COUNTERFEITS

The climax of the flood tide of these deceiving spirits sweeping upon the church is described by the apostle Paul in his second letter to the Thessalonians, where he spoke of the manifestation of one who will eventually gain entrance into the very sanctuary of God, so that he "sitteth in the temple of God" (2 Thess. 2:4), setting himself up as God. The presence of this one will be a presence like God, and yet he will be "after the working of Satan with all power and signs and lying wonders, and with all

27

deceivableness of unrighteousness" (2 Thess. 2:9–10).

The Lord's words recorded by Matthew are reaffirmed in the revelation He gave to John on Patmos, that, at the close of the age, the main weapon used by the Deceiver for obtaining power over the people of the earth will be supernatural signs from heaven, when a counterfeit "lamb" does "great wonders" and even "maketh fire come down from heaven" to deceive those on earth, and exercises such control over the whole world that "no man might buy or sell, save he that had the mark, or the name of the beast" (Rev. 13:11–17). Through this supernatural deception, the full purpose of the deceiving army of Satan will reach completion in the prophesied worldwide authority. The deception of the world with deepening darkness and the deception of the church through "teachings" and "manifestations" will reach the highest flood tide at the close of the age.

"BELIEVE NOT EVERY SPIRIT"

It is striking to note that the apostle who was chosen to transmit the revelation in preparation for the last days of the church militant should be the one to write to the Christians of his day, "Believe not every spirit" (1 John 4:1–6), and to earnestly warn his "children" that the "spirit of antichrist," the "spirit of error," was already actively at work among them. They were to "believe not"—that is, to doubt—every supernatural teaching and teacher until they were proved to be of God. They were to test the teachings to determine if they came from a "spirit of error" and were part of the Deceiver's campaign as antichrist.

If this attitude of neutrality and doubt toward supernatural teachings was needed toward the end of the apostle John's life—some fifty-seven years after Pentecost—how much more is it needed in the "latter times" (1 Tim. 4:1) foretold by the Lord and by the apostle Paul—times that were to be characterized by a clamor of voices of "prophets" (those whom we call speakers and teachers today) using the sacred name of the Lord, and during which teachings received supernaturally from the spiritual realm would abound. These teachings would be accompanied by such wonderful proofs of their so-called divine origin that they would perplex even the most faithful of the Lord's people, and even, for a time, deceive some of them.

WE MUST FACE THE TRUTH

The prophet Daniel, in writing about these "latter times," said that some of the teachers "shall fall, to try them, and to purge, and to make them white, even to the time of the end" (Dan. 11:35). The truth must be faced: the elect may be deceived. We learn from Daniel's words that they are apparently *permitted* to be deceived for a season, so that in the test of fire they may be "tried" or refined (the word refers to the expulsion of dross by the smelting fire), "purged" or purified (the removal of dross already expelled), and made "white" (the polishing and brightening of the metal after it has been freed from its impurities). It is probably in connection with this solemn word, *tried*, that one strange statement about the war at the close of the age is made, when it is said of the attack of the leopard-like beast, that "it was given unto him to make war with the saints, and to overcome them" (Rev. 13:7).

Daniel also speaks of the prevailing of the Enemy for a season: the horn "made war with the saints, and prevailed against them" (Dan. 7:21). Daniel adds: "Until the Ancient of days came...and the time came that the saints possessed the kingdom" (v. 22). It appears, therefore, that in the "time of the end" (Dan. 11:35), God will permit Satan to prevail for a season against His saints, even as he prevailed over Peter when the apostle was handed over to him to be sifted (Luke 22:31); as he seemed to prevail over the Son of God at Calvary, when the "hour, and the power of darkness" (Luke 22:53) closed around Him at the Cross (Matt. 27:38–46); as he is shown to overcome the "two witnesses" described in Rev. 11:3–7; and as in the last great manifestation of the Dragon-deceiver's triumph over the saints and his power over the whole inhabited earth. (See Revelation 13:7–15.)

GOD'S TRIUMPHS HIDDEN IN APPARENT DEFEAT

All these instances take place at different periods of time in the history of Christ and His church (and in the description in Revelation, the prevailing of the leopard-like beast may refer to the saints on the earth *after* the rapture of the church), but they show the principle that God's triumphs are often hidden in apparent defeat. The elect of God must therefore pay careful attention, at all stages of the war with Satan as Deceiver, not to be swayed or moved by appearances. For the apparent triumph of supernatural powers, which appears to be divine, may prove to be satanic; and appearances of outward defeat, which appear to be the Devil's victory, may prove to hide the triumph of God.

"Success" or "defeat" is therefore not an accurate criterion that a work is of God or Satan. Calvary stands forever as the revelation of God's way of working out His redemption purposes. Satan works for time, for he knows his time is short, but God works for eternity. Through death to life, through defeat to triumph, through suffering to joy, is God's way.

The key point to remember is that knowledge of truth is the primary safeguard against deception. Christians must know—and must learn to prove the spirits until they do know—what is of God, and what is of Satan. The words of the Master, "Behold, I have told you" (Matt. 24:25), plainly imply that our personal knowledge of danger is part of the Lord's way of guarding His own. Believers who blindly rely upon what they refer to as "the keeping power of God," without seeking to understand how to escape deception when they have been forewarned by the Lord, will surely find themselves entrapped by the subtle Foe.

In chapter two, we will explore what the Bible reveals about the nature of Satan and his evil spirits, and how Christ exposed and defeated the powers of darkness.

Chapter 2

The Powers of Darkness

*I pray not that thou shouldest take them out of the
world, but that thou shouldest keep them
from the evil.*
—John 17:15

A survey of biblical history shows that the rise
and fall in the spiritual power of the people of
God has been linked to their recognition of
the existence of evil spiritual forces. When believers
in the Old and New Testaments were at the highest
point of their spiritual power, it was because their
leaders recognized and drastically dealt with the
invisible forces of Satan. And when they were at
their lowest point, it was because these forces were
ignored, or allowed to have free access to the people.

In this chapter we will review what the Bible
tells us about the powers of darkness and their
strategies against both the unregenerate world
and the people of God. In this way, we will see how
the history of mankind may be viewed as the story
of a war—a spiritual war.

The Bible gives us more knowledge about the
workings of Satan and his principalities and powers than many realize. The work of Satan as Deceiver of the world can be traced from Genesis to
Revelation, until the climax is reached, and the
full results of the deception in the Garden of Eden
are unveiled in the book of Revelation.

SATAN'S SUBTLE DECEPTION

In Genesis we have the simple story of the
Garden, where the innocent pair are unaware of

any danger from evil beings in the unseen world. Here we encounter Satan's first work as Deceiver, and the subtle form of his method of deception. We see him using "good" to bring about evil, and suggesting evil to bring about supposed good. We see him working upon an innocent creature's highest and purest desires by using the godward desires of Eve to bring about her captivity and bondage to himself, while disguising his own destructive purpose under the pretense of seeking to lead a human being nearer to God. Caught with the bait of the promise of being "wise" and "as gods" (Gen. 3:5–6), Eve was blinded to the principle involved in being obedient to God and was deceived. (See 1 Timothy 2:14.)

This shows us that goodness is no guarantee of protection from deception. The shrewdest way in which the Devil deceives the world and the church is when he comes in the guise of somebody, or something, which seems to cause them to go godward and goodward. Satan said to Eve, "Ye shall be as gods" (Gen. 3:5), but he did not add, "and ye shall be like demons."

Angels and men did not know evil until they fell into a state of evil. Satan did not tell Eve this when he said that she would know good *and evil*. His true objective in deceiving Eve was to get her to disobey God, but his deception was, "you shall be like gods." Had she thought about it, she would have realized that the Deceiver's own suggestion exposed itself, for his "reasoning" amounted to: disobey God to be more like God!

Unfallen man in his pure state was not perfect in knowledge. Eve was ignorant of "good and evil" (Gen. 3:5), and her ignorance was a condition that contributed to her deception by the Serpent. The fact that a highly organized alliance of evil spirits was in existence is not revealed in the story of the Garden. Only a "serpent" is there, but the Serpent is spoken to by God as an intelligent being, carrying out a deliberate purpose in the deception of the woman.

The serpent disguise of Satan is exposed by God as He makes known the decision of the triune God in view of the catastrophe that had taken place. The Seed of the deceived woman (see Genesis 3:15) would eventually bruise the head of the supernatural being, who had used the form of the serpent to carry out his plan. From that time on, the name of "serpent" is attached to him. This is the very name throughout the ages that has been associated with the climactic action of his revolt against his Creator in beguiling and deceiving the woman in Eden and blasting the human race.

AN ONGOING WAR

Satan triumphed, but God overruled! The victim was made the vehicle for the coming of a Victor, who would ultimately destroy the works of the Devil and cleanse the heavens and the earth from every trace of his handiwork. The Serpent was cursed; but, in effect, the deceived victim was blessed, for through her would come the Seed which would triumph over the Devil and his seed. And through her, a new race would arise through this promised Seed that would be antagonistic to the Serpent to the end of time. "And I will put enmity between thee and the woman, and between thy seed and her seed; it shall bruise thy head, and thou shalt bruise his heel" (Gen. 3:15).

From that time on, the story of the ages has consisted of the record of a war between these two seeds—the Seed of the woman (Christ and His redeemed) and the seed of the Devil (see John 8:44; 1 John 3:10)—which will continue right on to the final commitment of Satan to the lake of fire (Rev. 20:10).

SATANIC ACTIVITY IN THE OLD TESTAMENT

When we clearly comprehend that there is an unseen army of evil spirits, all actively engaged in deceiving and misleading men, their actions in the Old Testament become evident to us. We can discern the work of Satan as the Deceiver penetrating everywhere.

David was deceived by Satan into numbering Israel because he failed to recognize that the suggestion to his mind came from a satanic source. (See 1 Chronicles 21:1.)

Job was also deceived when he believed the report that the "fire" that had fallen from heaven was from God (Job 1:16), and that all the other calamities that came to him in the loss of his wealth, home, and children, came directly from the hand of God. However, the early part of the book of Job clearly shows that Satan was the primary cause of all his troubles; as "prince of the power of the air" (Eph. 2:2), he used the elements of nature and the wickedness of men to afflict the servant of God. The Enemy hoped that ultimately he could force Job into renouncing his faith in God, who seemed to be unjustly punishing Job. That this was Satan's aim is suggested in the words of Job's wife, who became a tool for the Adversary in urging the suffering man to "curse God, and die" (Job 2:9). She also was deceived by the Enemy into believing that God was the primary cause of all the trouble and unmerited suffering that had come upon her husband.

35

In the history of Israel during the time of Moses, we learn even more about satanic powers. The world had sunken into idolatry—which the New Testament reveals to be the direct work of Satan (see 1 Corinthians 10:20)—and into actual dealings with evil spirits. The whole inhabited earth was in a state of deception and was held by the Deceiver in his power. Even though they knew the laws of God, and had seen His clear judgments among them, numbers of God's own people, through contact with others who were under satanic power, were deceived into communicating with "familiar spirits" and into using "divination" and other similar arts, implanted by the powers of darkness. (See Leviticus 17:7; 19:31; 20:6, 27; Dueteronomy 18:10–11.)

The reality of the existence of Satan and wicked spirits cannot be proved more strongly than by the fact that the statutes given by God to Moses on Mount Sinai included strict measures for dealing with the attempts of evil spirit beings to make inroads into the lives of the people of God. Moses was instructed by God to keep Israel free from their assaults by the drastic penalty of death for all who had dealings with them.

The very fact that the Lord gave statutes in connection with such a subject, along with the extreme penalty enforced for disobedience to His law, shows the existence of evil spirits, their wickedness, their ability to communicate with and influence human beings, and the necessity for uncompromising hostility toward them and their works. God would not make laws about dangers that had no real existence, nor would He command the extreme penalty of death, if contact with evil spirits did not necessitate such drastic measures. The severity of the penalty obviously implies, also, that the leaders of Israel must have been given acute "discerning of spirits" (see 1 Corinthians 12:10), so sure and so clear that they could have no doubt when deciding cases brought before them.

While Moses and Joshua were alive to enforce the strong measures decreed by God to keep His people free from satanic inroads, Israel remained in allegiance to God and at the highest point of its history. But when these leaders died, the nation sank into darkness brought about by evil spirit powers, who drew the people into idolatry and sin. In the years that followed, Israel continually went back and forth, from allegiance to God to idolatrous worship, and fell into all the sins resulting from worshipping Satan—the true meaning of idolatry—instead of the Lord God. (See Judges 2:19; 1 Kings 14:22–24; compare 2 Chronicles 33:2–5; 34:2–7.)

In the book of Daniel we discover additional revelation concerning the hierarchy of evil powers, when in the tenth chapter we are shown the existence of the princes of Satan, who actively oppose the angel God had sent to Daniel to make His servant understand His counsels for His people. There are also other references to the workings of Satan, his princes, and the hosts of his wicked spirits scattered through the Old Testament. But, on the whole, their activities are concealed as if by a veil, until the great hour arrives, when the Seed of the woman, who would bruise the head of the Serpent, is manifested on earth in human form. (See Galatians 4:4.)

CHRIST'S COMING EXPOSES SATANIC POWERS

With the coming of Christ, the veil that had hidden the active workings of the supernatural powers of evil since the Garden catastrophe is re-moved even further, and their deception and power over man is clearly revealed. The Arch-deceiver himself appears in the wilderness conflict of the Lord to challenge the Seed of the woman. It is not recorded that Satan himself had appeared on earth since the time of the Fall—the Garden of Eden and the wilderness of Judea being parallel periods for the testing of the first and Second Adam. In both cases Satan worked as Deceiver. However, in the second instance he completely failed to manipulate and deceive the One who had come as his Conqueror. Moreover, Jesus recog-nized the existence of the satanic powers of evil and showed uncompromising hostility toward them and their works.

SATANIC ACTIVITY IN THE NEW TESTAMENT

Examples of the characteristic work of Satan as Deceiver can be seen among the disciples of the Christ. He deceives Peter into speaking words of temptation to the Lord, suggesting that Christ turn from the path of the Cross (Matt. 16:22–23). Later on, he takes hold of the same disciple (Luke 22:31), prompting him to lie, "I know not the man" (Matt. 26:74), for the very purpose of deception. Further evidence of the work of the Deceiver may be found in the epistles of Paul, in his references to "false apostles" and "deceitful workers," as well as to Sa-tan's workings as an "angel of light" and "his min-isters...as the ministers of righteousness" among the people of God (2 Cor. 11:13–15). In the messages to the churches given by the ascended Lord to John in the book of Revelation, false apostles and false teaching of many kinds are spoken of. A "synagogue of Satan" (Rev. 2:9) consisting of deceived ones is mentioned, and "depths of Satan" (Rev. 2:24) are described as existing in the church.

THE FULL MEANING OF THE WAR

Then the veil is lifted completely at last. The full revelation of the satanic alliance against God and His Christ is given to the apostle John. He is told to write all that he is shown of the worldwide work of this Deceiver, that the church of Christ might know the full meaning of the war with Satan in which the redeemed would be engaged. This war would continue right on to the time when the Lord Jesus would be revealed from heaven in judgment upon these vast and terrible powers, which are full of cunning malignity and hatred to His people.

THEY HAVE BEEN AROUND A LONG TIME

As we read the book of Revelation, it is important to remember that the organized forces of Satan described there were in existence at the time of the Fall in Eden, and were only partially revealed to the people of God until the advent of the promised Seed of the woman. This Seed was to bruise the Serpent's head until the fullness of time came when God, manifest in the flesh, would meet the fallen archangel and leader of the evil angelic host in mortal combat at Calvary, and, putting them to open shame, would shake off from himself the vast masses of the hosts of darkness who would gather around the Cross from the furthermost realms of the kingdom of Satan. (See Colossians 2:15.)

The Scriptures teach us that when God reveals truths concerning Himself and the spiritual realm, He always times these disclosures to be of greatest possible help to His people. The full revelation of the satanic powers disclosed in the Apocalypse was not given to the church in its infancy. Forty years passed following the Lord's ascension before the book of Revelation was written. Perhaps it was necessary that the church of Christ fully understand the fundamental truths revealed to Paul and the other apostles before she could safely be shown the extent of the war with the powers of evil upon which she had entered. Whatever the reason for the delay, it is striking that it was the last of the apostles who was chosen to transmit, at the very end of his life, the full "war message" to the church, which would serve as a foreshadowing of the contest until its close.

WAR IN HEAVEN

In the revelation given to John, the name and character of the Deceiver is more clearly revealed, along with the strength of his forces, the extent of the war, and its final outcomes. We are shown that in the invisible realm there is war between the forces of evil and the forces of light. John wrote that "the dragon fought and his angels" (Rev. 12:7). The Dragon is explicitly described as the "serpent" (from his disguise in Eden) who is "called the Devil, and Satan" (v. 9), the Deceiver of the whole earth. His worldwide work as Deceiver is fully revealed, along with the war in the earthly realm caused by his deception of the nations and the world powers who act under his instigation and rule. We also learn of the highly organized alliance of principalities and powers that acknowledge the headship of Satan, along with their power "over all kindreds, and tongues, and nations"—who are deceived by these supernatural and invisible forces of evil—and of their "war with the saints." (See Revelation 13:7.)

WAR ON AN UNPRECEDENTED SCALE

War is the keyword of the Apocalypse: war on a scale undreamed of by mortal man; war between vast angelic powers of light and darkness; war by the Dragon and the deceived world powers upon the saints; war by the same world powers against the Lamb; war by the Dragon upon the church; war in many phases and forms, until the end when the Lamb overcomes, and those who are with Him also overcome, those who "are called, and chosen, and faithful" (Rev. 17:14).

The world is now drawing nearer to the "time of the end" (Dan. 11:35), characterized by this worldwide deception depicted in Revelation, when there will be a deception of both nations and individuals on such a vast scale that the Deceiver will practically have the whole earth under his control. Before this climax is reached, there will be preliminary stages of the Deceiver's working, marked by the widespread deception of individuals, both within and outside of the church, beyond the ordinary condition of deception in which the unregenerate world is lying.

HOW WILL SATAN DECEIVE THE WHOLE WORLD?

The worldwide deception depicted in Revelation will permit the supernatural powers to carry out their will and to drive nations and men into active rebellion against God. In order to understand why the Deceiver will be able to deceive the whole world, we first need to clearly grasp what the Scriptures say about unregenerate men in their normal condition, and the world in its fallen state. To do this, let us take a brief look at how human beings have fallen into deception, how God has intervened to protect us from deception, and how the early church dealt with the powers of darkness.

Satan is described in Revelation as the Deceiver of the whole earth (Rev. 20:7–8), and he has been so since the beginning of human history. "The whole world lieth in wickedness," said the apostle (1 John 5:19) to whom the revelation was given. John depicted the world as already lying deep in darkness through the Enemy's deception, and blindly led by vast multitudes of evil spirits who are under Satan's control.

Therefore, the word *deceived* is, according to Scripture, the description of every unregenerate human being, without distinction of person, race, culture, or sex. The apostle Paul said, "We ourselves also were...deceived" (Titus 3:3); although, in his deceived condition he was a religious man, walking blameless according to the righteousness of the law. (See Philippians 3:6.) Every unregenerate person is deceived by his own deceitful heart (Jer. 17:9; Isa. 44:20) and by sin (Heb. 3:13). To these things the god of this world adds the blinding of the mind, to keep the light of the Gospel of Christ from shining through the darkness (2 Cor. 4:4).

WILL THE CHURCH RISE TO FIGHT THE ENEMY?

From the time of Christ up to the giving of Revelation and the death of John, the power of God worked in varying degrees among His people, and the leaders of the church recognized and dealt with the spirits of evil. Then the forces of darkness gained. With intermittent intervals and exceptions, the church sank down under their power, until, in the darkest hour, which we call the Middle Ages, all the sins that spring up through the deceptive workings of evil spirits were as widespread as in the time of Moses, when he wrote by God's command,

> There shall not be found among you any one...that useth divination, or an observer of times, or an enchanter, or a witch, or a charmer, or a consulter with familiar spirits, or a wizard, or a necromancer.
> (Deut. 18:10–11)

Now, at the close of the age, will the church of Christ again arise and reach God's intended power? It will arrive at this place of spiritual strength only when its leaders recognize, as did Moses in the Old Testament and Christ (and His apostles) in the New, the existence of evil spirit powers of darkness, and take toward them and their works the same uncompromising attitude of hostility and aggressive warfare. Each recognized the existence of Satan and evil spirit beings. Each drastically dealt with them as beings who were able to enter and possess men. And each waged war against them as enemies who were actively opposed to God. In the next chapter, we will explore how to recognize our Adversary today.

Chapter 3

Recognizing Our Adversary

For we wrestle not against flesh and blood, but
against principalities, against powers, against the
rulers of the darkness of this world, against spiri-
tual wickedness in high places.
—Ephesians 6:12

Why the church today has not recognized the existence and workings of evil super-natural forces, can only be attributed to its low condition of spiritual life and power. But the Holy Spirit is already at work, opening the eyes of believers. God is awakening the church in the West—as in the recent revival in Wales—by an outpouring of the Spirit of God. This revival has not only manifested the power of the Holy Spirit at work today, as in the days of Pentecost, but has also unveiled the reality of satanic powers in active opposition to God and His people, and the need among the Spirit-filled children of God for the resources to deal with them.

The Welsh Revival has also thrown fresh light on Scripture, showing that the highest points of God's manifested power among men are always the occasion for concurrent manifestations of the working of Satan. It was this way when Jesus came out of the wilderness conflict with the Devil and found that hidden demons in many people were aroused to vicious activity, so that from all parts of Palestine, crowds of victims came to Him, and the possessing spirits trembled in impotent rage.

The awakened part of the church today has no doubt about the real existence of evil spirits, and that there is an organized alliance of supernatural powers in opposition to Christ and His kingdom, bent upon the eternal destruction of every member of the human race; and all who have been delivered and set free from satanic deception have become witnesses, from their own experience, to their existence and power.

They know that things were done to them by spirit beings, and that those things were evil; therefore, they recognize that there are spirit beings who do evil, and they know that the symptoms, effects, and manifestations of demonic influence have active, personal agencies behind them. From experience they know that they were hindered by spirit beings, and therefore they know that these things were done by evil spirits who are hinderers. By reasoning from experience, as well as the testimony of Scripture, they know that these evil spirits are murderers, tempters, liars, accusers, counterfeiters, enemies, haters, and wicked beyond comprehension. These believers know that God is calling them to seek all the resources available for withstanding and resisting these enemies of Christ and His church.

THE AUTHORITY OF CHRIST

The hour of need always brings the corresponding measure of power from God to meet that need. The church must lay hold of the same resources that the early Christians had, in order to deal with the influx of evil spirit hosts among her members.

First, all believers may receive the equipping of the Holy Spirit to overcome demons through the authority of Christ. The New Testament shows us this by the example of Philip in Acts 8:5–7. We also have the writings of the church Fathers from the early centuries of Christianity, which show that the Christians of that time recognized the existence of evil spirits; understood that they influenced, deceived, and possessed men; and knew that Christ gave His followers authority over them through His name. This authority through the name of Christ, applied by the believer who is walking in living and vital union with Him, is available for the servants of God today, at the close of the age.

GAIN KNOWLEDGE ABOUT YOUR ENEMY

After recognizing their authority in Christ, believers need to search the Scriptures thoroughly in order to obtain knowledge about the Enemy's character and how evil spirits are able to possess and use men. To many Christians the Adversary is merely a tempter. They hardly imagine his power as a deceiver (Rev. 12:9), hinderer (1 Thess. 2:18), murderer (John 8:44), liar (John 8:44), accuser (Rev. 12:10), and false angel of light (2 Cor. 11:14). They know even less about the host of spirits under his command, constantly blocking their path— a vast host who are completely given up to wickedness and who delight to do evil (Matt. 12:43–45), to slay (Mark 5:2–5), to deceive (Matt. 24:11), and to destroy (Mark 9:20)—prompting people of all walks of life to all kinds of wickedness, only satisfied when success accompanies their wicked plans to destroy the children of men (Matt. 27:3–5).

There is a distinction between Satan, the Prince of the Demons (Matt. 9:34), and his legion of demonic angels. This fact is clearly recognized by Christ and can be seen in many parts of the Gospels. (See Matthew 25:41.) We find Satan, in person, challenging the Lord in the wilderness temptation, and Christ answering him as a person, word for word and thought for thought, until he leaves, foiled by Christ's astute recognition of his tactics (Luke 4:1–13).

WHO IS SATAN?

The Lord described Satan as the "prince of this world" (John 12:31; 14:30; 16:11); recognized him as ruling over a kingdom (Matt. 12:26); used imperative language to him as a person, saying, "Get thee hence" (Matt 4:10); and designated him as being a "murderer from the beginning," a "liar," and the "father of [lies]," who "abode not in the truth" (John 8:44) that he once held as a great archangel of God. The Devil is also called "that wicked one" (1 John 3:12), the "adversary" (1 Peter 5:8), and "that old serpent" (Rev. 12:9).

Regarding the ways in which he works, the Lord spoke of him as sowing "tares," which are "children of the wicked one," among the "good seed," or the "children of the kingdom" (Matt. 13:38–39). In this way Christ shows us that the Adversary possesses the skill of a mastermind, who leads and directs his work as "prince of this world" throughout the whole earth, and who has power to place men who are called his "children," wherever he wills.

In the parable of the sower, Jesus depicted Satan as watching to snatch away the seed of the Word of God from all who hear it. (See Matthew 13:19; Mark 4:14–15; Luke 8:11–12.) This description again indicates the Enemy's leadership role in the worldwide direction of his agents, whom the Lord described as "fowls of the air" (Matt. 13:3–4; Mark 4:3–4; Luke 8:5). Jesus plainly indicated that these "fowls" represented the "wicked one" (Matt. 13:19) or the "devil" (Luke 8:12), who we know, from other parts of the Scriptures, conducts his work through the wicked spirits he has at his command. Satan himself is not omnipresent, although he is able to transpose himself with lightning speed to any part of his worldwide dominions.

The Lord was always ready to meet the antagonist whom He had foiled in the wilderness, but who had only left Him "for a season" (Luke 4:13). Christ quickly discerned Satan at work in Peter and exposed him by one swift sentence, mentioning his name. (See Matthew 16:23.) With the Jews, He stripped aside the mask of the hidden Foe and said, "Ye are of your father the devil" (John 8:44), and with sharp-edged words spoke of him as the "murderer" and the "liar," prompting the evil spirits to seek to kill Him (vv. 40, 59), and to lie to the Jews about Jesus and His Father in heaven (vv. 40–41). Fast asleep in a boat on the lake during a storm, Jesus was awakened suddenly, and was immediately alert to meet the Foe. He stood with calm majesty to rebuke the storm that the "prince of the power of the air" (Eph. 2:2) had roused against Him. (See Mark 4:38–39.)

Starting with the wilderness victory, the Lord continually unveiled the powers of darkness as He went forward in steady aggressive mastery over them. Behind what appeared natural, He sometimes discerned a supernatural power that demanded His rebuke. He rebuked the fever in Peter's mother-in-law (Luke 4:39), just as He rebuked the evil spirits in other, more manifest, forms (Mark 1:25; Mark 9:25). In other instances He simply healed the sufferer by a word (Matt. 8:13, 16).

The difference between Satan's attitude to the Lord and the attitude of the spirits of evil should also be noted. Satan, the Prince of Darkness, tempted Him, sought to hinder Him, prompted the Pharisees to oppose Him, hid behind a disciple to divert Him, finally took hold of a disciple to betray Him, and then swayed the multitude to put Him to death. But the spirits of evil bowed down before Him, begging Him to let them alone and not to command them to go into the abyss (Luke 8:31).

The realm of this Deceiver-prince is specifically mentioned by the apostle Paul in his description of him as "prince of the power of the air" (Eph. 2:2)— the "heavenly places" (Eph. 3:10) being the special sphere of the activity of Satan and his hierarchy of powers. The name of the Prince of the Demons, "Beelzebub" (Luke 11:18), meaning the "god of flies," suggests the aerial character of the "power of the air." The word *darkness* (Luke 22:53) describes their character and their doings. The Lord's description of Satan working through "fowls of the *air*" (Mark 4:4; Luke 8:5, italics added) strikingly corresponds to these descriptions.

The Gospels are full of references to the workings of evil spirits. They reveal that wherever the Lord moved, the emissaries of Satan sprang into active manifestation, and that the ministry of Christ and His apostles was actively directed against them, so that again and again the record reads: "He preached in their synagogues throughout all Galilee, and cast out devils" (Mark 1:39); "He...cast out many devils; and suffered not the devils to speak, because they knew him" (Mark

1:34); "Unclean spirits, when they saw him, fell down before him, and cried, saying, 'Thou art the Son of God'" (Mark 3:11). When Jesus sent out the twelve disciples, He again took the spirits of evil into account, for He "gave them power over unclean spirits" (Mark 6:7). Later, He appointed seventy other messengers, and as they went forward in their work, they, too, found the demons subject to them through His name (Luke 10:17).

THE PRIMARY CAUSE OF SIN AND SUFFERING

Were Jerusalem, Capernaum, Galilee, and all Syria at that time filled with people who were "insane" and "epileptic"? Or was evil spirit possession a common fact? Either way, it is evident from the Gospel records that the Son of God dealt with the powers of darkness as the active, primary cause of the sin and suffering of this world, and that the aggressive part of His and His disciples' ministry was directed persistently against them. On the one hand He dealt with the Deceiver of the world and bound the "strong man" (Matt. 12:29; Mark 3:27), while on the other He taught the truth about God to the people, to destroy the lies that the Prince of Darkness had placed in their minds (2 Cor. 4:4) about His Father and Himself.

We find, too, that the Lord clearly recognized the Devil behind the opposition of the Pharisees (John 8:44) and the "hour, and the power of darkness" behind His persecutors at Calvary (Luke 22:53). He said that His mission was to "preach deliverance to the captives" (Luke 4:18). He revealed who the Captor was on the eve of Calvary when He said, "Now is the judgment of this world: now shall the prince of this world be cast out"

(John 12:31). Later on he revealed that this "prince" would come to Him once more, but would have no hold on Him (John 14:30).

It is striking to find that the Lord did not attempt to convince the Pharisees of His claims as the Messiah, nor take the opportunity to win over the Jews by yielding to their desires for an earthly king. His one work in this world was clearly to conquer the satanic Prince of the World by His death on the cross (Heb. 2:14), to deliver the captives from the control of the Enemy, and to deal with the invisible hosts of the Prince of Darkness who are working against mankind. (See 1 John 3:8.)

The commission He gave to the Twelve and to the seventy was exactly in line with His own. He sent them out and "gave them power against unclean spirits, to cast them out, and to heal all manner of sickness and all manner of disease" (Matt. 10:1), to "first bind the strong man" (Mark 3:27) and then take his goods: to deal with the invisible hosts of Satan first, and then preach the Gospel.

ONLY ONE SATAN BUT MANY EVIL SPIRITS

From all this we learn that there is one Satan, one Devil, one Prince of the Demons, directing all the opposition to Christ and His people, but there are a myriad of wicked spirits—called demons, lying spirits, deceiving spirits, foul spirits, and unclean spirits—personally at work in people's lives. Who they are, and where they came from, no one can definitely say. However, it is beyond all doubt that they are spirit beings who are evil. The names of these wicked spirits describe their character, for they are called "foul," "lying," "unclean," "evil," and "deceiving" spirits, since they are completely given up to lies and every form of wickedness and deception.

Evil spirits are generally looked upon as "influences" and not as intelligent beings. However, their personality and entity, and difference in character as distinct intelligences, can be seen in the Lord's direct commands to them (Mark 1:25; 3:11–12; 5:8; 9:25); their power of speech (Mark 3:11); their replies to Him, couched in intelligent language (Matt. 8:29); their emotions of fear (Luke 8:31); their definite expression of desire (Matt. 8:31); their need of a dwelling place of rest (Matt. 12:43); their intelligent power of decision (Matt. 12:44); their power of agreement with other spirits and their degree of wickedness (Matt. 12:45); their power of rage (Matt. 8:28); their strength (Mark 5:4); their ability to possess a human being, either as one (Mark 1:26) or in a thousand (Mark 5:9); and their use of a human being as their medium for divination or foretelling the future (Acts 16:16) or as a great miracle worker by their power (Acts 8:11).

When evil spirits act in a rage, they act as a combination of the most insane and wicked persons in existence, but all their evil is done with complete intelligence and purpose. They know what they do; they know it is evil, terribly evil; and they *want* to do it. They do it with rage, and with a full measure of malice, enmity and hatred. They act with fury, like an enraged bull, as if they had no intelligence, and yet they carry on their work with full intelligence, showing the extent of their wickedness. They act from an absolutely depraved nature, with diabolical fury and with an undeviating perseverance. They act with determination, persistence, and with skillful methods, forcing themselves upon mankind, upon the church, and still more upon the mature believer.

Their manifestations, through the persons in whom they gain a foothold, vary according to the degree and kind of ground they secure. In one biblical case, the only manifestation of the evil spirit's presence was dumbness (Matt. 9:32); in another case, the person held by the spirit was "deaf and dumb" (Mark 9:25), and the symptoms included foaming at the mouth and the grinding of teeth— all connected with the head—but the spirit had such a long-standing hold (v. 21) that he could throw his victim down and convulse his whole body (vv. 20–22).

In another situation we find merely an "unclean spirit" (Mark 1:23) in a man in a synagogue. The evil spirit was probably so hidden that no one may have known the man was possessed until the spirit cried out with fear when he saw Christ, saying, "Art thou come to destroy us?" (v. 24). Or, we find a "spirit of infirmity" (Luke 13:11) in a woman of whom it might be said today that she simply required healing of some disease, or that she was always tired, and only needed rest.

But then we find a very advanced case in the man with the "legion," which shows that the evil spirits' possession had reached such a climax that they made the person appear insane, for his own personality was so mastered by the malignant spirits in possession that he had lost all sense of decency and self-control in the presence of others (Luke 8:27). The unity of purpose in the spirits of evil to carry out the will of their prince is especially clear in this case, as with one accord they sought to be allowed to enter the swine, and with one accord they rushed the whole herd into the sea (vv. 32–33).

That there are different kinds of spirits is evident from all the instances given in the gospel records. The manifestation of evil spirits beyond the Gospels may be seen in the Acts of the Apostles, in the story of the girl at Philippi who was possessed by a "spirit of divination" (Acts 16:16), and again in the account of Simon the Sorcerer, who was so energized by satanic power for the working of miracles that he was considered to be a "great power of God" by the deceived people (Acts 8:10).

SPIRITUALISM

In the same way that they use a "spirit of divination" (Acts 16:16), deceiving spirits can use palmists and fortune tellers to deceive. For in their work of watching human beings, they inspire the mediums to foretell not what they know about the future—for God alone has this knowledge—but things that they themselves intend to do; and if they can get the person to whom these things are told to cooperate with them by accepting or believing their "foretelling," they try to eventually bring these things about.

For example, the medium says such and such a thing will happen, the person believes it, and by believing, opens himself up to the evil spirit to bring that thing to pass. Or else the person admits the spirit, or gives free opportunity to one already in possession, to bring about the thing foretold. The evil spirits cannot always succeed, and this is the reason there is so much uncertainty about responses through mediums. Many things may hinder the workings of evil spirits, especially prayer by friends or intercessors in the church.

These are some of the "depths of Satan" (Rev. 2:24) mentioned by the Lord in His message to Thyatira, clearly referring to far deeper, more subtle workings among the Christians of that time than all that the apostles had seen in the cases recorded in the Gospels. "The mystery of iniquity doth already work," wrote the apostle Paul (2 Thess. 2:7), showing that the deeply laid schemes of deception through "doctrines" (1 Tim. 4:1), which it was foretold would reach their full culmination in the last days, were already at work in the church of God.

Evil spirits are at work today, inside as well as outside the church. And even spiritualists today are deceived, insofar as they really believe they are communicating with the spirits of the dead. It is easy for spirits of evil to impersonate any of the dead, even the most devoted and godly Christians, for they have watched them (Acts 19:15) all their lives and can easily counterfeit their voices, or say anything about them or their actions when they were on earth.

Moreover, Christians think they are free from spiritualism because they have never been to a séance, not knowing that evil spirits attack and deceive every human being, and that they do not confine their working to the church or the world; they work wherever they can find conditions fulfilled to enable them to manifest their power.

SYMPTOMS OF DEMON POSSESSION

The control of the spirits over the bodies of those they possess can be seen in the Gospels. The man with the legion was not master over his own body or mind. The spirits would catch him, drive him (Luke 8:29), compel him to cut himself with stones (Mark 5:5), strengthen him to burst every shackle and chain (v. 4), and cause him to cry out (v. 5) and fiercely attack others (Matt. 8:28). The boy with the dumb spirit would be thrown to the ground (Luke 9:42) and convulsed; the spirit forced him to cry out, and tore him, so that his body became bruised and sore (v. 39). Teeth, tongue, vocal organs, ears, eyes, nerves, muscles, and breath would be affected and interfered with by evil spirits in possession. They produced both weakness and strength through their workings, and men (Mark 1:23), women (Luke 8:2), boys (Mark 9:17), and girls (Mark 7:25) were equally open to their power.

The Jews were familiar with the fact of evil spirit possession. This is clear from their statement when they saw the Lord Christ cast out the blind and dumb spirit from a man. (See Matthew 12:24.) It is also clear that there were men among them who knew some method of dealing with such cases (v. 27). "By whom do your sons cast them out?" the Lord asked the Jews (Luke 11:19).

Yet, this kind of dealing with evil spirits was not very effective. From some of the examples given in Scripture, it appears that alleviation of the sufferings of evil spirit possession was the most that could be done. Note, for instance, the case of King Saul, who was soothed by David's harp playing (see 1 Samuel 16:23; 19:9–10), or the example of the sons of Sceva (see Acts 19:13–16), who were professional exorcists and yet recognized a power in the name of Jesus that their exorcism did not possess.

AUTHORITY OVER EVIL SPIRITS

In both these cases, the danger of attempted alleviation and exorcism, and the power of the evil spirits, is in striking contrast to the complete command manifested by Christ and His apostles. David, in the midst of playing to Saul, was suddenly aware of a javelin being flung at him by the hand of the man he was seeking to soothe; and the sons of Sceva found the evil spirits upon them and mastering them as they used the name of Jesus without the divine coworking given to all who exercise personal faith in Him. Incidentally, among the heathen today who know the venom of these wicked spirits, the propitiation and soothing of their hate by obedience is the most that they know.

How striking to contrast all this with the calm authority of Christ, who needed no adjuration or methods of exorcism and no prolonged preparation before dealing with a spirit-possessed man. "What a word is this! for with authority and power he commandeth...and they come out" (Luke 4:36) was the amazed testimony of the awe-struck people. "They" were the evil spirits whom the people knew to be real identities who were governed by Beelzebub, their prince. (See Matthew 12:24–27.) It was also the testimony of the seventy, sent out by Him to use the authority of His name, as they found that the spirits were subject to them even as they were to the Lord. (See Luke 10:17–20.)

The Lord's complete mastery over the demons compelled the Jewish leaders to find some way of explaining His authority over them. And so, by that subtle influence of Satan—with which all who have had insight into his devices are familiar—they suddenly charge the Lord with having satanic power Himself, saying, "This fellow doth not cast out devils, but by Beelzebub the prince of the devils" (Matt. 12:24), suggesting that Christ's authority over evil spirits was derived from their chief and prince.

This reference to the kingdom of Satan was left uncontradicted by the Lord. He simply declared the truth in the face of Satan's lie: that He cast out demons "with the finger of God" (Luke 11:20), and that Satan's kingdom would soon fall were he to act against himself (v. 18) and dislodge his demons from their presence in human bodies, where alone they can achieve their greatest power and do the greatest harm among men. Satan does apparently sometimes fight against himself, but when he does so, it is for the purpose of hiding some scheme that will bring greater advantage to his kingdom.

That the apostles after Pentecost recognized and dealt with evil spirits is evident from accounts in Acts and other references in the Epistles. The disciples were prepared for Pentecost and the opening of the supernatural world through the coming of the Holy Spirit by their three years' training with the Lord. They had watched Him deal with the wicked spirits of Satan and had themselves learned to deal with them too, so that the power of the Holy Spirit could safely be given to men who already knew the workings of the Foe. We see how quickly Peter recognized Satan's work in Ananias (Acts 5:3) and how "unclean spirits" came out at his presence, as they had with his Lord (Acts 5:16). Philip, too, found the evil hosts subservient (Acts 8:7) to the word of his testimony as he proclaimed Christ to the people. Paul also knew the power of the name of the risen Lord (Acts 19:11–12) in dealing with the powers of evil.

It is clear from the Bible that the manifestation of the power of God invariably meant aggressive dealing with satanic hosts; that the manifestation of the power of God at Pentecost, and through the apostles, meant an aggressive attitude to the powers of darkness; and, therefore, that the growth and maturity of the church of Christ at the end of the age will mean the same recognition, the same attitude toward the satanic hosts of the "prince of the power of the air" (Eph. 2:2), and the same authority in the name of Jesus, as in the early church. In brief, the church of Christ will reach its high water mark when it is able to recognize and deal with demon possession, when it knows how to "bind the strong man" (Matt. 12:29; Mark 3:27) by prayer, and when it can command the spirits of evil in the name of Christ and deliver men and women from their power.

The church must recognize that the existence of deceiving, lying spirits is as real today as in the time of Christ, and that the attitude of these spirits toward the human race remains unchanged. Their one ceaseless aim is to lie to and deceive every human being; they are given up to wickedness all day and all night; and they are ceaselessly and actively pouring a stream of wickedness into the world. Again, they are satisfied only when they succeed in their wicked plans to deceive and ruin people.

ADDRESS THE CAUSE, NOT THE SYMPTOMS

Even so, the servants of God have only been concerned with destroying their works and dealing with sin, and have not recognized the need to use the power given to us by Christ to resist—by continual faith and prayer—this ever flowing flood of satanic power that is pouring in among men. The result is that men and women, young and old, Christian and non-Christian, become deceived, oppressed, and possessed through the guile of evil spirits and because of their ignorance about them and their wiles.

These supernatural forces of Satan are the true causes of hindrance to revival. The power of God that broke forth in Wales with all the characteristics of the days of Pentecost has been stopped and prevented from going on to its fullest purpose by the same influx of evil spirits that met the Lord Christ and the apostles of the early church, with this difference: that the powers of darkness found the Christians of the twentieth century, with few exceptions, unable to recognize and deal with them. Evil spirit deception and attack have followed, and have stopped every similar revival throughout the centuries since Pentecost.

Therefore, evil spirit activity must now be understood and dealt with if the church is to advance to maturity. It must be understood not only in the kind of possession recorded in the Gospels, but in the special forms of manifestations suited to the close of the age, which will be disguised as counterfeits of the Holy Spirit. These manifestations, while especially connected with end-time deception, will still retain some of the very characteristic marks of those in the gospel records, when all who saw them knew they were the work of the spirits of Satan.

Chapter 4

You Are at Risk

Let him that thinketh he standeth
take heed lest he fall.
—1 Corinthians 10:12

In the special onslaught of the Deceiver, which will come upon all of the true church of Christ at the close of the age, there are some, more than others, who will be especially attacked by the powers of darkness. These believers need spiritual wisdom and insight regarding the Enemy's deceptive workings so that they may pass through the trial of the last hour and be counted worthy to escape that Hour of greater trial which is coming upon the Earth. (See Luke 21:34–36; Revelation 3:10.)

MATURE BELIEVERS ARE MORE
SUSCEPTIBLE TO DECEPTION

There are degrees of growth among Christians, and there are therefore degrees of testing permitted by God, who provides a way of escape for those who know their need and, through watchful prayer, take heed lest they fall. (See 1 Corinthians 10:12–13.) God is the Sovereign Lord of the universe, and He limits Satan in what he is permitted to do in the life of a redeemed believer. (See Job 1:12; 2:6; Luke 22:31.) Some Christians are still in the stage of babyhood, and others do not even know the initial reception of the Holy Spirit. But there are others, who may be described as the "advance guard" of the church of Christ, who have been baptized with the Holy Spirit or who are seeking that baptism—honest and earnest believers who are distressed over the powerlessness of the true church of Christ and who grieve that her witness is so ineffective and that spiritualism and other "isms" are sweeping thousands into their deceptive errors.

These dedicated believers do not imagine that as they themselves go forward in the spiritual realm, the Deceiver, who has misled others, has special wiles prepared for them, in order to render ineffective their aggressive power against him. Yet these are the ones who are in danger of the special deception of counterfeit "Christs" and false prophets, and the dazzling lure of "signs and wonders" and "fire out of heaven," designed to meet their longing for the mighty intervention of God in the darkness settling upon the earth. They do not recognize that such subtle, deceptive workings of the spirits of evil are possible, and so, they are unprepared to meet them.

These are the ones, also, who are recklessly ready to follow the Lord at any cost and yet do not realize their unpreparedness for warfare with the spiritual powers of the unseen world as they press on into fuller spiritual things. They often have certain assumptions about the spiritual life that have been ingrained in them from earlier years but which hinder the Spirit of God from preparing them for all they will meet as they press on to their cherished goal of a deeper life and service in God. These preconceived ideas also hinder others from giving them, from the Scriptures, much that they need to know of the spiritual world into which they are so blindly advancing—preconceived ideas that lull them into a false security and give an opportunity for, and even bring about, that very deception that enables the Deceiver to find them an easy prey.

CAN SINCERE CHRISTIANS BE DECEIVED?

One idea that is widely believed, and which many such believers have deeply embedded in their minds, is that sincere seekers of God will not be allowed to be deceived. This is one of Satan's lies, to lure such seekers into a false position of safety. We see this demonstrated in the history of the church during the past two thousand years, for every demonic deception that has borne sad fruit throughout the church age first took hold of devoted believers who were sincere. The errors among groups of such believers all began among sincere children of God who were baptized with the Holy Spirit and who were very sure that they would never be caught by the wiles of Satan, even though they were aware that others had been sidetracked. Yet they, too, were deceived by lying spirits, who counterfeited the workings of God in the higher realms of the spiritual life.

Lying spirits have taken advantage of the determination of devoted believers to obey the Scriptures literally. By misusing the letter of the written Word, these evil spirits have pushed people into states of unbalanced truth, and this has resulted in erroneous practices. Many who have suffered for their adherence to these so-called biblical commands firmly believe that they are martyrs suffering for Christ. The world calls these devoted ones "cranks" and "fanatics." Yet they give evidence of the highest devotion and love for the Lord, and could be delivered, if they only understood why the powers of darkness have deceived them, and the path of freedom from their power.

The aftermath of the revival in Wales, which was a true work of God, revealed numbers of sincere believers who were swept off their feet by evil supernatural powers, which they were not able to distinguish from the true workings of God. And even more recently than the Welsh Revival, there have been other movements in which large numbers of earnest servants of God were swept into deception through the wiles of deceiving spirits who counterfeited the workings of God. All are sincere Christians, but they have been deceived by the subtle Foe. Now, they are certain to be led on into still deeper deception, despite their honesty and earnestness, if they are not awakened to recovery from the snare of the Devil, into which they have fallen. (See 2 Timothy 2:25–26.)

DECEPTION BASED ON IGNORANCE, NOT CHARACTER

The children of God need to know that to be true in motive, and to be faithful in the spiritual knowledge they have acquired, is not a sufficient safeguard against deception, and that it is not safe for them to rely upon their sincerity of purpose as a guarantee of protection from the Enemy's wiles. Instead, they must take to heart the warnings of God's Word and pray diligently.

Christians who are true and faithful and sincere can be deceived by Satan and his deceiving spirits for the following reasons:

1. When someone becomes a child of God by the regenerating power of the Spirit, he is given new life as he trusts in the atoning work of

Christ. However, he does not at the same time receive fullness of *knowledge*, either of God, himself, or the Devil.

2. The mind that by nature is darkened (Eph. 4:18) is only renewed, and the veil on the mind that is created by Satan (2 Cor. 4:4) is only destroyed, up to the extent that the light of truth penetrates it, and according to the measure with which the person is able to comprehend it.

3. Deception has to do with the mind. It means a wrong thought admitted to the mind, under the deception that it is truth. Since deception is based on ignorance and not on a person's moral character, a Christian who is true and faithful in the spiritual knowledge he has, is open to deception in the sphere where he is ignorant of the "devices" of the Devil (2 Cor. 2:11) and what he is able to do.

4. The thought that God will protect a believer from being deceived if he is true and faithful is itself a deception, because it throws a person off guard and ignores the fact that there are conditions on the part of the believer that have to be fulfilled in order for God to work. God does not do anything without the active participation and cooperation of a person. Neither does He attempt to make up for a believer's ignorance when He has provided him with knowledge that will prevent him from being deceived.

5. Christ would not have warned His disciples, "Take heed...be not deceived" (Luke 21:8), if there had been no danger of deception, or if God had undertaken to keep them from deception apart from their action of "taking heed" and their knowledge of such danger.

The knowledge that it is possible to be deceived keeps the mind open to spiritual truth and enlightenment from God. Having this knowledge is also one of the primary conditions we need to fulfill in order truly to remain in the keeping power of God. On the other hand, a mind that is closed to spiritual knowledge and truth is guaranteed to be deceived by Satan at his earliest opportunity.

As we glance back over the history of the church, and watch the rise of various "heresies," we can see that deception begins with some great spiritual event or crisis, such as what we have termed "the baptism of the Holy Spirit"—a spiritual crisis in which a person is brought to give himself up in full abandonment to the Holy Spirit, and in so doing opens himself up to the supernatural powers of the invisible world.

The reason the baptism of the Holy Spirit is a crisis point is that, up to this time, the believer has used his reasoning faculties to judge right and wrong, and has obeyed from principle what he believed to be the will of God. But now, in his abandonment to the Holy Spirit, he begins to obey an unseen person, and to submit his faculties and his reasoning powers in blind obedience to that which he believes is of God.

DISCERNING BETWEEN CONTRARY POWERS

We will discuss the nature of the baptism of the Holy Spirit in more detail in the last chapter. At this point, it is only necessary to say that it is a crisis in the life of a Christian that none but those who have gone through it can fully understand. It means that the Spirit of God becomes so real to a person that his supreme purpose in life from that time on is implicit obedience to the Holy Spirit.

The Christian's will is surrendered to carry out the will of God at all costs, and his whole being is made subject to the powers of the unseen world. The believer, of course, only intends to be subject to the power of God and does not take into account that there are other powers in the spiritual realm, and that there are aspects of the supernatural that are not of God. He does not realize that this absolute surrender of one's whole being to invisible forces, without knowing how to discern between the contrary powers of God and Satan, must be of the gravest risk to the inexperienced believer.

OBEYING THE SPIRIT?

The question of whether this surrender to "obey the Spirit" is one that is in accord with Scripture, should be examined in view of the way in which so many wholehearted believers have been misled, for it is strange that an attitude that is scriptural should be so grievously the cause of danger, and often of complete destruction, to many devoted children of God.

"The Holy Ghost, whom God hath given to them that obey him" (Acts 5:32), is the chief verse that gives rise to the expression, "obey the Spirit." It was used by Peter before the council at Jerusalem, but nowhere else in the Scriptures is the same thought given. The whole passage needs careful reading in order to arrive at a clear understanding of it. "We must obey God" (see Acts 5:29), Peter said to the Sanhedrin, for "we are his witnesses...and so is also the Holy Ghost, whom God hath given to them that obey Him" (v. 32).

Does the apostle mean "obey the Spirit," or "obey God," according to the first words of the passage? The distinction is important, and the context of the words can only be correctly understood by the insights of other parts of Scripture— that *the triune God in heaven* is to be obeyed through the power of the indwelling Spirit of God. For to place the Holy Spirit as the object of obedience, rather than God the Father, through the Son, by the Holy Spirit, creates the danger of leading the believer to rely upon, or obey, a spirit in or around him, rather than God on the throne in heaven, who is to be obeyed by the child of God united to His Son, the Holy Spirit being the means through whom God is worshipped and obeyed.

The baptism of the Spirit, however, brings the person of the Holy Spirit so vividly into the range of the believer's consciousness, that for the time being, the other persons of the Trinity, in heaven, are eclipsed. The Holy Spirit becomes the center and object of thought and worship and is given a place that He Himself does not desire, nor is it the purpose of the Father in heaven that He should have, or occupy. "He shall not speak of himself" (John 16:13), said the Lord before Calvary as He told of the Holy Spirit's coming at Pentecost. The Holy Spirit would act as Teacher (John 14:26), but would teach the words of Another, not His own; He would bear witness to Another, not to Himself (John 15:26); He would glorify Another, not Himself (John 16:14); He would only speak what was given Him to speak by Another (John 16:13). In brief, His entire work would be to lead souls into union with the Son and knowledge of the Father in heaven, while He Himself directed and worked in the background.

But when the spiritual world is opened up—which takes place through the incoming of the Spirit and with the work of the Spirit, which now occupies the attention of the believer—this is just the opportunity for the Arch-deceiver to commence his wiles under a new form. If the believer is untaught in the scriptural statements about the work of the triune God, to "obey the Spirit" is now his supreme purpose; and to counterfeit the guidance of the Spirit, and the Spirit Himself, is now the Deceiver's scheme. For the Deceiver must somehow regain power over this servant of God in order to render him useless for aggressive warfare against the forces of darkness, drive him back into the world, or in some way sidetrack him from active service for God.

TIME OF GREATEST DANGER FOR A BELIEVER

It is in this crucial moment that the ignorance of the believer about the spiritual world now opened to him, the workings of evil powers in that realm, and the conditions upon which God works in and through him, give the Enemy his opportunity. It is the time of greatest danger for every believer, unless he is instructed and prepared, as the disciples were by the Lord for three whole years.

The danger lies along the line of supernatural guidance: (1) when a believer does not know the conditions of cooperation with the Holy Spirit, and how to discern the will of God, and (2) when a believer does not have the "discerning of spirits" (1 Cor. 12:10) necessary to detect the workings of the false angel of light, who is able to bring about counterfeit gifts of prophesy, tongues, healing, and other spiritual experiences connected with the work of the Holy Spirit.

Those who have their eyes open to the opposing forces of the spiritual realm understand that very few believers can guarantee that they are obeying God, and God alone, in direct supernatural guidance, because there are so many factors liable to intervene, such as the believer's own mind, spirit, and will, and the deceptive intrusion of the powers of darkness.

Since evil spirits can counterfeit God as Father, Son, or Holy Spirit, the believer also needs to know very clearly the principles upon which God works, in order to distinguish between divine and satanic workings. There is a discernment that is a spiritual gift, enabling the believer to discern spirits, but this also requires knowledge of doctrine (see 1 John 4:1) in order to detect doctrine that is of God and doctrines, or teachings, of evil teaching spirits.

In other words, a believer is able to detect, by the gift of the discernment of spirits, which spirit is at work. There is also a test of spirits, which is doctrinal. In the first, a believer can tell through a spirit of discernment that lying spirits are at work in a meeting, or in a person, but he may not have the understanding needed for testing the doctrines set forth by the teacher. He needs knowledge in both cases: knowledge to read his spirit with assurance in the face of all contrary appearances, that the supernatural workings are "of God," and knowledge to detect the subtlety of teachings that have certain infallible indications that they emanate from the pit, while they appear to be from God.

In the same way, a believer needs this knowledge in his personal obedience to the Lord. He can detect whether or not he is obeying God when obeying some "command," by judging its fruits, and by knowledge of the character of God, such as the knowledge that God always has a purpose in His commands and that He will give no command out of harmony with His character and Word. Other factors needed for clear knowledge in this area will be dealt with later on.

FANATICAL BEHAVIOR

Another question of grave importance arises here. How can a believer be so especially open to the Deceiver's workings after the baptism in the Holy Spirit? The Enemy must find an opening (or, "grounds") in his life to work upon, and since the Holy Spirit so clearly dwells in him, how can grounds be possible, or how can the believer be open to the Deceiver's approach?

It is possible that, in earlier years, through yielding to sin, an evil spirit may have obtained access to a person's body or mind, and, hiding deeply in the structure of the person, never been detected or dislodged. The manifestation of this evil spirit might possibly have seemed so natural, or so identified with the person's character, that it had unhindered sway in his being. For instance, it may have come forth as some peculiar idea in his mind, so that it was considered an idiosyncrasy; or it may have been manifested as some bodily habit that was believed to be the result of the person's upbringing and was therefore "put up with" by others and looked upon by the person as something acceptable, or of trivial importance. Or, an evil spirit may have gained entrance through some secret sin known only to the person, or through some tendency which opened the person to its power.

To be baptized in the Spirit, a person's sin—that is, the "works of the devil" (see 1 John 3:8)—will necessarily have been dealt with. But the evil spirit, manifested in the peculiar idiosyncrasy, might have been left undetected. When the baptism of the Spirit takes place and the Holy Spirit fills the spirit of the person, the body and mind are surrendered to God, but hidden secretly in one, or both, may be the evil spirit, or spirits, which obtained lodgment years before, but who now break forth into activity and hide their manifestations under cover of the true workings of the Spirit of God, who dwells within the inner shrine of a person's spirit.

The result is that, for a time, the person's heart is filled with love, his spirit is full of light and joy, his tongue is released to witness; but before long a "fanatical spirit," or a subtle spirit of pride or self-importance and self-aggrandizement, may be seen creeping in at the same time as the pure fruits of the Spirit, which are undeniably of God.

We will deal with this in more detail in a later section. The fact to remember now is that sincere and earnest believers can be deceived and oppressed by lying spirits, so that for a time they go out of the mainstream into a fog of deception, or are left deceived to the end, unless spiritual light for their deliverance reaches them.

VIEWS OF TRUTH

In light of the activities of deceiving spirits and their methods of deception, it is also becoming clear that close examination is needed of current theories, conceptions, and expressions concerning the things of God and His way of working in man. For only the truth of God, not views of truth, will be effective for protection or offensive warfare in the conflict with wicked spirits in the heavenly sphere.

All that is in any degree the outcome of the mind of the "natural man" (1 Cor. 2:14) will prove to be only weapons of straw in this great battle. If we rely upon others' views of truth or upon our own human conceptions of truth, Satan will use these very things to deceive us, and will even build us up in these false theories and views so that, under cover of them, he may accomplish his purposes.

In view of the critical time through which the church of Christ is passing, we cannot overestimate the importance of believers having open minds to examine everything they have thought and taught in connection with the things of God and the spiritual realm: all the truths they have held, all the phrases and expressions they have used in teachings, and all the teachings they have absorbed through others.

For any wrong interpretation of truth, any theories and phrases which are man-conceived and which we may build upon wrongly, will have dangerous consequences to ourselves and to others in the conflict which the church, and the individual believer, are now passing through. Since, in the end times, evil spirits will come to us with deceptions in doctrinal form, believers must carefully examine what they accept as doctrine in light of the truth of God's Word, lest it should be from the emissaries of the Deceiver.

GOD INVITES US TO EXAMINE HIS WORKS

The apostle Paul again and again strongly urged believers to fulfill their responsibility to examine spiritual things. He wrote, "He that is spiritual judgeth all things" (1 Cor. 2:15). To "judge" in this case means to "examine." The Greek word means to "investigate" and "decide." The spiritual believer—one who is walking in fellowship with God—is to use his judgment, which is a renewed faculty if he is a spiritual man. This spiritual examination, or judging, operates in connection with "things of the Spirit of God" (v. 14), and shows that God Himself honors the intelligent personality of the one He recreates in Christ. He invites him to judge, or examine, His own workings by His Spirit, so that even the "things of the Spirit" are not to be received without being examined and "spiritually discerned" (v. 14) that they are of God.

REMAIN NEUTRAL UNTIL YOU KNOW

People sometimes say, in connection with supernatural and abnormal manifestations, that it is not necessary, nor even according to the will of God, for believers to understand or explain all the workings of God. Yet this does not agree with the apostle's statement that, "he that is spiritual judgeth all things."

Believers should remain neutral toward all supernatural workings that they are unsure of until they do know whether or not they are from God. Many have a wrong anxiety to know, as if knowledge alone would save them. They think that they must be either for or against certain things, which they cannot decide are from God or from the Devil, and want to know infallibly which is which, so that they may declare their position. However, believers can take the attitude of "for" or "against" without knowing whether the things they are in doubt of are divine or satanic. They can maintain the wisdom and safety of remaining neutral to the things themselves, until, by a means which cannot be fully described, they know what they have wanted to understand.

One effect of overeagerness in desiring knowledge is a feverish anxiety and a restless impatience, worry, and trouble that causes people to lose their moral poise and power. It is important in seeking one blessing not to destroy another. In seeking knowledge of spiritual things, the believer should not lose patience and calm, quiet restfulness; and in faith he should watch himself, lest the Enemy gain advantage and rob him of moral power while he is eager to get light and truth concerning the way of victory over the Adversary.

EXAMINE YOURSELF

Moreover, the believer is not only to judge all things in the spiritual realm. He is also to judge himself. For if we would "judge" ourselves (see 1 Corinthians 11:31-32)—the word in Greek refers to a thorough investigation—we would not need the Lord to deal with us to bring to light things that we have failed to discern by examining ourselves.

"Brethren, be not children in understanding; howbeit in malice be ye children, *but in understanding be men*" (1 Cor. 14:20, italics added), wrote Paul again to the Corinthians, as he explained to them the way the Spirit worked among them. The Greek word here means to be of "full, or mature, age." The believer is to be of "full age" in his understanding. That is, he is to be able to examine and "*prove* all things" (1 Thess. 5:21, italics added). He is to abound in "knowledge and in all judgment," in order to "approve things that are excellent," that he may be "sincere and without offence till the day of Christ" (Phil. 1:9-10).

Every criticism—just or unjust—should be humbly received and examined to discover its ground, apparent or real. Facts concerning spiritual truths from every segment of the church of God should be analyzed, independent of their pleasure or pain to us personally, either for our own enlightenment or for our equipment in the service of God.

For the knowledge of truth is the first essential for warfare with the lying spirits of Satan. Truth must be eagerly sought and faced with an earnest and sincere desire to know it and to obey it in the light of God: truth concerning ourselves, discerned by unbiased evaluation; truth from the Scriptures, uncolored, unstrained, unmutilated, undiluted; truth in facing facts about the experiences of all members of the body of Christ, and not one section alone.

There is a fundamental principle involved in the power of truth to free us from the deceptions of the Devil. Deliverance from believing lies must come from believing truth. Nothing can remove a lie but truth. "Ye shall know the truth, and the truth shall make you free" (John 8:32) is applicable to every aspect of truth, as well as to the special truth referred to by the Lord when He spoke these pregnant words.

A sinner must know the truth of the Gospel if he is to be saved. Christ is the Savior, but He saves us through certain instruments and means, for example, our faith in Him, who is the Truth. Likewise, if the believer needs freedom, he must ask the Son of God for it. The Son sets the believer free by the Holy Spirit, and the Holy Spirit does it by the instrumentality of truth. Or we may say, in brief, freedom is the gift of the Son, by the Holy Spirit working through truth.

There are three stages of apprehending truth: perception of truth by the understanding; perception of truth for use and personal application; and perception of truth for teaching and passing on to others. Truth that does not seem to have been grasped may lie dormant in the mind, but in the hour of need may suddenly emerge into experience, when what has been lying dormant becomes clear to the mind. Then it is only by continual application and assimilation of truth in experience that it becomes clarified in the mind in order to teach others.

EAGERLY SEEK TRUTH

The great need of all believers is that they should eagerly seek truth. In this way, they will become progressively free from all of Satan's lies, for knowledge and truth alone can give victory over Satan as the Deceiver and Liar. Even when truth is resisted, it has at least reached the mind, and at any time may bear fruit into experience.

There are three attitudes of mind in regard to knowledge: (1) assumption of knowing a certain thing; (2) neutrality toward it ("I do not know."); and (3) certainty of real knowledge. When believers first hear of the possibility of counterfeits of God and of divine things, they almost invariably ask, "How are we to *know* which is which?" First, they must know that such counterfeits are possible. Then, as they mature and seek spiritual wisdom from God, they learn to know for themselves, for no human being can explain it to them.

Since truth removes the deceptions of lies, let us look briefly at some misinterpretations of truth that are giving ground to the powers of darkness, and which need examination in light of Scripture.

MISCONCEPTION: A mistaken idea concerning the "shelter of the blood of Jesus"—that if it is claimed over an assembly, it guarantees absolute protection from the workings of the powers of darkness.

TRUTH: The New Testament truths concerning the application of the blood, by the Holy Spirit, are as follows. (1) The blood of Jesus cleanses us from all sin "if we walk in the light" and "if we confess our sins" (1 John 1:7, 9). (2) The blood of Jesus gives us access to the Holy of Holies because of its power to cleanse us from sin (Heb. 10:19). (3) The blood of Jesus is the ground of victory over Satan because it cleanses us from every confessed sin, and because at Calvary, Satan was conquered. (See Revelation 12:11.) Yet we do not read that any can be put under the blood apart from their own will and individual condition before God.

For example, if the "shelter of the blood" is claimed over an assembly of people, and one who is present is giving ground to Satan, the claiming of the blood does not serve to prevent Satan from working on the ground that he has a right to in that person. A misconception, therefore, about the protecting power of the blood is serious. For those who are present in a meeting where Satan, as well as God, is working, may believe they are personally safe from Satan's workings, regardless of their individual condition and relationship with God, while through the ground they have given—even unknowingly—to the Adversary, they are open to his power.

MISCONCEPTION: Mistaken ideas concerning "waiting for the Spirit to descend." Here again we find statements and theories misleading and opening the door to satanic deceptions. "If we want a manifestation of the Spirit like at Pentecost," we have said to each other, "we must 'tarry' as the disciples did before Pentecost," and we have seized upon the verses in Luke 24:49, and Acts 1:4, and passed the word along. "Yes, we must 'tarry,'" we have said, until, compelled by the inroads of the Adversary in "waiting meetings," we have had to search the Scriptures once more to discover that the Old Testament admonition to "wait on the Lord," so often used in the Psalms, has been strained beyond New Testament truth. It has been exaggerated into a waiting on God for the outpouring of the Spirit that has even gone beyond the ten days which preceded Pentecost, into four months, and even four years, and which, to our knowledge, has ended in an influx of deceiving spirits that has rudely awakened some of the waiting believers.

TRUTH: The scriptural truth concerning "waiting for the Spirit" may be summed up as follows. (1) The disciples waited ten days, but we have no indication that they waited in any passive state, but rather in simple prayer and supplication until the fullness of time came for the fulfillment of the promise of the Father. (2) The command to wait, given by the Lord (Acts 1:4), was not carried over after the Holy Spirit had come, for in no single instance, either in the Acts or in the Epistles, do the apostles command the disciples to wait for the gift of the Holy Spirit. They use the word *receive* in every instance. (See Acts 2:38; 19:2; 2 Corinthians 11:4; Galatians 3:14.) The Greek word used for receiving the Holy Spirit carries the forceful idea of "grasping."

It is true that at this time the church is, as a whole, living experientially on the "wrong" side of Pentecost, in that they are not living in the power and gifts of the Holy Spirit. But when individuals pray to God to receive the Holy Spirit, this does not put these seekers back in the position of the disciples before the Holy Spirit had been given. The risen and ascended Lord poured forth the stream of the Spirit again and again after the day of Pentecost, but in each instance it was without "tarrying" as the disciples did at the first. The Holy Spirit, who proceeds from the Father through the Son to His people, is now among them, waiting to give Himself unceasingly to all who will appropriate and receive Him. (See John 15:26; Acts 2:33, 38–39.)

A "waiting for the Spirit," therefore, is not in accord with the general tenor of the truth given in the Acts and the Epistles, which instead show the imperative call to the believer to put in his claim, not only to his identification with the Lord Jesus in His death and to union in life with Him in His resurrection, but also to the empowerment for witnessing that came to the disciples on the day of Pentecost.

A believer may need to wait for God while the Holy Spirit deals with him and prepares him until he is in the right attitude for the inflow of the Holy Spirit into his spirit, but this is different from the "waiting for Him to come" that has opened the door so frequently to satanic manifestations from the unseen world. The Lord does take the believer at his word when he puts in his claim for his share of the gift of the Holy Spirit, but the "manifestation of the Spirit" (1 Cor. 12:7)—the evidence of His indwelling and outworking—may not be according to any preconceptions of the seeker.

"Waiting for the Spirit" until He descends in some manifested way has been very profitable to deceiving spirits. It is not in accord with the written Word, which says that the Holy Spirit is not to be prayed to, or asked to come, as He is the Gift of Another (see Luke 11:13; John 14:16), and that the Holy Spirit is not to be "waited for," but is to be taken, or received, from the hand of the risen Lord (see John 14:26; 20:22), of whom it is written, "He shall baptize you with the Holy Ghost, and with fire" (Matt. 3:11). Because it is out of line with the truth of the Scriptures, prayer to the Spirit, trust in the Spirit, obeying the Spirit, and expecting the Spirit to descend, may all become prayer, trust, and obedience to evil spirits when they counterfeit the working of God. We will explore this in more detail later on.

Other mistaken conceptions of spiritual truth center around thoughts such as these:

1. *God can do everything. If I trust Him, He must protect me.* This shows a lack of understanding that God works according to laws and conditions, and that those who trust Him should seek to know the conditions upon which He can work in response to their trust.

2. *If I were wrong, God would not use me.* If a man is right in his will, God will use him to the fullest extent possible, but this being "used" of God is no guarantee that any man is absolutely right in all that he says and does.

3. *I have no sin, or sin has been entirely removed.*
   This statement indicates a lack of knowledge
   of how deeply the sinful life of Adam is ingrained in the fallen creation, and how the assumption that sin has been eliminated from
   the whole being enables the Enemy to keep the
   fallen nature from being dealt with by the continual power of the Cross.

4. *God, who is love, will not allow me to be deceived.* This thought is itself a deception based
   on ignorance of the depths of the Fall, and the
   misconception that God works regardless of
   spiritual laws.

5. *I have been a Christian too long to need teaching,* or *I must be taught by God directly, because
   it is written, "Ye need not that any man teach
   you"* (1 John 2:27). This is another misused passage of Scripture, which some believers interpret to mean that they are to refuse all spiritual
   teaching through others. But the apostle's
   words, "Ye need not that any man teach you,"
   did not rule out the fact that God teaches us
   through anointed teachers, as can be seen in the
   inclusion of "teachers" in the list of gifts to the
   church, "for the edifying of the body of Christ"
   through "that which every joint supplieth"
   (Eph. 4:11–16). For God is sometimes able to
   teach His children more quickly through indirect means—that is, through others—than directly, because men are so slow to understand
   how to be taught directly by the Spirit of God.

Many other similar misconceptions of spiritual things by Christians today give opportunity
for the Enemy to deceive, because they cause believers to close their minds to the statements of

God's Word, the facts of everyday existence, and the help of others who could provide spiritual knowledge and insight. (See 1 Peter 1:12.) Other dangers center around the coining of phrases to describe some special experience, and words that are commonly used among dedicated Christians who attend conventions, words such as *possess*, *control*, *surrender*, and *let go*. All of these contain truth in relation to God, but, in the interpretation of them in the minds of many believers, are liable to bring about conditions for evil spirits to control those who "surrender" and "let go" to the evil powers of the spiritual world—those who do not know how to discern between the working of God and Satan.

Various preconceptions of the way God works also give evil spirits their opportunity, such as the idea that when a believer is supernaturally *compelled* to act, it is a special indication that God is guiding him, or that if God brings "all things" to our "remembrance" (John 14:26) we do not need to use our own memories at all.

Other thoughts that are liable to bring about a passive condition, which evil spirits need for their deceptive workings, may also be cultivated through the following misconceptions of truth:

1. Christ lives in me; therefore, *I* do not now live at all (erroneously based on Galatians 2:20).

2. Christ lives in me; therefore, I have lost my personality because Christ is now personally in me (erroneously based on Galatians 2:20).

3. God works in me; therefore, I do not need to work, only to surrender and obey (erroneously based on Philippians 2:13).

4. God wills instead of me; therefore, I must not use my will at all (erroneously based on Philippians 2:13).

5. God is the only one to judge; therefore, I must not use my judgment (erroneous interpretation of verses such as 1 Corinthians 4:4–5).

6. I have the mind of Christ; therefore, I must not have any mind of my own (erroneously based on 1 Corinthians 2:16).

7. God speaks to me, so I must not think or reason, only obey what He tells me to do (erroneous interpretation of verses such as Proverbs 3:5–6 and John 16:13).

8. I wait on God, and I must not act until He moves me (erroneous interpretation of verses such as Psalm 25:5 and Philippians 2:13).

9. God reveals His will to me by visions, so I do not need to decide and use my reason and conscience (erroneous interpretation of verses such as Acts 2:17).

10. I am crucified with Christ; therefore, I am "dead," and must "practice death," which I conceive of as passivity of feeling, thinking, etc. (erroneous interpretation of verses such as Galatians 2:20).

To carry out in practice these various misconceptions of truth, the believer must quench all personal action of mind, judgment, reason, will, and activity, in order to allow the "divine life" to flow through him. In reality, God needs the fullest freedom of the faculties of a person, and the active and intelligent cooperation of his will, for the working out of spiritual truths in experience.

HOW TO BE SAFE FROM DECEPTION

The conditions, then, which will keep us safe from deception by evil spirits include:

1. the knowledge that they exist

2. an awareness that they can deceive the most sincere believers

3. an understanding of the conditions and ground necessary for them to work, so that they are not allowed to gain a foothold or any opportunity to work

4. intelligent knowledge of God through His Word and of how to cooperate with Him in the power of the Holy Spirit

We will explore these four essential points in the following chapters.

Chapter 5

The Danger of Passivity

Be sober, be vigilant; because your adversary the
devil, as a roaring lion, walketh about, seeking
whom he may devour.
—1 Peter 5:8

The primary causes of the deception and oppression of believers must now be made
clear. These are to be distinguished from
satanic attacks that come from yielding to sins of
the flesh, or to any sin that gives evil spirits a hold
in the fallen nature.

Christians are as open to deception by evil
spirits as other people. They become deceived because they have, in most cases, unknowingly fulfilled the conditions upon which evil spirits work,
and have given ground to deceiving spirits through
accepting counterfeits of divine workings and cul-
tivating passivity and nonuse of their faculties
through a misconception of the spiritual laws that
govern the Christian life.

GIVING GROUND TO THE ENEMY

It is this matter of "giving ground" that is the
most crucial point of all. All believers acknowledge
known sin—even unknown sin in their lives—to
be ground given to the Enemy, but they do not realize that every thought suggested to the mind by
wicked spirits, and accepted, is ground given to
them; and every unused faculty invites their attempted use of it.

The primary cause of deception in surrendered believers may be condensed into one word:

passivity. This means a cessation of the active exercise of the will in control over spirit, soul, and body, or any of the three, as may be the case. It is, practically, a counterfeit of surrender to God. The believer who "yields" his "members" or faculties to God and ceases to use them himself (based on a false understanding of Romans 6:13), thereby falls into passivity, which enables evil spirits to deceive and influence any part of his being that has become passive.

The kind of deception connected with passive surrender may be seen in the following example. A believer surrenders his arm to God. He permits it to hang passively, waiting for God to use it. He is asked, "Why do you not use your arm?" and replies, "I have surrendered it to God. I must not use it now; God must use it." But will God lift the arm for the man? No, the man himself must lift it, and use it, while seeking to understand intelligently the mind of God in doing so.

The word *passivity* simply describes the condition opposite to activity; and in the experience of the believer it means, briefly, loss of self-control, in the sense of the person himself controlling any or all of his mental or physical faculties; and loss of free will, in the sense of the person himself exercising his will as the guiding principle of personal control, in harmony with the will of God.

The danger of passivity comes when the powers of darkness take advantage of the passive condition. Apart from these evil forces and their workings through the passive person, passivity is merely inactivity, or idleness. In normal inactivity, the inactive person is always holding himself ready for activity, whereas in passivity, which has given place to the powers of darkness, the passive person is unable to act by his own volition.

GOD REQUIRES INTELLIGENT ACTION

The chief condition, therefore, for the working of evil spirits in human beings, apart from sin, is passivity. This is exactly the opposite of the condition that God requires from His children in order to work in them. Along with surrendering his will to God and actively choosing to do His will as it may be revealed to him, God requires a believer to cooperate with His Spirit and to fully use every faculty of the whole man. In brief, the powers of darkness aim at obtaining a passive slave, or captive, to their will. God desires a regenerated man, intelligently and actively willing and choosing and doing His will, with a spirit, soul, and body liberated from slavery.

The powers of darkness would make a man a machine, a tool, a robot; the God of holiness and love desires to make him a free, intelligent sovereign in his own sphere—a thinking, rational, renewed creation, created after His own image. (See Ephesians 4:24.) Therefore, God never says to any faculty of man, "Be idle."

God does not need or demand nonactivity in the believer in order to work in and through him, but evil spirits demand the utmost nonactivity and passivity. God asks for intelligent action (see Romans 12:1-2, "your reasonable service") in cooperation with Him. Satan demands passivity as a condition for his compulsory action, and in order to compulsorily subject men to his will and purpose.

God requires believers to stop any evil actions, primarily because they are sinful, and secondarily

88

because they hinder cooperation with His Spirit. Passivity must not be confused with quietness, or the "meek and quiet spirit" which, in the sight of God, is "of great price." (See 1 Peter 3:4.) Quietness of spirit, heart, mind, manner, voice, and expression may be coexistent with the most effective activity in the will of God. (See 1 Thessalonians 4:11.)

SURRENDER OR PASSIVITY?

Ironically, people who are open to passivity are those who become fully surrendered to God and are brought into direct contact with the supernatural world by receiving the baptism of the Holy Spirit. There are some who use the word *surrender*, and think they are surrendered to fully carry out the will of God, but are only so in sentiment and purpose; for actually they walk by the reason and judgment of the natural man, although they submit all their plans to God, and, because of this submission, sincerely believe they are carrying out His will. But those who are really surrendered give themselves up to implicitly obey, and carry out at all costs, what is revealed to them supernaturally as from God, and not what they themselves plan and reason out to be the will of God.

Again, believers who surrender their wills and all that they have and are to God, yet who walk by the use of their natural minds, are not the ones who are open to the passivity that gives ground to evil spirits, although they may, and do, give ground to them in other ways. These belong to the first group of believers described below.

Group One are surrendered in will but not truly surrendered in the sense of being ready to carry out obedience to the Holy Spirit at all costs. They consequently know little of conflict, and nothing of the Devil, except as a tempter or accuser. They do not understand those who speak of the "onslaughts of Satan," for, they say, they are not attacked in this way. But the Devil does not always attack when he can. He reserves his attack until it suits him. If the Devil does not attack a man, it does not prove that he could not.

Group Two are believers who are surrendered in such a measure of abandonment that they are ready to obey the Spirit of God at all costs, with the result that they become open to a passivity that gives ground for the deception and possession of evil spirits. These surrendered believers fall into passivity after the baptism of the Holy Spirit because of their determination to carry out their surrender at all costs; because of their relationship with the spiritual world, which opens them to supernatural communications that they believe to be all of God; and because of their surrender, which leads them to submit, subdue, and make all things subservient to this supernatural plane.

WRONG INTERPRETATION OF SCRIPTURE

The origin of the passivity that gives evil spirits an opportunity to deceive is generally a wrong interpretation of Scripture, or wrong thoughts or beliefs about divine things, some of which we have already referred to in the previous chapter. Passivity may affect the whole man, in his will, mind, spirit, and body, when it has become very deep and is of many years' standing. The progress is generally very gradual and insidious in growth, and consequently, the release from it is gradual and slow.

The *will* is the helm, so to speak, of our lives. Passivity of the will originates from a wrong conception of what full surrender to God means. Thinking that a surrendered will to God means no use of the will at all, the believer ceases to choose, determine, and act on his own volition. The serious effect of this is that he is not allowed by the powers of darkness to discover his state, for at first the consequences are trivial and scarcely noticeable. In fact, at first it appears to be most glorifying to God. The strong-willed person suddenly becomes passively yielding. He thinks that God is "will"-ing for him in circumstances and through people, and so he becomes passively helpless in action. After a time, no choice can be gotten from him in matters of daily life, no decision, or initiative, in matters demanding action. He is afraid to express a wish, much less a decision. Others must choose, act, lead, decide, while the person drifts as a cork upon the waters.

Later on, the powers of darkness begin to make capital out of this surrendered believer and to work around him evil of various kinds, which entangles him through his passivity of will. He now has no power of will to protest or resist. Things going on around him that are obviously wrong, and which this believer alone has a right to deal with, flourish and grow strong and blatant. The powers of darkness have slowly gained—in him personally and through external circumstances—upon the ground of the passivity of his will, which at first was merely passive submission to his environment, under the idea that God was "will"-ing for him in all things around him. The

Scripture verse that such believers misinterpret is Philippians 2:13: "For it is God which worketh in you both to will and to do of His good pleasure." The passive person reads it, "God who works in me the willing and the doing," i.e., "wills instead of me."

The verse means that God works in the soul up to the point of the action of the will. However, the person who is in passivity assumes that He actually wills instead of and acts instead of the believer. This wrong interpretation causes people not to use their wills because they conclude, "God wills instead of me," and this brings about passivity of will. The truth to be emphasized is that God never wills instead of man, and whatever a man does, he is himself responsible for his actions.

The believer whose will has become passive finds, after a time, the greatest difficulty in making decisions of any kind, and he looks outside and all around him for something to help him to decide the smallest matters. When he has become conscious of his passive condition, he has a painful sense of being unable to meet some of the situations of ordinary life. The tactic of the Enemy now may be to drive him into situations where these demands may be made, and thus torture or embarrass him before others.

Little does the believer know that in this condition he may, unknowingly, rely upon the assistance of evil spirits who have brought about the passivity for this very purpose. The unused faculty of the will lies dormant and dead in their grip, but if used, it is an occasion for them to manifest themselves through it. They are too ready to "will" instead of the person, and they will put within his reach many supernatural props to help him in his "decision," especially Scripture texts used apart from their context and supernaturally given, which the believer, seeking longingly to do the will of God, seizes upon and firmly grasps as a drowning man does a rope. He is blinded, by the apparently divinely-given help, to the principle that God only works through the active volition of a man, and not for him in matters requiring his action.

PASSIVITY OF THE MIND

Passivity of the mind is produced by a wrong conception of the place of the mind in the life of surrender to God and obedience to Him in the Holy Spirit. Christ's call of unschooled fishermen is used as an excuse for passivity of the mind, for some believers say that God has no need for the use of the brain and can do without it! But God's choice of Paul, who had the greatest intellect of his age, shows that when God sought a man through whom He could lay the foundations of the church, He chose one with a mind capable of vast and intelligent thinking. The greater the brain power, the greater the use God can make of it, provided it is submissive to truth.

Passivity of mind is sometimes caused by the idea that using the brain is a hindrance to the development of the divine life in the believer. However, the truth is that the nonworking of the brain hinders, the evil working of the brain hinders, but the normal and pure working of the brain is essential, and helpful, for cooperation with God. This is dealt with fully in chapter eight, where we examine the various tactics of the powers of darkness in their efforts to get the mind into a condition of passivity, and therefore incapable of action to discern their wiles.

The effects of passivity of the mind may be seen in inactivity when there should be action; overactivity beyond control, which seems to suddenly break out into ungovernable action; hesitation, or rashness; indecision (similar to that of a passive will); unwatchfulness; lack of concentration; lack of judgment; and bad memory. Along with passivity of the mind is passivity of the imagination, which places the imagination outside personal control and at the mercy of evil spirits who throw at it what they please. One danger is to take these visions, and call them "imaginations."

Passivity does not change the nature of a faculty; rather, it hinders its normal operation. In pure inactivity of the mind, the mind can be used at the will of the person, but in evil passivity of the mind, the person is helpless and says he cannot think. He feels as if his mind were bound, and held by a weight or pressure on his head.

PASSIVITY OF JUDGMENT AND REASON

The person in this condition has closed his mind to all arguments and statements upon which he has come to settled conclusions; all efforts to give him further truth and spiritual insight are regarded as interference, and the person attempting to give them is considered ignorant, or intrusive. The believer in this stage of passivity lapses into a state of evil confidence and has feelings of infallibility, and nothing can release his judgment and reason but the rude shock of seeing that he has been deceived and influenced by evil spirits. A believer in this condition almost needs to reestablish the very foundations of his spiritual life in order to overcome his deception. That is why we have the few—called "fanatics" and "cranks" by the world—who have been saved out of this degree of the deception of the Enemy.

Passivity of the reasoning powers occurs when believers have accepted words spoken to them supernaturally as if they were God's expressed will, and have taken them as law, so that they cannot be persuaded to reason over them. If they receive a "commandment" (supernaturally) about anything, they will not examine it or think it over, and they steadfastly determine to absolutely close themselves off from any further spiritual wisdom in this area. This brings about what may be described as "passivity of conscience."

PASSIVITY OF CONSCIENCE

The conscience becomes passive when believers think that they are being guided by a higher law of being told to do this or that directly from God, that is, by direct guidance through voices and Scripture texts.

When believers sink into passivity of conscience, there is a manifestation of moral degradation in some and stagnation in others, or there is regression in life or service. Instead of using their minds or conscience in deciding what is good and evil, and right and wrong, they walk, as they believe, according to the "voice of God," which they make the deciding factor in all their decisions. When this takes place, they will not listen to their reason or conscience or the words of others, and having come to a decision through the supposed direction of God, their minds become as a closed and sealed book on the matter in question.

Ceasing to use their true reasoning powers, they become open to all kinds of suggestions from evil spirits, and false reasonings. For example, in regard to the coming of Christ, some have falsely reasoned that because Christ is coming soon they do not need to carry on their usual work, overlooking the words of the Lord on this very matter:

> Who then is a faithful and wise servant, whom his lord hath made ruler over his household, to give them meat in due season? Blessed is that servant, whom his lord when he cometh shall find so doing.
>
> (Matt. 24:45–46)

Because of what he will gain through it, therefore, the Devil will do anything to engender passivity in any form whatsoever: in spirit, mind, or body.

PASSIVITY OF THE SPIRIT

Passivity of the spirit is closely associated with passivity of the mind because there is a close relationship between mind and spirit; a wrong thought generally means a wrong spirit, and vice versa. The human spirit is often spoken of in the Scriptures as having activities and is described as being in various conditions. It can be moved or be inactive; it can be loosed, bound, depressed, faint, free, and moved from three sources: God, the Devil, or the man himself. It can be pure, filthy (2 Cor. 7:1), or in a mixed condition.

By the cleansing power of the blood of Christ (1 John 1:9) and the indwelling of the Holy Spirit (John 20:22), the spirit is brought into union with Christ (1 Cor. 6:17) and should actively dominate a person in full cooperation with the Holy Spirit. But passivity of spirit can be brought about by so many causes that a believer may be scarcely conscious of having any spirit at all. Or, through the baptism of the Holy Spirit, which releases the human spirit into freedom and buoyancy, a person may become acutely conscious of the spirit life for a season, and, afterwards, unknowingly sink into passivity of spirit. This condition means absolute powerlessness in the believer's warfare with the powers of darkness. For, full liberty and use of the spirit in coworking with the indwelling Holy Spirit, is a supreme essential for personal victory, and for wielding the authority of Christ over the powers of evil. (See the example of Paul in Acts 13:9–10.)

Again, passivity of spirit generally follows the baptism of the Spirit. The will and the mind become passive through lack of use, and the believer then wonders why he has lost the buoyant light and liberty of his joyous experience.

There are four ways this may come about. First, through ignorance of the laws of the spirit and how to keep in the freedom of the spirit.

Secondly, through wrong mental conclusions or wrong thoughts, and not knowing what feelings are physical, soulish, or spiritual. For example, a person may attribute to the spiritual what is soulish and physical, or attribute to the spiritual that which is natural and physical.

Thirdly, through drawing upon the soulish life instead of the spirit, through a lack of knowledge of the difference between them, and by quenching the spirit through ignoring the spiritual sense. For the mind should be able to read the sense of the spirit as clearly as it does all the senses of the body. There is a knowledge of the mind and a knowledge in the spirit. There is also a "sense" of the spirit, which we should learn to understand. It should be read, used, and cultivated, and when there is a weight on the spirit, we should be able to recognize it and know how to get rid of it.

Lastly, through drainage and exhaustion of the mind or body by constant and excessive activity of the mind. In short, the mind and body must be released from strain before the spirit can be fully operative. (Compare the experience of Elijah in 1 Kings 19:4–5, 8–9.) Worry or trouble over the past or future inhibits the free action of the spirit by making the outer man and outer affairs dominant; it keeps the inner man from being at liberty for the will of God at the moment.

The result of all these is that the spirit becomes locked up, so to speak, so that it cannot act or fight against the powers of darkness, either in their indirect attacks through the environment or in aggressive warfare against them. A believer can sink into passivity at any moment when the resisting attitude ceases, as fast as a stone sinks in water.

PASSIVITY OF THE BODY

This condition practically means a cessation of consciousness, as passivity affects sight, hearing, smell, taste, and feeling. Assuming a person is in normal health, he should be able to focus his eyes on any object he chooses, either for vision or work, and he should have the same control over all the other senses, as avenues of knowledge to his mind and spirit.

But with all, or some, of these senses in a passive condition, the consciousness becomes dulled or deadened. The believer is unconscious of what he should be keenly alive to, and is automatic in his actions. Unconscious habits, repulsive or peculiar, are manifested. It is easier for persons in this condition to see these things in others than to know what is going on in themselves, while they may be hyperconscious of external things relating to their own personality.

When the passive condition brought about by evil spirits reaches its climax, passivity of other parts of the body may result, such as stiff fingers, lost elasticity of the frame in walking, lethargy, heaviness, stooping of the back and spine. The handshake is flabby and passive, the eyes will not look straight into the eyes of others, but move from side to side, all indicating passivity brought about by deepening interference of the powers of darkness with the whole man, resulting from the initial passive condition of the will and mind, in which the person gave up his self-control and the use of his will.

At this stage, every department of the whole being is affected. The person acts without using, or using fully, the mind, will, imagination, or reason—that is, without thinking (volitionally), deciding, imagining, reasoning. The affections, as well as all the faculties of mind and body, seem dormant. In some cases, bodily needs are also dormant, or else the person suppresses them and deprives himself of food, sleep, and bodily comfort at the dictation of the spirits in control, thus carrying out a severity to the body that is not of any real value against the indulgence of the flesh. (See Colossians 2:23.) The animal part of the person may also be awakened, and while he is stoical in sensibilities and feeling, he may be gluttonous in his demand to have his bodily needs supplied. That is, the machinery of his bodily frame goes on working independently of the control of his mind or will, for the body now dominates his spirit and soul.

Men may live in the body, soul, or (human) spirit. For example, the glutton lives in, or after, the body; the student, in the mind, or soul; the spiritual man, "in the spirit." Incidentally, spiritualists are not really spiritual, for they generally live in the sense realm. They only deal with the "spirit" through their contact with evil spiritual forces, by understanding the laws through which they work and fulfilling them.

When the believer is in any degree oppressed by evil spirits, he is liable to live in the body, to give way to the sensuous, and to be dominated by the physical realm. This can become the case through "spiritual" experiences felt in the physical frame, but which are not really spiritual because they are not from the spirit. A sense of fire in the body, "glow," "thrills," and all exquisite bodily sensations from apparently spiritual causes, really feed the senses; and, unconsciously to themselves, while they have these experiences, believers live in the sense realm, practically walking "after the flesh" (Rom. 8:4–5), though they call themselves spiritual. Bringing the body into subjection (1 Cor. 9:27) is practically impossible because the sense life is aroused in all kinds of ways and the sensations of the body are forced upon the consciousness of the person. The spirit sense is practically lost in the acute realization of all the sensations in the bodily consciousness.

RECOGNIZING PASSIVITY

The cultivation of this condition of passivity may be ignorantly and actively carried out for years by the believer, so that it deepens its hold upon him to an incredible extent until, when it reaches its highest point, he may be so under the bondage of it that he awakens to his state. He may then think that natural causes alone explain his condition, or that, in some unaccountable way, his acute sensitivity to God and divine things has become dulled beyond the power of restoration or renewal. The physical feelings become deadened or atrophied, and the affections seem petrified and stoical. This is the time when deceiving spirits suggest that he has grieved God beyond repair, and he goes through agonies of seeking the presence of God that he thinks he has grieved away.

The cultivation of passivity may come about when a person relies upon the many helps he has unknowingly contrived to counteract or prevent the inconvenience of the passive state, such as the provision of, and dependence upon, outward helps to the eye for assisting the passive memory; utterance in speech to assist the thinking of the passive mind; and what may be termed "crutches" of all kinds, known only to the individual, elaborately constructed and multiplied to meet his different needs, but all of which keep him from recognizing his true condition, even if he has the knowledge to do so.

But this truth about the working of evil spirits among believers, and the causes and symptoms of their power upon mind or body, has been so veiled in ignorance that multitudes of children of God are held in bondage to their power without knowing it. The manifestations are generally taken as natural idiosyncrasies or infirmities. The believer puts the Lord's work to one side, or never even takes it up, because he is "overstrained," or "without gifts" for doing it. He is "nervous," "timid," has no "gift of speech," no "power of thought" where the service of God is concerned. However, in the social sphere these apparent deficiencies are forgotten, and the "timid" ones shine out at their best. It does not occur to them to ask why it is that they are so incapable only in God's service. But it is only in respect to such a service that the hidden workings of Satan interfere.

The shock is great when the believer first comprehends the truth that deception and oppression are possible in himself. Yet, as the ultimate issue is realized, the joy of the one who sets himself to understand and fight through to full deliverance, is more than words can tell. Light pours in upon the unsolved problems of years, both in his personal experience and in the perplexities of his environment, as well as on conditions in the church and in the world.

As the open-minded believer seeks light from God, the subtle inroads of the deceiving spirits into his life slowly become clear; and their many devices to deceive him stand revealed, as the searchlight of truth goes far back into the past, revealing the cause of unaccountable difficulties in experience and life and many mysterious happenings that had been accepted as "the inscrutable will of God."

Passivity! How many have fallen into it, little knowing their state. Through passivity, much time is lost as people become dependent upon the help of outward circumstances and environment. In the lives of so many there is much "doing," with so little accomplished—many beginnings, and few endings.

WHY ARE CHRISTIANS APATHETIC?

How familiar we are with the words, "Yes, I can do that." A passive person may be inspired and motivated, but by the time the need for action comes, he has lost his momentary interest. This is the key to much of the lamented apathy and dulled sympathy of Christians to really spiritual things, while they are keenly alive to the social or worldly elements around them. The unbeliever can be stirred with deep feeling for the sufferings of others, but many of the children of God have, unknowingly, opened themselves to a supernatural power which has dulled them in thought and mind and sympathy. Always craving comfort and happiness and peace in spiritual things, they have sung themselves into a passivity, that is, a passive state of "rest" and "peace," which has given the powers of darkness an opportunity to lock them up in the prison of themselves and to make them almost incapable of clearly understanding the needs of a suffering world.

This condition of passivity may come about by wrong interpretations of truth, even the truth of "death with Christ" set forth in Romans 6 and Galatians 2:20, when it is carried beyond the true balance of the Word of God. God calls upon true believers to "reckon" themselves "dead indeed unto sin" (Rom. 6:11) and also to the evil self-life, even in a religious form. That is, to consider themselves dead to the life that came from the first Adam, the old creation. However, this does not mean a death to the human personality, for Paul said, "Nevertheless I live," although, "Christ liveth in me" (Gal. 2:20). There is a retention of the personal being, the ego, the will, the personality, which is to be dominated by the Spirit of God as He energizes the man's individuality, held by him in "temperance" (Gal. 5:23) or self-control.

In light of the fact that some believers misunderstand the concept of death with Christ, thinking that it means passivity and suppression of the actions of the personality, it is easy to see why a false application of the truths connected with Romans 6 and Galatians 2:20 have been the prelude, in some cases, to supernatural manifestations of the powers of darkness. The believer, through the misconception of these truths, actually fulfills the primary conditions for the working of evil spirits. These are the very conditions understood by spiritualist mediums to be necessary for obtaining the manifestations they desire. In such cases it may be said that truth is the Devil's fulcrum for launching his lies.

The powers of darkness are defeated as long as Romans 6 is understood to be a momentary declaration of an attitude to sin, as long as Galatians 2:20 is considered another declaration of an attitude to God, and as long as 2 Corinthians 4:10–12 and Philippians 3:10 are seen to be the outworking of the Spirit of God in bringing the believer into actual conformity to the death of Christ as he maintains these attitudes. For this moment-by-moment declared attitude demands an active decision of the will, active cooperation with the risen Lord, and active acceptance of the path of the Cross.

But when these truths are interpreted to mean a loss of personality, an absence of will and self-control, and a passive letting go into a condition of mechanical, automatic obedience, which the believer thinks is mortification or the working of death in him, it distorts the truth of death with Christ into a fulfillment of conditions for evil spirits to work, and causes an absence of conditions upon which God can alone work. In this way, supernatural manifestations, which take place on the basis of passivity, can have no other source than lying spirits, however beautiful and godlike they may be. This counterfeit of death to self may be manifest in regard to spirit, soul, or body. How the truth of death with Christ can be misconstrued, and made the occasion for evil spirits to gain the foothold of passivity, may be seen in some of the following ways.

MISCONCEPTION OF SELF-EFFACEMENT

A believer who understands surrender of self to God in terms of self-effacement, self-renunciation, and almost self-annihilation, aims at an unconsciousness of personality; personal needs; personal states, feelings, desires; external appearance, circumstances, discomforts, opinions of others, etc., in order to be conscious of God alone moving, working, and acting through him. To this end he gives his self-consciousness over to death and prays that he might have no consciousness of anything in the world, except the presence of God. Then, in order to carry out this absolute surrender of self to death and this entire self-effacement, he consistently, in practice, yields to death every trace of the movement of self he becomes aware of and sets his will steadily to renounce all consciousness of personal wishes, desires, tastes, needs, feelings, etc.

All this appears to be so "self-sacrificing" and "spiritual" but really results in an entire suppression of his personality and gives a foothold to evil spirits through a passivity of his whole being. This permits the powers of darkness to work and to bring about an unconsciousness that becomes, in time, a deadness and dullness of the sensibilities and an inability to feel, not only for himself, but for others, so that he does not to know when they suffer or when he himself causes suffering.

This conception of self-effacement and loss of self-consciousness is the exact opposite of a believer's full use of his faculties, which the Spirit of God requires for cooperation with Him. Therefore, evil spirits gain ground on the basis of this deception about death to self. This occurs because the person is ignorant of the possibility of being deceived when he is in wholehearted surrender to God. Yet, he has actually accepted a subtly-given "doctrine of devils." (See 1 Timothy 4:1.) The teachings of demons can, therefore, be based on truth that is misunderstood or misinterpreted, even while the believer is honestly holding the truth itself.

The unconsciousness produced by evil spirits is hard to break. In this state, a believer has no ability to discern, recognize, feel, or know things around him, or in himself. He is unconscious of his actions, ways, and manners, and has a "hyperself-consciousness" that he does not recognize in himself, and which makes him easily hurt. However, he is not aware when he hurts others. He has practically become stoical, unable to see the effect of his actions in causing others to suffer. He acts without exercising his will in thinking, reasoning, imagining, and deciding what he says and does. His actions are consequently mechanical and automatic. He is unconscious of sometimes being a channel for the transmission of words, thoughts, and feelings that pass through him apart from the action of his will and his knowledge of the source.

"Unconsciousness" becomes a formidable stumbling block to deliverance, for the evil spirits may hold, hinder, attack, divert, suggest, impress, draw, or do any other equally offensive and injurious thing, in or through the person, while he is unaware of their workings.

WRONG ACCEPTANCE OF SUFFERING

The believer consents to accept "suffering with Christ" in the "way of the Cross" (see 1 Peter 4:1), and, in fulfillment of this surrender, passively yields to suffering in whatever form it may come, believing that suffering with Christ means reward and fruitfulness. He does not know that evil spirits can give counterfeit suffering, and that he may accept suffering from them, believing it to be from the hand of God, and, by so doing, may give ground to them.

Oppression explains both sin that cannot be gotten rid of and suffering that cannot be explained. By understanding the truth, the first can be gotten rid of, and the second explained. Suffering is a great weapon to control and compel a person into a certain course. In this way, it is a great weapon for evil spirits to control people, because through suffering they can drive someone to do what he would not do, apart from its compulsion.

Not knowing these things, the believer may entirely misinterpret the suffering he goes through. Believers are often deceived over what they think is "vicarious" suffering for others or for the church. They look upon themselves as martyrs when they are really victims, not knowing that suffering is one of the chief symptoms of oppression.

Suffering directly caused by evil spirits may be distinguished from the true fellowship of Christ's sufferings by a complete absence of result, either in fruit, victory, or ripening of spiritual growth. If carefully observed, it will be seen to be entirely purposeless. On the other hand, God does nothing without a definite purpose. He does not delight in causing suffering for the sake of suffering, but the Devil does. Suffering caused by evil spirits is acute and diabolical in character, and there is no inward witness of the Spirit that tells the suffering believer that it is from the hand of God. To a discriminating eye, it can be as clearly diagnosed as coming from an evil spirit as any physical pain can be discriminated from a mental one by a skillful physician.

The suffering caused by evil spirits can be spiritual, by causing acute suffering in the spirit, injecting repugnant or poignant "feelings" into the spirit; soulish, by bringing acute darkness, confusion, chaos, horror in the mind, or anguished, knifelike pain in the heart or other innermost vital parts of the being; or physical, in any part of the body.

The ground given for evil spirits to produce counterfeit suffering in such an acute degree as this may be traced back to the time when the believer, in his absolute surrender to God for the "way of the Cross," deliberately willed to accept suffering from Him. Then, afterwards, in fulfillment of this surrender, he gave ground to the Enemy by accepting some specific suffering as if it were from God, suffering that really came from the spirits of evil. In this way, the believer opened the door to them by receiving their lie and admitting their actual power, manifested in the suffering (and by continuing to give more ground by believing their interpretation of the suffering as "the will of God"), until his whole life became one prolonged "yielding to suffering" that seemed unreasonable, unaccountable in its origin, and purposeless in its results. In this way,

God's character is often slandered to His children, and the deceiving spirits do their utmost to arouse rebellion against Him for what they themselves are doing.

WRONG IDEAS OF HUMILITY

When a believer consents to accept "death," so that he allows it be carried out in his life in a kind of "nothingness" and self-effacement, this gives him no opportunity for proper and true self-estimation whatsoever. (Compare 2 Corinthians 10:12–18.) If the believer accepts the self-depreciation, suggested to him and created by evil spirits, it brings an atmosphere of hopelessness and weakness about him, and he conveys to others a spirit of darkness and heaviness, sadness and grief. His spirit is easily crushed, wounded, and depressed. He may attribute the cause to sin, without being aware of any specific sin in his life; or he may even look upon his suffering experience as vicarious suffering for the church, whereas an abnormal sense of suffering is one of the chief symptoms of oppression.

This counterfeit of the true elimination of pride may be recognized by (1) the believer imposing his self-depreciation at very inopportune moments, bringing a painful perplexity to those who hear it; (2) a shrinking back from service for God, with an inability to recognize the interests of the kingdom of Christ; (3) a laborious effort to keep "I" out of sight, both in conversation and action, which actually forces the "I" more into view in an objectionable form; (4) a deprecatory, apologizing manner, which gives opportunity to the "rulers of the darkness of this world" (Eph. 6:12) to instigate their subjects to crush and put aside this "not I" person in moments of strategic importance to the kingdom of God; and (5) an atmosphere of weakness, darkness, sadness, grief, lack of hope, easily-wounded touchiness. All of these conditions may be the result of the believer's willingness, in some moment of "surrender to death," to accept an effacement of his true personality, because he knows that God requires the personality to be a vessel for the manifestation of the Spirit of Christ. The believer, by his wrong understanding and submission to evil spirits, suppresses into passivity a personality that could not, and was not meant to, "die." Then, through this passivity, he opens the door to the powers of darkness to gain ground for oppression.

A WRONG CONCEPT OF WEAKNESS

This occurs when a believer consents to a perpetual condition of weakness, under the misconception that it is a necessary state for the manifestation of divine life and strength. This false concept is generally based upon Paul's words, "*When* I am weak, then am I strong" (2 Cor. 12:10, italics added). The believer does not comprehend that the apostle was simply stating that when he was weak, he found God's strength to be sufficient for doing all His will. It is not an exhortation to God's children to deliberately will to be weak, and therefore to be unfit for service in many ways, instead of saying, "I can do all things through Christ which strengtheneth me" (Phil. 4:13). That the will to be weak in order to have a claim on Christ's strength is a wrong idea, can be seen in many people's lives, where weakness is passively accepted and results in these people becoming a burden and care to others. This clearly shows that such an attitude is not in accordance with God's plan and provision. The will to be weak actually hinders God's strengthening, and by this subtle deception of the Enemy in the minds of many, God is robbed of much active service for Him. By this attitude the believer thought he would ascend to a higher plane of spiritual life, but when he eventually discovers the truth, he has a battle to recover his true normal condition.

PASSIVITY COMBINED WITH SATANIC ACTIVITY

Passivity in its full extent does not mean "no activity," for once a person becomes passive in volition and mind, he is either held by deceiving spirits without any power to act or is driven into satanic activity, that is, uncontrollable activity of thought, restlessness of body, and wild, unbalanced action of all degrees. The actions are fitful and intermittent; the person sometimes dashes ahead, and at other times is sluggish and slow like a machine in a factory, with the wheels whirring aimlessly, because the switch at the center control is out of the hand of the master. The man cannot work, even when he sees so much to be done, and is feverish because he cannot do it. During the time of passivity, he appears to be content; but when he is driven into satanic activity, he is restless and out of accord with all things around him. When his environment should lead to a state of full contentment, something (may it not be "somebody"?) makes it impossible for him to be in harmony with his external circumstances, however pleasant they may be. He is conscious of a restlessness and activity that is painfully feverish, or

111

of passivity and weight from doing "work" and yet no work: all manifestations of a demoniacal destruction of his peace.

WHAT IS NORMAL?

The believer needing deliverance from the condition of passivity must first seek to understand what should be his normal or right condition, and then examine himself in light of it to discern if evil spirits have been interfering. To do this, let him recollect a moment in his life that he would call his "best," either in spirit, soul, or body, or in his whole being; and then let him look upon this as his normal condition that he should expect is possible to be maintained, and never rest satisfied below it.

As the passivity has come about gradually, it can only end gradually, as it is detected and destroyed. The full cooperation of the person is necessary for its removal, and this is the reason for the long period needed for deliverance. Deception and passivity can only be removed as he understands his condition, refuses to give ground, and rejects the deception which came through his giving ground in the past.

It is important to keep the standard of the normal condition perpetually in mind. If at any time the believer drops below it, the cause must be discovered in order to remove it. Whatever faculty or part of the being has been surrendered into passivity, and therefore lost for use, must be retaken by the active exercise of the will, and brought back into personal control.

The believer must maintain a steady resistance to the spirits of evil, remembering that the powers of darkness fight against the loss of any part of their kingdom in man as much as any earthly government would fight to protect its own territory and subjects. Yet the "stronger than he" (Luke 11:22) is the Conqueror, and He strengthens the believer for the battle and to recover all the spoil. The way that the "stronger" than the "strong man" works with the believer in practical deliverance, we will deal with later on.

Chapter 6

Discerning Good and Evil

*But strong meat belongeth to them that are of full
age, even those who by reason of use have their
senses exercised to discern both good and evil.*
—Hebrews 5:14

The following is a glimpse into the mixed
manifestations that have come upon the
church of God since the revival in Wales.
For almost without exception, in every land where
revival has since broken forth, a counterfeit
stream has mingled with the true within a very
brief period of time. And almost without exception,
true and false have been accepted together because
people are ignorant of the possibility of concurrent
streams.

Sometimes both true and false have been rejected by those who could not detect one from the
other; or, it has been believed that there was no
"true" at all because the majority of believers fail
to understand that there can be mixed workings of
the divine and satanic, divine and human, satanic
and human, soul and spirit, soul and body, and
body and spirit: the three former in regard to
source and power, and the three latter in regard to
feelings and consciousness.

Therefore, it is vitally important that believers
know how to discern good and evil. Multitudes are
oppressed in various degrees but do not know it because they attribute the manifestations to natural
causes, or to self or sin, and they attribute them to
these causes because they do not appear to bear the
characteristics of demoniacal attack. In some cases,

the counterfeit manifestations have been accepted with such reckless abandonment that deception has quickly developed into oppression in a most acute, yet subtle and highly refined, form. There is no apparent trace of the presence of evil, yet the peculiar "double personality," characteristic of fully developed demon possession, is easily recognizable to trained spiritual discernment, although it may be hidden under the guise of the most beautiful "angel of light" manifestation, with all the fascinating attraction of "glory light" upon the face, exquisite music in song, and powerful effect in speech.

The dual personality of fully developed demon possession is generally only recognized when it takes the form of objectionable manifestations, such as when a distinct other-intelligence obscures the personality of the possessed one and speaks through the vocal organs in a distinctly separate or altered voice, expressing thoughts or words unintended or only partially willed by the subject. The victim is compelled to act in ways contrary to his natural character, the body is manipulated by a foreign power, and nerves and muscles are twisted in contortions and convulsions, such as are described in the Scripture records. (See Luke 9:39.) Another characteristic of the dual personality of demon possession is that the manifestations are usually periodic and the victim is comparatively natural and normal between what are described as attacks, but which are really periods of manifestations of the intruding power.

Evidences are now available that prove that this dual personality has taken place in believers who are not disobedient to light or yielding to any known sin, but who have become oppressed through deception in their abandonment to supernatural power which they believed to be of God. Again, such cases have all the symptoms and manifestations described in the gospel records. The demon answers questions in his own voice, and speaks words of blasphemy against God through the person while that person is, in spirit, in peace and fellowship with God. This shows that the Holy Spirit is in the believer's spirit, and that the demon or demons are in his body, using the tongue and throwing the body about at their will.

This same dual personality, under entirely different manifestations, is easily recognizable by any who have the "discerning of spirits" (1 Cor. 12:10). Sometimes the environment of the person is more favorable than at other times for the spirit manifestations, and then they can be detected in both beautiful and objectionable forms.

These facts destroy the theory that only people in "heathen" countries, or persons deep in sin, can be "possessed" or oppressed by evil spirits. This unexamined, unproved theory in the minds of believers, serves the Devil well as a cover for his activities to gain possession of the minds and bodies of Christians in the present time. But the veil is being stripped off the eyes of the children of God by the hard path of experience. Knowledge is dawning upon the awakened section of the church that a believer, baptized in Holy Spirit, and indwelt by God in the inner shrine of the spirit, can be deceived into admitting evil spirits, and be oppressed, in varying degrees, by demons.

TWO SOURCES OF POWER

From such believers there can proceed, at intervals, streams from the two sources of power—one from the Spirit of God in the center, and the other from an evil spirit in the outer man—with two parallel results to those who come in contact with the two streams of power. In preaching, all the truth spoken by such a believer may be of God, and, according to the Scriptures, correct and full of light—since the spirit of the man is right. But in the meantime, evil spirits may be working in his mind or body, making use of the cover of the truth to insert their manifestations, so that their deceptions will find acceptance with both speaker and hearers. In other words, there may pour through a believer, at one moment, a stream of truth from the Word, giving light and love and blessing to receptive ones among the listeners; and the next moment, a foreign spirit may send forth a streamlet through the soulish or physical part of the man, producing corresponding effects in soul or body among the listeners, who respond in their soulish or physical part to the satanic stream, either by emotional or physical manifestations, or in nervous or muscular actions.

One or the other of the streams of power, from the Holy Spirit in his spirit or from the deceiving spirit, may predominate at different times, thus making the same man appear dual in character at different periods of time. "See how he speaks! How he seeks to glorify God! How sane and reasonable he is! What a passion he has for souls!" may be said with truth about a worker, until some moments later some peculiar change is seen in him, and in the meeting. A strange element comes in, possibly only recognizable to some with keen spiritual vision, or else plainly obvious to all. Perhaps the speaker begins to pray quietly and calmly, with a pure spirit, but suddenly the voice is raised, it sounds hollow or has a metallic tone, the tension of the meeting increases, an overwhelming, overmastering "power" falls upon it, and no one thinks of resisting what appears to be such a manifestation of God!

The majority of those present may have no idea of the mixture that has crept in. Some fall upon the ground unable to bear the strained emotion, or effect upon the mind, and some are thrown down by some supernatural power. Others cry out in ecstasy. The speaker leaves the platform and passes by a young man, who becomes conscious of a feeling of intoxication upon him that does not leave his senses for some time. Others laugh with the exuberance of the intoxicating joy.

Some have had real spiritual help and blessing through the Word of God which was expounded before this climax came, and during the pure outflow of the Holy Spirit; consequently, they accept these strange workings as coming from God because, in the first stage of the meeting, their needs have been truly met by Him, and they cannot discern the two separate "manifestations" coming through the same channel. If they doubt the latter part of the meeting, they fear they are untrue to their inner conviction that the earlier part was of God. Others are conscious that the manifestations are contrary to their spiritual vision and judgment; but, because of the blessing of the earlier part of the meeting, they stifle their doubts and say, "We cannot understand the physical manifestations, but we must not expect to understand all that God does. We only know that the wonderful outpouring of truth and love and light at the beginning of the meeting was from God and met our need. No one can mistake the sincerity, the pure motive of the speaker; therefore, although I cannot understand, or say I 'like' the physical manifestations, yet, it *must* be all of God...."

MIXING LIES WITH TRUTH

There must be more than one quantity to make a mixture, at least two. The Devil mixes his lies with the truth, for he must use a truth to carry his lies. The believer must therefore discriminate and judge all things. He must be able to see what is impure and what he can accept.

Again, Satan is a "mixer." If he finds anything to be ninety-nine percent pure, he tries to insert one percent of his poisonous stream, and this grows, if undetected, until the proportions are reversed. Where it is known that certain meetings will contain a mixture of good and evil when supernatural manifestations take place, believers should keep away from them until they are able to discern truth from error.

When a believer accepts satanic counterfeits, he believes he is yielding to God in order to ascend to a higher life. In reality, he is complying with conditions for satanic attacks in his life, and therefore descends into a pit of deception and suffering, even though his spirit and motive are pure.

THE WORKINGS OF EVIL SPIRITS

We will now examine how evil spirits deceive, obtain ground for deception, gain access, and keep the believer in ignorance of their presence and the ground they hold. We will also examine the effect on a deceived person and the symptoms of demonic attack. Taking these one by one, we shall see how subtly the evil spirit works, first to deceive, and then to gain access to the believer.

One principle governs both the working of God and the working of Satan in seeking access to a person. In the creation of a human being with a free will, God, who is Sovereign Lord of the universe and of all angelic powers, has limited Himself in that He does not violate man's freedom in order to obtain his allegiance. Satan's evil spirits cannot influence any part of a person aside from that person's consent, given either consciously or unconsciously. When someone "wills" a good thing, God makes it fact. In the same way, when he "wills" an evil thing, evil spirits make it fact. Both God and Satan need the will of man in order to work in man.

In the unregenerate man, the will is enslaved to Satan, but in the man who has been regenerated and delivered from the power of sin, the will is liberated to choose the things of God. In one who has been brought into fellowship with God, Satan can only gain ground by strategy, or, in biblical terms, by "wiles" (Eph. 6:11), for he knows he will never get a believer to deliberately consent to being controlled by evil spirits. The Deceiver can only hope to obtain that consent by guile. For example, he may pretend to be God Himself, or a messenger from Him. He knows that such a believer is determined to obey God at all costs and values the knowledge of God above anything else on earth. There is therefore no other way to deceive him but by counterfeiting God Himself, and His presence and workings, and, while pretending to be God, by obtaining the cooperation of the man's will in accepting further deceptions, so that he may control some part of the believer's life, injuring or hindering his usefulness to God as well as that of others who will be affected by him.

The counterfeit of God in and with the believer, is the basis on which the whole after-structure of deception is built. Believers desire and expect God to be with and in them. They expect God's presence with them, and this is counterfeited. They expect God to be in them as a person, and evil spirits counterfeit the three persons of the Trinity.

THE PRESENCE AND THE PERSON

In order to understand the counterfeiting methods of evil spirits, we must distinguish between the "presence" and the "person" of God. The presence may be described as "giving forth an influence," while the person is manifested as Father, Son, or Holy Spirit. Simply put, the distinction may be understood as the difference between God as light, and a person having light from God, or God as love, and having love from God. The One is the person Himself in His nature, and the other is the outshining, or giving forth, of what He is.

Many believe that the person of Christ is in them, but in reality, Christ *as a person* is in no man. He dwells in believers *by His Spirit*—the "Spirit of Christ" (Rom. 8:9; 1 Pet. 1:11), as they receive the "supply of the Spirit of Jesus" (Phil. 1:19).

It is necessary, also, to understand the teaching of the Scriptures on the Trinity, and the different attributes and work of each person of the Trinity, in order to discern the counterfeiting work of the Deceiver. God the Father, as a person, is in the highest heaven; His presence is manifested in men as the "Spirit of the Father." Christ the Son is in heaven as a person; His presence in men is by

His Spirit. The Holy Spirit, as the Spirit of the Father and of the Son, is on earth in the church, which is the body of Christ; He manifests the Father or the Son, in, and to, believers as they are taught by Him to comprehend the triune God. That is why Christ said to those who loved and obeyed Him, "*I*...will manifest myself" (John 14:21, italics added), and, "*We* will come...and make our abode with him" (John 14:23, italics added). This would be accomplished by the Holy Spirit who would be given on the day of Pentecost.

The person of God is in heaven. However, His *presence* is manifested on earth, in and with believers, through and by the Holy Spirit, in and to the human spirit. The spirit is the organ of the Holy Spirit for the manifested presence of God.

The believer's misconceptions of the manner in which God can be in, and with, him, and his ignorance that evil spirits can counterfeit God and divine things, form the ground upon which he can be deceived into accepting the counterfeit workings of evil spirits and give them access into and influence over his inner being.

If God, who is Spirit, can be in and with a man, evil spirits can also be in and with men, if they can obtain access by consent. Their aim and desire is possession and control. These are terms that are often used in regard to God's work in believers, but which are not really scriptural, in the way they are defined today. God "possesses" a man in the sense of ownership, and then He asks for cooperation, not control. The believer is to control himself, by cooperation in his spirit with the Spirit of God; but never does God "control" the person as a machine is controlled by a person, or by some dynamic force.

We must also make a distinction between God and divine things. All that is divine is not God Himself, just as all that is satanic is not Satan himself, and all that is human is not the man himself. Divine, satanic, and human things are those that emanate from God, Satan, and man, respectively.

These three sources must always be taken into account in everything. Guidance can be divine, satanic, or human. Obedience may be given to God, Satan, or men. Visions may have their source in God, evil spirits, or the man himself. Dreams can come from God, evil spirits, or the man's own condition. Writing, in its source, may be from God, evil spirits, or the man's own thoughts. Counterfeits by evil spirits may therefore be of God and divine things, Satan and satanic things, or men and human things.

In order to obtain control over believers who will not be attracted by sin, the deceiving spirits must first counterfeit the manifestation of the presence of God, so that under cover of this "presence" they can get their suggestions into the mind and their counterfeits accepted without question. This is their first, and sometimes their long, piece of labor. It is not always an easy task, especially when the soul has been well-grounded in the Scriptures and has learned to walk by faith upon the Word of God. Nor is it easy when the mind is sharp through use, well guarded in thought, and healthily occupied.

From the counterfeit presence comes the influence that causes the counterfeit to be accepted. Evil spirits must manufacture something to imitate the presence of God, as their presence is not, and cannot be, a counterfeit of it. The counterfeit presence is a work of theirs, made by them, but is not the manifestation of their own persons. For instance, they may give sweet or soothing feelings, or feelings of peace, love, etc., with the whispered suggestion, adapted to suit the victim, that these indicate the presence of God.

When a counterfeit presence, or influence, is accepted, they then go on to counterfeit a person, such as one of the persons of the Trinity. This deception is again adapted to the ideals or desires of the victim. If the believer is drawn to one more than another of the persons of the Trinity, the counterfeit will be of the One he is attached to most: the Father, to those who are drawn to Him; the Son, to those who think of Him as "Bridegroom" and crave love; and the Holy Spirit, to those who crave power.

Therefore, the counterfeit presence, as an influence, precedes the counterfeit of the person of God, through which evil spirits gain much ground. The period of greatest danger is, as we have already seen, at the time when a believer is seeking the baptism of the Holy Spirit, when others have told him a great deal about manifestations of God to the consciousness or some "coming upon" of the Spirit that is felt by the senses. This is the opportunity for the watching spirits.

What believer is there who does not long for the conscious presence of God and would not give up all to obtain it? How difficult it is to walk by faith when passing through the dark places of life! If the conscious presence of God is to be obtained by the baptism of the Spirit, and if there can be supernatural effects upon our senses, so that God is really *felt* to be at hand, then who would not be tempted to seek it? It seems to be an absolutely necessary equipment for service, and it appears from the Bible story of Pentecost as if the believers at that time must have physically felt this conscious presence.

Here lies the danger point that first opens the door to Satan. Working upon people's senses in the sphere of religion has long been Satan's special mode of deceiving men throughout the whole world, of which he is the god and Prince. He knows how to soothe and move and work upon the senses in every possible way and in every form of religion ever known, deceiving unregenerate men with the form of godliness, while denying its power. (See 2 Timothy 3:5.) Among truly converted and committed believers, the senses are still his way of approach. Let the soul admit a craving for beautiful emotions, happy feelings, overwhelming joy, and the idea that manifestations, or "signs," are necessary to prove the presence of God, especially in the baptism of the Spirit, and the way is open for Satan's lying spirits to deceive.

The Lord said, on the eve of His Cross, concerning the coming of the Holy Spirit to the believer, "I...will manifest myself to him" (John 14:21), but He did not say how He would fulfill His promise. To the woman at the well He said, "God is a Spirit: and they that worship him must worship him in spirit and in truth" (John 4:24). The manifestation of Christ is, therefore, to the spirit, and not in the realm of the senses or soul.

Therefore, the craving for sense-manifestation opens the door to deceiving spirits to counterfeit the real presence of Christ; but they must obtain the consent and cooperation of the believer's will, and this they seek to get under the guise of an "angel of light"—a messenger of God apparently clothed with light, not darkness, for light is the very nature and character of God.

125

The believer is deceived because of his ignorance of the principles on which God works in man, the true conditions for His manifested presence in the man's spirit, and the conditions upon which evil spirits work, especially through a passive surrender of the will, mind, and body to supernatural power. In his ignorance of the true working of God, the believer comes to depend upon Him to move on his physical being, so that He is continually manifested to the senses. He expects God to use his faculties apart from him, as a proof of His presence and control, whereas God only moves in, and through, the man himself by the active cooperation of his will—the will being the ego, or center, of the man. God does not act instead of the man, but with him.

The counterfeit presence is an influence from outside upon the believer. In some cases, it can begin not only at the time of the baptism of the Spirit, but also when a believer "practices" the "presence of God," defined as seeking the consciousness of God through one's senses. The true presence of God is not always felt by the physical senses, but in the spirit. The same is true of "feeling" the presence of evil spirits, or Satan. The spirit sense alone can discern the presence of God or Satan; the body only feels indirectly.

Evil spirits persistently disturb and besiege believers in order to gain control. They oppress their minds with some dominating idea that destroys their peace and clouds their life, or they counterfeit some divine experience that seems to come from God, and which the believer accepts without question. One dangerous form of oppression today is when evil spirits seek to gain control over a believer by counterfeiting some exterior manifestation of

God, such as a "presence" that fills the room and is felt by the physical senses; "waves of power" pouring upon, and through, the physical being; or a feeling of wind, air, or breath upon the outer man, apparently from divine sources.

COUNTERACT DECEPTION WITH TRUTH

The deliverance of persons under oppression of any degree comes from counteracting deception with truth. Deliverance comes, for example, (1) by giving people knowledge about how to detect what is of God or the Devil, through an understanding of the principles distinguishing the workings of the Holy Spirit and evil spirits; (2) by showing them that God the Holy Spirit works from within the spirit of the man, illuminating and renewing his mind and bringing the body under the believer's own control; and (3) by teaching them how to stand in Christ and to resist all besieging attacks of the powers of darkness.

Much knowledge of God and of spiritual things is needed for the deliverance of souls under the bondage of evil spirits. The main principle of deliverance is to be undeceived. Believers should therefore seek spiritual insight concerning the foothold the evil spirits have obtained, and then give it up. Evil spirits gain access through the foothold that is given to them. Likewise, it is through the removal of the foothold that they depart. It is for this reason that emphasis is placed in this book upon the understanding of truth, as it is written for the deliverance of believers who are deceived and oppressed because they have accepted counterfeits of the workings of God.

Believers should also be taught the fundamental principle of the attitude of the human will in relation to God and in relation to Satan and his deceiving spirits. The Scriptures are full of this truth. "If any man will do his will, he shall know" (John 7:17). "Whosoever will, let him take" (Rev. 22:17). Deliverance requires the active exercise of the will, which must, in reliance upon the strength of God, and in the face of all beguilements and suffering, be kept steadily set against the powers of darkness, in order to nullify previous consent to their working.

Deceiving spirits also counterfeit God in His holiness and in His righteousness. The effect in such a case is to make the believer afraid of God and to make him shrink away from, and loathe, all spiritual things. They try to terrorize those who are timid and fearful, to influence those who yearn for power, or to draw into their control those who are open to the attraction of love and happiness.

It may be said, deliberately, that it is never safe in any case to totally rely upon feeling God's presence with the physical senses. This is one reason why some who have urged upon other believers their need for a "realization of God"—meaning, a felt presence in the atmosphere or within them—have, to their grief and dismay, at some point lost the "realization" themselves and have sunk into darkness and numbness of feeling. These believers do not realize that this loss of feeling is the natural result of all supernatural manifestations to the senses; yet they look for the cause of the breakdown or deadness to spiritual things in "overstrain" or "sin," and not to the realization experience they rejoiced in.

The normal condition of a Christian's mind or body can be plainly seen in all the biblical accounts of men who were in direct communication with

God. Paul, in a "trance" (Acts 22:17–19), had full possession of his faculties and intelligent use of his mind and tongue. This is also particularly recognizable in John on Patmos. His physical being was prostrate from the weakness of the natural man in the unveiled presence of the glorified Lord; but after the quickening touch of the Master, his full intelligence was in use and his mind was clearly at work, with the ability to grasp and retain all that was being said and shown to him. (See Revelation 1:10–19.)

The difference between the biblical records of the revelations of God to men and the records of many of the supernatural manifestations today, can be seen in principles that reveal the striking contrast between pure divine working and the satanic counterfeits of God. They are the contrasting principles of the retention of the use of the will and faculties, and the loss of personal control through passivity.

Take, for example, what is called "clairvoyance" and "clairaudience"—the power to see supernatural things and to hear supernatural words. There is a true seeing and hearing and a false seeing and hearing of supernatural things, and they result either from a divine gift, which is the true gift (see Revelation 1:10–12), or an evil passive state, which admits the counterfeit.

It is said that clairvoyance and clairaudience are "natural gifts," but they are really the result of an evil state in which evil spirits are able to manifest their power and presence. Crystal gazing is also merely a means of inducing this passive state, and it is the same with all the various methods in vogue in the East and elsewhere to bring about the manifestations and workings of supernatural powers. The principle is the same. The key to all these and other satanic workings in human beings, is the need for the suspension of mental activity, whereas in all divine revelations, the mental faculties and powers are unhindered and in full operation.

The people at the foot of Mount Sinai "saw God" (Exod. 24:11), yet they were not passive. Vision—whether mental or physical—is really active and not passive. That is, it is not separated from the will and personal action, and "visions" may be either physical, mental, or spiritual.

In supernatural writing under the control of evil spirits, the same principle of suspending the will and mental action is manifested. The person writes what he hears, dictated audibly in a supernatural way; what he sees, presented to his mind supernaturally, sometimes with rapidity as if compelled; and automatically, as his hand is moved, without any mental or volitional action.

In "descriptive" writing, or writing from what is supernaturally presented to the mind, the words may pass before the mental vision as clearly as if they were seen by the physical eye, sometimes in letters of fire or light. The same may take place in public speaking, when the speaker may describe what is presented to his mental vision—that is, if his mind is in a passive state—thinking that it is all "illumination by the Holy Spirit."

This may take place in such a refined degree that a person may be deceived into thinking that it comes from his "brilliant mind," "gifts of imagination," or "delicate power of poetic description," while none of it is the real product of his own mind, for it is not the outcome of thought. Rather, it comes because he seizes subtly-presented "pictures," which are given to him at the moment he is writing or speaking. These may be tested by their fruits. They will be empty of tangible results, or mischievous in suggestion. Certain false sentences will be intermingled with words of truth, which subvert the pure Gospel, while the message as a whole has no spiritual substance behind the beautiful words, or any permanent result in the salvation of the unregenerate or the building up of believers.

The powers of darkness have nothing to fear from words—even words of gospel truth—if there is no fructifying life in them from the source of the Spirit of God. That spurious conversions are permitted, or perhaps even brought about on a wide scale by the spirits of evil, is now beyond question. It is apparently easy for them to release their captives when it suits their plans to deceive the people of God, and there is much in the religious movements of today that absorbs the energy of Christians and appears to extend the kingdom of God, but leaves the kingdom of the spirits of the air undisturbed.

Ignorant of the existence of evil spirits and their unceasing schemes to deceive every child of God, and equally ignorant of the danger of fulfilling the conditions for their working, a great number of believers do not know that in the ordinary circumstances of life they can be opening themselves to the deceptions of supernatural beings who are keenly watching to gain a foothold in order to use the servants of God. For instance, a public speaker who seeks to depend on "supernatural help," and does not use his mind keenly in alert spiritual thinking, practically cultivates a passive condition which the Enemy may make use of to the fullest degree. Unknown to him, the Enemy may then gain an influence in his life, manifested in unaccountable attacks of all kinds, even though it seems as if he has not given Satan any reason—through his life or actions—to gain a foothold.

The same may be true of an author, who, in some way, unknown to himself, has become passive—or bluntly put, *mediumistic*—in some faculty or part of his inner life, and has thereby opened his speaking or writing to the supernatural presentations of evil spirits, which he thinks is illumination from God.

In writing under divine guidance, three factors are required: a spirit indwelt by, and moved by, the Holy Spirit (2 Peter 1:21); an alert and renewed mind, acute in active power of apprehension and intelligent thinking (see 1 Corinthians 14:20); and a body under the complete control of the spirit and will of the person. (See 1 Corinthians 9:27.)

In writing or speaking under the control of evil spirits, a person is not truly spiritual, for his spirit is not in use; what appears spiritual is actually the work of supernatural powers manifesting their spirit power on, and through, the passive mind of the person, apart from his spirit. But in writing under the guidance of God, since it is not given by dictation, as if to a machine, but by the movement of the Holy Spirit in his spirit, the person must be truly spiritual, the source being *in the spirit,* and not in the mind, as it is when men write the products of their own thoughts. The Scriptures bear the marks of their having been written in this way. "Holy men of God spake as they were moved by the Holy Ghost" (2 Pet. 1:21). They "spake from God," but as men they received and uttered or wrote the truth given in the spirit, transmitted through the full use of their divinely enlightened faculties.

Paul's writings all show the fulfillment of the three requirements mentioned: his *spirit* open to the movement of the Holy Spirit, his *mind* in full use, and his *body* an obedient instrument under the control of the spirit. His letters also reveal the capacity of the renewed mind for comprehending the deep things of God. In Paul, too, we see the clear discernment held by a spiritual man, able to recognize what came from God in his spirit and what was the product of his own thought in the exercise of his judgment as a servant of God. (See 1 Corinthians 7:10–12.)

The records of most "supernatural revelations" today almost entirely show the absence of the requirements for true divine manifestations, and they show the fulfillment of the law for the workings of evil spirits—the suspension of the use of the mental faculties—with the consequent emptiness, and sometimes childish folly, of words said to have been "spoken by God," and the purposelessness of the "visions" and other manifestations.

If the conditions necessary for evil spirits to work are fulfilled, no experience of the past, no dignity of position, no intellectual training or knowledge, will protect the believer from their counterfeit manifestations. Consequently, the Deceiver will do anything and everything to engender passivity in the children of God, in any form whatsoever, either in spirit, soul, or body, for he knows that sooner or later he will gain a foothold. It can therefore be said, unhesitatingly, that if the law for evil spirits to work is fulfilled through the nonuse of the mind and faculties, evil spirits will work, and they will deceive the very elect of God.

Why do evil spirits work so persistently to gain access and control? First, because in it they find "rest" (see Matthew 12:43), and seem to find some relief for themselves in a way we do not know. But even more, because the body is the outlet of the soul and spirit, and if they can control the exterior, they can thereby control the inner man at the center by hindering his freedom of action manward, although they may not do so godward. In the case of the believer, they do not destroy the life at the center, but they can imprison it, so that the inner man, indwelt by the Holy Spirit, is unable to attack and destroy their kingdom and works. All previous spiritual growth is practically of no value for service.

A great number of mature believers in the church of Christ need spiritual light in order to be liberated from this bondage. Their spiritual growth is checked and hindered by the dulling of their faculties, the clog of misconceptions and deceptions in their minds, or weakness and disease in their bodies. These conditions also prevent the outflow of the Holy Spirit who indwells their spirits, so that the life of Jesus cannot be manifested through them in using their minds for the transmission of truth or in the strengthening and use of their bodies in active, effective service.

Therefore, when the outer man becomes undeceived, it does not bring the center life into existence, but into freedom of operation. All this may occur in various degrees, for all believers are not in the same degree of bondage. There are degrees of inner spiritual growth; in the mixture of the workings of God from the spirit and of evil spirits in the outer man; and in passivity of spirit, soul, and body, resulting in degrees of deception and oppression.

The moment ground is given to evil spirits in any degree, the faculties are dulled by them, or become passive through nonuse. Their aim then is to substitute themselves for the person in all his actions. The person, meanwhile, believes that he is admitting divine substitutions for himself—that it is God working and acting instead of himself—and therefore he believes he is becoming "God-possessed."

These believers then have supernatural power, and can, in a supernatural way, receive from the spirits that control them. They give forth, as their transmitters, many supernatural workings or manifestations, such as the

- getting and transmitting of false revelations
- power of counterfeit prophecy
- power of divination
- receiving and giving of impressions
- getting of specific guidance
- foretelling of events
- power of writing, automatically or otherwise
- receiving and giving of information
- receiving of interpretations
- getting of visions

Such believers may also obtain the power of

- listening to spirit beings
- concentration necessary for listening
- getting knowledge, supernaturally
- translating, criticizing, correcting, judging
- getting and giving suggestions
- getting and giving messages
- dealing with obstacles

- receiving and giving so-called interpretations of facts and imaginations
- giving supernatural meanings to natural facts, and natural meanings to supernatural facts
- being led and controlled

Many of these manifested workings of evil spirits appear to be the workings of the man himself, but they are actions of which he is incapable naturally. For example, he may have no natural power of "translating," "criticizing," etc. Yet the spirits in possession can give him power for doing so, thus creating a false personality in the eyes of others, who think that he possesses such and such "gifts" (naturally) and are disappointed when he will not use them, not realizing that he is unable to manifest or use such supposed gifts, except at the will of the spirits in control of him.

Also, when the deceived believer discovers that such manifestations are the fruit of evil spirits and refuses any longer to be their slave, such gifts cease to exist. This is the time when the undeceived man is persecuted by the revengeful spirits of evil through their suggestions to others that he has "lost his power" or "backslidden" in his spiritual life, when in reality he is being liberated from the effects of their wicked and malicious workings.

The following examples show how evil spirits substitute their own working in a believer's life, through his misconceptions of spiritual truth.

SUBSTITUTION IN SPEAKING

"It is not ye that speak" (Matt. 10:20). Some believers think that this verse means divine substitution for their speaking, that God *Himself* will speak through them. A believer may say, "I must not speak, God is to do so," thereby "surrendering" his mouth to God to be His mouthpiece, abandoning his powers of speech to the supernatural power that he thinks is God. The result: the believer does not speak; God does not speak because He makes no one a machine; evil spirits speak because the door has been opened for their doing so through the believer's passivity. The outcome is that evil spirits substitute themselves in the place of the believer, particularly in the form of supernatural "messages" that increasingly demand his passive obedience and which, in due time, bring about a mediumistic condition wholly unforeseen by him.

SUBSTITUTION IN MEMORY

"The Holy Ghost...shall...bring all things to your remembrance" (John 14:26). Some Christians believe this means that they do not need to use the memory, that God will bring all things to their minds. The result is that the believer himself does not use his memory; God does not use the person's memory because He will not do so apart from the believer's coaction; evil spirits use it, and substitute their workings in the place of the believer's volitional use of his memory.

SUBSTITUTION IN CONSCIENCE

"Thine ears shall hear a word behind thee, saying, This is the way" (Isa. 30:21). Believers look upon supernatural guidance that directs them, through a voice or scripture text, as a higher form of guidance than the conscience. With this mindset, a person then thinks that he does not need to reason or think, but simply obey. He follows this so-called "higher guidance," which he substitutes for his conscience. The result is that he does not use his conscience; God does not speak to him to mechanically obey; evil spirits take the opportunity, and supernatural voices are substituted for the action of the conscience. The outcome is the substitution of evil spirit guidance in his life.

From this time, he is not influenced by what he feels or sees or by what others say, and he closes himself to all questions, and will not reason. This substitution of supernatural guidance for the action of the conscience explains the deterioration of the moral standard in persons with supernatural experiences because they have really substituted the direction of evil spirits for their conscience. They are quite unconscious that their moral standard has been lowered. Yet their conscience has become seared because they have deliberately ceased to heed its voice and have listened to the voices of the teaching spirits in matters that should be decided by the conscience, matters regarding right or wrong, good or evil.

SUBSTITUTION IN DECISION

"It is God which worketh in you...to will" (Phil. 2:13). Many believers think this means that they are not to use their own wills, that God is to will through them. The result is that the believer does not exercise his will; God does not exercise the person's will because the believer would cease to be a free agent; evil spirits seize upon the passive will and either hold it in a paralyzed condition of inability to act, or else make it domineering and strong. In this way, the emissaries of Satan gain a hold on the very center of his life, eventually making the believer a victim of indecision and weakness in the action of his will, or else energizing his will into a force of mastery, even over others, which is fraught with disastrous results.

In a similar way, evil spirits will not only endeavor to substitute their own workings in a person's life in the place of God, through the believer's misconception of the true way of working together with God, but they will also seek to substitute their workings for all his mental faculties: mind, reason, memory, imagination, judgment. This is a counterfeit of self through substitution. The person thinks it is himself all the time.

The evil spirits' substitution of themselves through the believer's passivity on any point is the basis of deep deception and oppression among the most surrendered children of God. The deception takes an entirely spiritual form at first, such as the man having an exaggerated sense of his importance in the church, his "worldwide ministry," his lofty position of influence arising out of his "divine commission," his unusual height of spirituality, and his definite and almost unprecedented "experience," which makes him feel he has been placed far above others. But a tremendous and inevitable fall awaits such a one. He ascends his pinnacle, pushed by the Enemy, without any power whatsoever to control the inevitable descent which must follow when he is undeceived.

A spiritual "crash" is the result, shaking the things that can be shaken. Then he experiences awful darkness. The effect of deception in its fullest climax is darkness, nothing but darkness; darkness within, darkness without; intense darkness; darkness over the past; darkness enveloping the future; darkness surrounding God and all His ways.

Here many sink under the horror that they have committed the "unpardonable sin." Some, however, discover that their bitter experience may be turned into light for the church in its fight with sin and Satan, and as those who have been in the camp of the Enemy and heard all his secrets, they become a terror to the forces of evil upon their emergence to liberty, with the result that they are assailed with intensified malignity because of their knowledge of the Foe.

Chapter 7

Counterfeits of the Divine

For false Christs and false prophets shall rise, and shall show signs and wonders to seduce, if it were possible, even the elect.
—Mark 13:22

In seeking to obtain control over a believer, evil spirits make a great effort to cause him to accept their suggestions and workings as the speaking, working, or leading of God. Their initial method is to counterfeit a "divine presence," through which they can mislead their victim as they will.

The deceiving spirits find an opportunity to counterfeit the presence of God when believers have a false understanding of where God is in relation to them, when they think of Him as being in or around them so that they can actually, consciously, feel or sense Him. When they pray, they pray to God in themselves, or they pray to Him as if He is around them, in the room or atmosphere. They use their imagination and try to realize His presence, and they desire to feel His presence in them or upon them.

This locating of God in or around the believer, usually comes at the time of the baptism of the Holy Spirit. For up to that time of spiritual crisis in his life, the believer lives more by accepting facts declared in the Scriptures, which he understands by his intelligence. With the baptism of the Spirit he becomes more conscious of the presence of God by the Spirit, and in his spirit, and so he begins to "locate" the person of God in, around, or

141

upon him. When he turns inward, and begins to pray to God as within him, this, in time, really results in prayer to evil spirits, if they succeed in gaining admittance under this counterfeit idea.

Prayer to God in this way can be pressed to absurdity. For example, if a person prays to God in himself, why should he not pray to God in another believer who is elsewhere? The limitation of viewing God as a person within and all the possible dangers arising from this misconception of truth are obvious.

Some believers live so inwardly in communion, worship, and vision, that they become spiritually introverted, and cramped and narrowed in their outlook. The result is that their spiritual capacity and mental powers become dwarfed and powerless. In its extreme form, people become victims to the "inner voice" and the introverted attitude of listening to it, so that, eventually, the mind becomes fixed in the introverted condition with no outgoing action at all.

In fact, any form of turning inward to God, as if He indwells, speaks, communes, and guides from a subjective location within us, in a physical or conscious sense, opens a person to gravest danger. For upon this thought and belief, the most serious deceptions and final outworkings of deceiving spirits have taken place. This mistaken idea of the location of God is actively cultivated by the powers of darkness; they use it as the groundwork for manifestations to support and deepen their deception. It is through this misconception that the delusions of believers, who assert themselves to be "Christ," have come about—whether during past ages or in recent years. The same false doctrine will bring about the great deceptions at the end of the age, foretold by the Lord in Matthew 24:24, by the "false Christs" and "false prophets," and the claims of "I am Christ" (see Matthew 24:5) by the leaders of groups of side-tracked believers. It is also the cause of the delusions of the thousand others who have been sent to asylums, although they are not mentally ill at all. The Devil's richest harvest is from the effects of his counterfeits, and, unknowingly, many sober and faithful teachers have aided him in his deceptions through using language that gives a materialistic idea of spiritual things, onto which the natural mind eagerly grasps.

Those who locate God personally and wholly in themselves, practically make themselves, by their assertions, "divine" persons. God is not wholly in any man. He dwells in those who receive Him, by His own Spirit. "God is a Spirit" (John 4:24), and mind or body cannot hold communion with spirit. Feelings in the senses, or conscious physical enjoyment of some supposed spiritual presence, is not true communion of spirit with Spirit such as the Father seeks from those who worship Him. (See John 4:24.)

The location of the God we worship is of supreme importance. God is in heaven. Christ the glorified Man is in heaven. If we think of our God as in us and around us, for our worship and for our enjoyment, we unwittingly open the door to the evil spirits in the atmosphere that surrounds us. Instead, we need to penetrate in spirit through the lower heavens (see Hebrews 4:14; 9:24; 10:19–20) to the throne of God, which is in the highest heaven, "above all principality, and power, and might, and dominion, and every name that is named, not only in this world, but also in that which is to come" (Eph. 1:21).

The Word of God is very clear on this point, and we need only to ponder such passages as Hebrews 1:3; 2:9; 4:14–16; 9:24, and many others, to see it. The God we worship, the Christ we love, is in heaven. It is as we approach Him there, and by faith apprehend our union with Him in spirit there, that we, too, are raised with Him and seated with Him above the plane of the lower heavens, where the powers of darkness reign. And as we are seated with Him, we see them under His feet. (See Ephesians 1:20–23; 2:6.)

The Lord's words recorded in the gospel of John, chapters fourteen through sixteen, state the truth very clearly concerning His indwelling in the believer. The truth that the believer is to comprehend and have faith in, is that we are in Him, in His heavenly position. This can be seen in John 14:20, which says, "At that day ye shall know that I am in my Father, and ye in me, and I in you." The result of this in the life of the individual believer—which Christ spoke about to His company of disciples and therefore to the body of Christ as a whole—is that Christ is in us. Union with Christ in glory results in the inflow and outflow of His Spirit and life through the believer on earth. (See Philippians 1:19.) In other words, the "subjective" is the result of the "objective." The objective fact that Christ is in heaven is the basis of faith for the subjective inflow of His life and power by the Holy Spirit of God.

The Lord said, "If ye abide in me, and my words abide in you, ye shall ask what ye will" (John 15:7). Christ abides in us by His Spirit and through His words; but He Himself, as a person, is in heaven, and it is only as we abide in Him there that His Spirit and His life, through His Word, can be manifested in us here.

When a believer "abides," it means he has an attitude of trust and dependence on a person in heaven. However, if his attitude changes into a trust and dependence upon a Christ within, he is really resting upon an inward experience and turning from the Christ in heaven. This actually blocks the avenue for the inflow of Christ's life, and disassociates the believer from cooperation with Him by the Spirit. Any manifestation, therefore, of a presence within, cannot be a true manifestation from God if it sidetracks the believer from his right attitude toward the Christ in heaven. There is a true knowledge of the presence of God, but it is in the spirit, when joined to Him: a knowledge of spiritual union and fellowship with Him that lifts the believer, so to speak, out of himself to abide with Christ in God.

THE COUNTERFEIT PRESENCE OF GOD

A false presence of God is nearly always manifested as a counterfeit love to which the believer opens himself without hesitation. The deceived one finds that it fills and satiates his innermost being, but he does not know that he has opened himself to evil spirits in the deepest need of his inner life. The powers of darkness counterfeit the presence of God to those who are ignorant of His ways, in a manner similar to the following example.

At some moment when the believer is yearning for a sense of God's presence, either alone or in a meeting, and certain conditions (of passivity) are fulfilled, the subtle Foe approaches, wraps the believer's senses with a soothing, lulling feeling—sometimes filling the room with light, or causing what is apparently a "breath from God" by a movement of the air—and whispers, "This is the presence you have longed for," or leads the believer to infer that it is what he has desired. Then, off his guard, and lulled into a false security that Satan is far away, some thoughts are suggested to his mind that are accompanied by manifestations that appear to be divine; a sweet voice speaks, or a vision is given, which is at once received as "divine guidance," given in the "divine presence," and therefore "unquestionably" from God. If accepted as from God, when from the spirits of evil, the first foothold is gained.

The person is now very sure that God has instructed him to do this or that. He is filled with the thought that he has been highly favored by God and chosen for some high place in His kingdom. His deeply hidden self-centeredness is fed and strengthened by this, and he is able to endure all things by the power of this secret strength. He has been spoken to by God! He has been singled out for special favor! His support now comes from within, based upon his experience, rather than upon God Himself and the written Word.

Through this secret confidence that God has specially spoken to him, the man becomes unteachable and unyielding, with a confidence bordering on feelings of infallibility. He cannot listen to others now, for they have not had this "direct" revelation from God. He is in direct, special, personal communion with God, and to question any direction given to him becomes the height of sin. Obey he must, even though the direction given is contrary to all enlightened judgment and the action commanded is opposed to the spirit of the Word of God. In brief, when a person at this stage believes he has a command from God, he will not use his reason because he thinks it would be "carnal" to do so; common sense is considered a lack of faith, and therefore sin. Conscience, for the time being, has ceased to speak.

Some of the suggestions made to the believer by deceiving spirits at this time may be: "You are a special instrument for God," which serves to feed self-centeredness; "You are more advanced than others," which works to blind his soul to sober knowledge of itself; "You are different from others," which causes him to think he needs special dealing by God; "You must take a separate path," which feeds an independent spirit; and "You must give up your occupation and live by faith," the purpose of which is to cause the believer to launch out on false guidance, which may result in the ruin of his home and sometimes the work for God in which he is engaged. All these suggestions are made to give the man a false conception of his spiritual state, for he is made to believe that he is more advanced than he actually is, so that he may act beyond his measure of faith and knowledge (compare Romans 12:3) and consequently be more open to the deceptions of the beguiling Foe.

Upon the basis of the supposed revelation of God and the special manifestation of His presence, and the assumption of His consequent full possession of the believer, the lying spirits afterwards build their counterfeits. For the true indwelling of God is in the shrine of the spirit alone; and the soul vessel, or personality of the believer, is purely a vehicle for the expression of Christ, who is enthroned within by His Spirit, while the body, quickened by the same Spirit, is governed by God from the central depths of the human spirit through the self-control of the man, acting by his renewed will.

The counterfeit presence of God is deepened as the evil spirits repeat the false manifestations to the senses—manifestations given so gently that the person goes on yielding to them, thinking this is truly communion with God. For believers too often look upon communion with God as only something they can sense or feel, and not something in their spirits. In this way, a person begins praying to evil spirits in the belief that he is praying to God. His self-control is not yet lost, but as the believer responds to, or gives himself up to, these false manifestations, he does not know that his willpower is being slowly undermined.

At last, through these subtle, delicious experiences, the belief is established that God Himself is consciously in possession of his body, quickening it with thrills that can be felt; filling it with warmth and heat or even with agonies which seem like fellowship with the sufferings of Christ and travail for souls; or giving it the experience of death with Christ, with the conscious feeling of nails being driven into the body, etc. From this point the lying spirits can work as they will, and there is no limit to what they may do to a believer who is deceived to this extent.

When evil spirits want to intrude, they work by sudden suggestion, which is not the ordinary way the mind works. They give suggestions that come from outside the mind, like "flashes of memory" (again, not the ordinary way the memory works). They give sensations of touch, twitchings of the nerves, feelings of drafts and sensations of wind blowing upon the body, etc.

When evil spirits are in control, the whole body is affected, at times with the pleasant sensations referred to, but at other times with pains in the head and body that have no physical cause, or that work with the natural in such a way that the supernatural cannot easily be distinguished from it (such as an accelerated heartbeat and other physical causes), so that part has a natural reason and part is from the intensifying force of evil. Depression then ensues in proportion to the previous exhilaration. Exhaustion and fatigue come in reaction to the demand upon the nervous system from the hours of ecstasy. There is a sense of being drained of strength without any visible cause. Grief and joy, heat and cold, laughter and tears, all rapidly succeed each other in varied degrees. In brief, the emotional sensibilities seem to have full play.

The senses are aroused and are in full mastery of the person, apart from his will. Or, they may be apparently under control, so that the evil spirit's presence may be hidden from the person's knowledge, his workings being carefully measured to suit the victim he has studied so well; for he knows he must not go a shade too far, lest he awaken suspicion of the cause of the abnormal movements of the emotions and of the sensitive parts of the bodily frame.

It can easily be seen that, in time, the health of the deceived one must be affected by this play upon mind and body. That is the reason for the breakdown that so often follows experiences of an abnormal kind. There may be a snapping of the tension by a sudden end to all conscious feelings, and the apparent withdrawal of the "conscious presence of God." This is followed by an entire change of tactics by the deceiving spirits, who may now turn upon their victim with terrible accusations and charges of having committed the "unpardonable sin," producing in the person as acute anguish and real suffering as he once experienced of the "bliss of heaven."

PUBLIC CONFESSIONS

Here the evil spirits may push the person to confessions of all kinds, however public and painful, which he hopes may result in regaining the "experience" he apparently lost. All this is in vain, however. These confessions, instigated by deceiving spirits, may be recognized by their compulsory character. The person is forced to confess sin, sin which often exists only in the accusations of the Enemy. It does not dawn upon the person that evil spirits will push people to do what looks like the most meritorious thing and which the Scriptures declare is the one condition for obtaining forgiveness, and so he yields to the drive upon him, simply to get relief.

True confession of sin should come from deep conviction, and not compulsion, and should be made only to God, if the sin is one only known by God; to man personally, and in private, when the sin is against man; and to the public only when the sin is against the public. Confession should never be made under the impulse of any compulsory emotion but should be a deliberate act of the will choosing the right, and putting things right, according to the will of God.

That Satan's kingdom gains by public "confessions" is evident by the devices the Enemy uses to push men into them. Evil spirits drive a man into sin and then compel that man to publicly

confess the sin which they forced him to commit—
contrary to his true character—in order to make
the sin that they forced him into a stigma upon
him for the remainder of his life.

Oftentimes the sins confessed are the result of
wicked spirits inserting feelings into the person as
consciously abhorrent and loathsome as were his
former conscious feelings of heavenly purity and
love. At that time, the person who experienced
them had declared that he knew of no sin to confess to God, nor any rising of an evil impulse whatsoever, leading him to believe that sin had been
completely eliminated from his being.

In short, counterfeit manifestations of the divine presence, through agreeable and heavenly
feelings, can be followed by counterfeit feelings of
sinful things, wholly repugnant to the will and
central purity of the believer, who is as faithful to
God now in his hatred to sin as in the days when
he reveled in the sense of purity that was given to
him as a conscious feeling in his body.

The deceiving spirit may now reveal his malice through attacks of apparent disease or acute
pain without physical cause, counterfeiting or producing consumption, fever, nervous breakdown,
and other illnesses, through which the life of the
victim may be lost unless the activities of the
"murderers" acting under Satan are discerned and
dealt with by prayer against them, and unless the
body is cared for in the natural way.

HOW DOES GOD GUIDE?

Counterfeit guidance is one of the fruits of
deception. Many believers think the guidance or
leading of God occurs only through a voice saying,
"Do this," or, "Do that," or by a compulsory

movement or impulse apart from the action or will of the person. They point to the expression used about the Lord, "the Spirit driveth him into the wilderness" (Mark 1:12), but this was not the norm in the life of Christ, for the statement implies intense spirit conflict in which the Holy Spirit departed from His ordinary guidance. We have a glimpse into a similar intense movement in the Spirit of the Lord Jesus in the account given in John 11:38, when, "groaning in himself," He moved to the grave of Lazarus. In both instances He was moving forward to direct conflict with Satan—in the case of Lazarus, with Satan as the Prince of Death. The Gethsemane agony was of the same character.

But, normally, the Lord was guided, or led, in simple fellowship with the Father. He decided, acted, reasoned, thought, as One who knew the will of God, and He intelligently (speaking reverently) carried it out. The "voice" from heaven was rare and, as the Lord Himself said, was for the sake of others and not for Himself (John 12:30). He knew the Father's will, and with every faculty of His being as Man, He did it. (See John 5:30; 6:38.)

As Christ is a pattern or example for His followers, guidance in its perfect and true form is shown in His life, and believers can expect the coworking of the Holy Spirit when they walk after the pattern of their Example. When they are out of line with the Pattern, they cease to have the working of the Holy Spirit and they become open to the deceptive counterfeit workings of evil spirits. If the believer ceases to use his mind, reason, will, and all his other faculties, and depends upon voices and impulses for guidance in every detail of life, he will be "led" or guided by evil spirits pretending to be God.

At first, after the baptism of the Spirit, the believer knows to a great extent the true guidance of the Spirit of God. He knows true inward constraint to act and restraint from action, such as when to speak to another about his soul, when to rise and testify in a meeting, etc. But, after a time, he ceases to watch for this pure inward moving of the Spirit, often through ignorance of how to read the warnings of his spirit, and he begins to wait for some other incentive or manifestation to guide him in action. This is the time for which the deceiving spirits have been watching.

At this point, the believer has ceased, unknown to himself, to cooperate with the inward spirit action, to use his will, and to decide for himself, and therefore he is now watching for some other supernatural indication of the way to go or the course to take. Hence, he must somehow have guidance, or some text, some indication, some providential circumstance, etc. This is the moment of opportunity for a deceiving spirit to gain his faith and confidence. And so, some word or words are whispered softly that are exactly in accordance with the inward "drawing" that he has had, but which he has not recognized as from a source other than the Holy Spirit, who works by a deep inner constraining and restraining of the spirit. The soft whisper of the deceiving spirit is so delicate and gentle that the believer listens to and receives the words without question and begins to obey this soft whisper, yielding more and more to it, without any thought of exercising mind, judgment, reason, or volition.

The feelings come from the body, but the believer is unconscious that he is ceasing to act from his spirit and by the pure, unfettered action of his will and his mind, which, under the illumination of the Spirit, is always in accord with the spirit. This is a time of great danger if the believer fails to discriminate the source of his feelings of being "drawn" and yields to them before finding out their source. The believer should examine the basic principles by which he makes decisions, especially when they have to do with feelings, so that he will not be led away by any feeling without being able to say where it comes from or whether it is safe for him to go by it.

From this point, deceiving spirits can increase their control, for the believer has begun an attitude of inward listening that can be developed acutely until he is always watching for an "inner voice," or a voice in the ear, which is an exact counterfeit of the voice of God in the spirit; thus, the believer moves and acts as a passive slave to supernatural guidance.

Evil spirits are able to counterfeit the voice of God because believers are ignorant that they can do so and are unaware of the true principle of God's way of communication with His children. The Lord said, "My sheep know My voice" (see John 10:14, 27), that is, His way of speaking to His sheep. He did not say this voice was an audible voice, nor a voice giving directions which were to be obeyed apart from the intelligence of the believer. On the contrary, the word *know* indicates the use of the mind, for although there is knowledge in the spirit, it must reach the intelligence of the man so that spirit and mind become of one accord. In any case, it is best and safest in these days of peril to keep in the path of faith and reliance upon the Holy Spirit of God, who works through the Word of God.

In order to detect which is the voice of God and which is the voice of the Devil, we need to understand that the Holy Spirit alone is charged to communicate the will of God to the believer, and that He works from within the spirit of the man, enlightening the understanding (Eph. 1:17–18) in order to bring him into intelligent coworking with the mind of God.

The purpose of the Holy Spirit is, briefly, the entire renewal of the redeemed one, in spirit, soul, and body. He therefore directs all His work to bring about the liberation of every faculty, and never in any way seeks to direct a man as a passive machine, even into good. He works in him to enable him to choose the good, and strengthens him to act, but never—even for "good"—dulls him or renders him incapable of free action. Otherwise, He would nullify the very purpose of Christ's redemption on Calvary, and the purpose of His own coming.

When believers understand these principles, the "voice of the Devil" is recognizable (1) when it comes from outside the man or within the sphere of his body and not from the central depth of his spirit where the Holy Spirit abides; (2) when it is imperative and persistent, urging sudden action without time to reason or intelligently weigh the issues; and (3) when it is confusing and clamorous, so that the man is hindered from thinking; for the Holy Spirit desires the believer to be intelligent, as a responsible being with a choice, and will not confuse him so as to make him incapable of coming to a decision.

The speaking of evil spirits can also be a counterfeit of the apparent inner speaking of the man, as if he himself were thinking, but with no concentrated action of the mind. For example, this may be manifest in a persistent and ceaseless commentary going on somewhere within, apart from an act of the will or mind, which comments on the man's own actions or the actions of others with thoughts such as, "You are wrong," "You are never right," "God has cast you off," "You must not do that," etc., etc.

The voice of the Devil as an angel of light is more difficult to detect, especially when it comes with wonderful strings of Scripture texts that make it appear like the voice of the Holy Spirit. A believer may reject outside voices which pretend to come from God or angels, yet he may be deceived by "floods of texts" which he thinks are from God. In this case, he needs more knowledge for discernment. For example:

1. Does the believer rely upon these texts apart from the use of his mind or reason? This indicates passivity.

2. Are these texts a prop to him, undermining his reliance on God Himself and weakening his power of decision and (right) self-reliance?

3. Do these texts influence him and make him elated and puffed up as "specially guided by God," or crush and condemn him and throw him into despair and condemnation, instead of leading him to deal seriously with God Himself regarding the course of his life? Does he have a keen and increasing knowledge of right and wrong, obtained from the written Word by the light of the Holy Spirit?

If these, and other similar results, are the fruit of the texts given, they may be rejected as from the Deceiver. Or, at the very least, an attitude of neutrality should be taken to them until further proof of their source is provided. In addition, the voice of the Devil, as distinguished from the voice of God, may also be recognized by its purpose and outcome. Obviously, if God speaks directly to a person, what he says or does must prove true.

THE METHODS OF EVIL SPIRITS

Deceiving spirits carefully adapt their suggestions and leadings to the idiosyncrasies of the believer so that they will not be found out. No leading will be suggested contrary to any strong truth of God firmly rooted in his mind, or contrary to any special bias of his mind. If his mind has a practical bent, no visibly foolish leading will be given; if he knows the Scriptures very well, nothing contrary to Scripture will be said; if he feels strongly on any point, the leadings will be harmonized to suit that point and, wherever possible, will be so adapted to previously true guidance from God that they will appear to be the continuance of that same guidance.

Here we see clearly the way the Enemy works. The soul begins in God's will, but the purpose of the evil spirit is to draw it off into carrying out his will by counterfeiting the guidance of God. Satanic guidance alters the points of a person's life, misdirects his energies, and lessens his service value. To frustrate this artifice of the Enemy, the believer should know that there are two distinct attitudes toward guidance that have serious results if their difference is not understood: trusting God to guide, and trusting that God is guiding.

The first means reliance upon God Himself, and the second is an assumption of being guided that can be taken advantage of by deceiving spirits. In the first, God does guide in response to definite trust in Him, and He guides through the spirit of the man who continues to cooperate with His Spirit, leaving every faculty free to act and the will free to choose intelligently the right step in the path before him.

In the second, when the spirits of evil take advantage of a believer's assumption that God is guiding, independent of a moment-by-moment watchful cooperation with the Holy Spirit, a slight compulsion may be noticed, which slowly increases in force until presently the believer says, "I was compelled" to do so-and-so and "I was afraid to resist." He takes this compulsion as an evidence of the guiding of God, instead of recognizing it as contrary to God's principle of dealing with His children.

OBEDIENCE OR COMPULSION?

If the compulsion is believed to be of God and is yielded to, the result is that the believer becomes a slave to a supernatural power which destroys all freedom of volition and judgment. He begins to be afraid to act on his own, for fear that he will not fulfill what he believes to be careful obedience to the will of God. He asks permission to do the most obviously simple duties of life, and fears to take a step without this so-called permission. As soon as the deceiving spirits have obtained perfect control, and the believer is so passively automatic that he is incapable of realizing his condition, they do not need to work under cover as much. They insidiously commence to direct him to do the most absurd or foolish things, carefully working inside the range of his passive obedience to their will, in order to avoid the danger of awakening his reasoning powers.

As a matter of "obedience," and not from any true conviction or true principle, he may be commanded to let his hair grow long, in order to be like Samson, a Nazarite; to go without his hat, to prove his willingness to obey in the smallest matters; to wear faded clothes as a test of pride or as a "crucifixion of self" or as a mark of implicit obedience to God. These things may seem like trifles to others, who use their reasoning powers, but they have great results in the purpose of the deceiving spirits who, by these directions, aim at making the believer a passive, unthinking, or unreasoning medium, pliable to their will, in obedience to which—even in these trivial matters—their hold deepens upon him.

When these foolish and absurd actions are publicly visible, the lying spirits know that they have destroyed the testimony of the deceived man in the eyes of sober people. However, there are vast numbers of devoted believers, known to the church at large, who are not pushed to such extremes of exterior action, but who are equally misled or in bondage to supernatural commands concerning matters of food, dress, manner, etc., which they think they have received from God. The spirit of judgment toward others, and the secret self-satisfaction for their "consecration to God" which accompanies their supposed obedience, betrays the subtle workings of the Enemy.

As long as the believer thinks it is God who is directing him, the deceiving spirits are safe from exposure, and they can lead him on into more and more deception. When the man reaches a very high degree of satanic deception, he finds himself unable to act unless the spirits in control allow him, so that he no longer even asks for permission to do this or that. In some cases they even establish communication with him. If he desires to know whether he should go here or there, he turns inward for guidance from the inner voice—assumed to be the voice of God—the answer yes given by a movement of his head caused by the spirit, or no, by no action at all. Evil spirits make use of the body of the person in the same way that they reply to those who consult them through a "planchette," showing their complete control over the nerves of the body and the whole being of the victim, who now believes that every supernatural movement in his body has a signification, since it may be originated by God in possession of him.

The deception by deceiving spirits at this stage is so great that no arguments, reasonings, or outward considerations of any kind influence the actions of the believer thus deceived, or turn him from obeying the guidance or permission of the inner voice, which he fully believes is of God. In fact, if he endeavors to go against it in the smallest matter, the condemnation and suffering are so great that he becomes terrified at any "disobedience," and would rather be condemned and misjudged by the whole world than go against it. His great horror is disobeying the Holy Spirit, and the evil spirits deceiving him take every occasion to deepen this fear in order to retain their hold upon him.

As the believer minutely obeys the evil spirit in this way, he relies more and more upon supernatural help, for the moment he does something apart from it he is accused—apparently by the Holy Spirit—of working apart from God. It is at this stage that all the faculties fall into deepening passivity, as the person lets go entirely to the voice of "guidance" and into a reliance upon the "divine" speakings, which keep his mind in complete inaction.

COUNTERFEIT REPRESENTATIONS

Here also *counterfeit* manifestations in miraculous gifts, prophecy, tongues, healing, visions, and supernatural experiences of every kind possible to the satanic powers, may be given to the believer, along with abundant Scripture texts and "proofs" to confirm their "divine origin." He experiences a lightness of the body that makes it appear as if he were being carried by invisible hands; he is lifted off his bed in what spiritualists know as "levitation"; he can sing and speak and do what he has never been capable of doing before. Constant contact with spirit forces gives the man a "mystical" look, but all lines of strength, which come from strenuous conflict and self-mastery, go out of the face, for the sense life is being fed and indulged in a spiritual way as much as by fleshly habits, yet these, such as smoking, etc., have for a time no power.

But counterfeits of God and divine things are not the only counterfeits the Angel of Light has at his command. There are also counterfeits of human things, such as the impersonation of others, and even of the believer himself. People may appear to be different from what they really are—jealous or angry, critical or unkind. Others may seem to have an inflated sense of "self" where there is really the very opposite manifestation of selflessness and love. In still others, wrong motives may appear to govern where none exist; simple actions may be colored, and words may be made to mean and suggest what is not in the minds of the speakers, and may sometimes seem to confirm the supposed wrongdoing of others.

People of the opposite sex may also be impersonated to a believer in times of prayer or leisure, either in repulsive or in beautiful form, with the purpose of arousing various dormant elements in the human frame, unknown to exist by the innocent believer. Sometimes the reasons for the impersonation are given as: "for prayer" or "fellowship" and "spirit-communion in the things of God."

The lying spirits' counterfeit representations of others may be in the realm of the passions and affections, seeking to rouse or feed these in the deceived one. People's faces, voices, and "presence" are presented as if they, too, were equally affected. This is accompanied by a counterfeit love or drawing to the other one, with a painful craving for their company that almost masters the victim.

This subject of love, and its painful arousing and communicating or counterfeiting by evil spirits, is one that touches multitudes of believers of all classes. Many are made to suffer poignant agonies of a craving for love, with no specific person involved; others are provoked in their thoughts so that they are not able to hear the word love mentioned without blushing. None of these manifestations are under the control of the will of the believer.

In counterfeiting the believer himself, the evil spirit gives him exaggerated views, almost visions, of his own personality. He is "wonderfully gifted," and is therefore puffed up; he is "miserably incapable," and so is in despair; he is "amazingly clever," and thus undertakes what he cannot do; he is "helpless," "hopeless," "too forward," or "too backward"—in brief, a countless number of pictures of himself, or others, are presented to his mind once the lying spirit has gained a foothold in the imagination.

So subtle is the identity of the deceiving spirit with a believer's individuality, that others see what may be described as a false personality. Sometimes the person appears to be full of self when the inner man is deeply selfless, or full of pride when the inner man is sincerely humble. In fact, the whole outer appearance of the man in manner, voice, actions, and words, is often quite contrary to his true character, and he wonders why others misunderstand, misjudge, and criticize. Some believers, on the other hand, are quite unconscious of the manifestation of this spurious self and go on happily satisfied with what they themselves know of their own inner motives and heart life, oblivious of the very contrary manifestation that others behold, and pity or condemn.

The false personality caused by evil spirits can also be in a beautiful form in order to attract or mislead others in various ways. This can happen without the knowledge of the victim or those who are being misled, and is sometimes described as "unaccountable infatuation." However, if it were recognized as the work of evil spirits, refused, and resisted, the infatuation would pass away. The work of evil spirits is so wholly apart from the action of the will in the persons concerned, that it can be clearly recognized, especially when the supposed infatuation follows supernatural experiences, and when deception through the accepting of counterfeits has resulted.

COUNTERFEIT SIN

Evil spirits can also counterfeit sin by causing some apparent manifestation of the evil nature in a person's life. Mature believers should know whether such a manifestation really is sin from the old nature or a manifestation from evil spirits. The purpose in the latter case is to get the believer to take what comes from them as if it came from himself. For whatever is accepted from evil spirits gives them a foothold.

When a believer knows the Cross and his position of death to sin, and in will and practice unflinchingly rejects all known sin, and a manifestation of sin takes place, he should at once take a position of neutrality to it, until he knows its source. For if he calls it sin from himself when it is not, he believes a lie as much as in any other way; and if he confesses as a sin what did not come from himself, he brings the power of the Enemy upon him to drive him into the sin which he has confessed as his own. Many believers are thus held down by supposed "besetting sins" which they believe are theirs, and which no confessing to God removes, but from which they would find liberty if they attributed them to their right cause. There is no danger of minimizing sin in the recognition of these facts, because, in either case, the believer desires to be rid of the sin or sins, or he would not trouble about them.

The believer is so acutely conscious of a "self" that he hates and loathes, that he is never free from the dark shadow of self-condemnation, self-accusation, or self-despair, which no appropriation of identification with Christ in death destroys. Or, he has a self-confidence that continually draws him forward into situations from which he has to retire abashed and disappointed. A false personality encompasses the true inner man, which few are aware is possible, but which is a sadly real thing among multitudes of the children of God.

COUNTERFEIT REVELATION

The person beset with constant demonic presentations to his mind only thinks he has a vivid imagination, or even more, that some of these things are visions from God and that he is favored of God, especially when the vision is of "great plans for God," or wide visions of what God is going to do. In these, the believer is always at the center, the special instrument of this service!

Many of the plans for "movements" in connection with revival, which have gone even as far as print, have been of such a character—plans given by "revelation," which have resulted in gaining only the few caught by them, and no others. The aftermath of revival, where men have left their regular calling and followed a will-o'-the-wisp revelation of "launching out on God," has been of such a character. Worldwide plans are conceived and dissipated in a few months. Such deceived believers become ultra-devotional, with an excess of zeal that blinds them to all things but the supernatural realm, and robs them of power to wisely meet the claims of other aspects of life. All this comes from an evil spirit's access to the mind and imagination through the deception of counterfeiting the presence of God.

COUNTERFEITS OF SATAN

Counterfeits of Satan himself also suit his purpose at times when he desires to terrorize a person from actions, or prayer, adverse to his interests.

There are also occasions when Satan appears to fight against himself, but this is only to hide deep schemes for obtaining fuller control of a victim or some greater advantage which he knows how to secure.

Fear of the Devil may always be regarded as from the Devil, to enable him to carry out his plans of hindering the work of God. This may be the reason believers fearfully shrink from hearing about him and his works, or are passive in regard to all scriptural truth concerning the forces of evil. Fear caused by reference to his name is given in order to frighten believers away from knowing the facts about him, while others who desire the truth may be given exaggerated impressions of his presence, and of "conflict," "clouds," "blocks," "darkness," etc., until they lose the clearness of the light of God.

The work of the Deceiver is especially manifest in his efforts to make the children of God believe in his nonexistence, and in the suggestion that it is only necessary to hear or know about God to be protected from any form of the Enemy's power. On the other hand, a deceived believer may be more deeply deceived by seeing nothing but Satan's counterfeits everywhere.

COUNTERFEIT VISIONS AND DREAMS

Supernatural visions and manifestations are also a fruitful source of profit for deceiving spirits. They have gained a strong foothold when these are given, especially when the believer relies upon and quotes more from these experiences than the Word of God. For the aim of the wicked spirit is to displace the Word of God as the rock-ground of his life.

It is true that the believer may refer to and quote the Scriptures, but often only as a basis for the experiences and to strengthen faith, not in God, but in His (apparent) manifestations. This covert drawing of the believer to put more faith in the manifestations of God than in the pure Word of God, is a keenly subtle deception of the evil one, and it is easily recognized in a believer thus deceived.

When evil spirits are able to give visions, the ground is not necessarily known sin, but a condition of passivity, that is, nonaction of the mind, imagination, and other faculties. As we have seen, this essential condition of passive nonaction as the means of obtaining supernatural manifestations, is well understood by spiritualist mediums, clairvoyants, crystal gazers, and others who know that the least action of the mind immediately breaks the clairvoyant state.

Believers who do not know these main principles can unknowingly fulfill the conditions for evil spirits to work in their lives, and they ignorantly induce the passive state by wrong conceptions of the true things of God. For example, they may: (1) in times of prayer, sink into a passive mental condition that they think is waiting on God; (2) deliberately will the cessation of their mental action in order to obtain some supernatural manifestation which they believe to be of God; (3) in daily life practice a passive attitude which they think is submission to the will of God; (4) endeavor to bring about a state of personal negation, in which they have no desires, needs, wishes, hopes, or plans, which they think is full surrender to God and a will lost in God.

The deceiving spirits are careful not to frighten the believer by doing anything that will open his eyes, but keep within the range of what he will receive without question. They will impersonate the Lord Jesus in the special way that will appeal to the person. To some He may appear as "Bridegroom," to others, as seated on a throne and coming in great glory. As in spiritualism, evil spirits will also impersonate the dead to those who grieve over their loved ones, and since they have watched these loved ones during life, and know all about them, they will give ample "proofs" to establish the deceived ones in their deception.

Visions may come from one of three sources: the divine, from God; the human, such as hallucinations and illusions, because of disease; and the satanic, which are false. Visions given by evil spirits also describe anything supernatural presented to and seen by the mind or imagination from outside it—such as terrible pictures of the future, the flashing of Scripture texts as if they were lit up, and visions of widespread movements—all counterfeiting either the true vision of the Holy Spirit given to the "eyes of [the] understanding" (Eph. 1:18), or the normal and healthy action of the imagination. The church is thus often made a whirlpool of division through believers relying upon "visions" for guiding their decisions, instead of the principle of right and wrong set forth in God's Word.

Apart from visions that are the result of disease, detecting divine from satanic visions depends a great deal upon knowledge of the Word of God and the fundamental principles of His working in His children. These principles may be briefly stated in this way:

1. No supernatural vision, in any form, which requires a condition of mental nonaction or

which comes while the believer is in such a condition, can be taken to be of God.

2. All of the Holy Spirit's enlightening and illuminating vision is given when the mind is in full use and when every faculty is awake to understand, the very opposite condition than that required by the working of evil spirits.

3. All that is of God is in harmony with the laws of the way God works, as set forth in the Scriptures.

Many a believer has been caught by a vision of a worldwide sweeping in of souls, given by Satan, whose malignant hatred and ceaseless antagonism is directed against the true seed of Jesus Christ, which, in union with Him, will bruise the Serpent's head. The Devil's aim is to delay the birth and growth of the holy seed. To this end he will encourage any widespread superficial work for God, knowing it will not really touch his kingdom nor hasten the full birth into the throne-life of the conquering seed of Christ. The safe path for believers at the close of the age is one of tenacious faith in the written Word as the sword of the Spirit to cut the way through all the interferences and tactics of the forces of darkness—to the end.

In addition, all dreams as well as visions can be classified as divine, human, or satanic. Each can be discerned, first, by the condition of the person and, second, by the principles distinguishing the working of God or Satan. Dreams arising from the natural condition of the person, and attributable to purely physical causes, may be recognized as natural when there is no deception and when such physical causes really exist and are not used as a cover by deceiving spirits to hide their workings.

Passivity of mind is an essential condition for the presentation of dreams by evil spirits. At night the brain is passive, and while the activity of the mind in the daytime hinders the workings of such spirits, they have their occasion at night when passivity is more pronounced in sleep. Believers who are fighting to regain the use of their mental faculties in normal action can refuse these night presentations by evil spirits as definitely as they refuse their workings during the day, and in due time find their complete cessation.

Apart from the condition of the person, divine dreams may be distinguished from satanic ones by their import and exceptional value. (See Genesis 37:5-9; Matt. 1:20; 2:12.) Satanic dreams are characterized by their mystery, absurdity, emptiness, folly, etc., as well as by their effects on the person. With divinely-given dreams, the recipient is left normal, calm, quiet, reasonable, and with an open, clear mind. With satanic ones, he is elated, or dazed, confused, and unreasonable.

The presentations of evil spirits at night is frequently the cause of morning dullness of mind and heaviness of spirit. The sleep has not been refreshing because of their power, through the passivity of the mind during sleep, to influence the whole being. Natural sleep renews, and invigorates the faculties and the whole system. Insomnia is, in a great degree, the work of evil spirits adapting their workings to the overwrought condition of the person, in order to hide their attacks.

Believers who are open to the supernatural world should specially guard their nights by prayer and by definite rejection of the first insidious workings of evil spirits along these lines. How many say, "The Lord woke me," and place their reliance upon "revelations" given in a state of half-consciousness, when mind and will are only partially alert to discern the issues of the guidance or revelations given to them. If such believers watch the results of their obedience to night revelations, they will find many traces of the deceitful workings of the Enemy.

They will find, too, how their faith is often based upon a beautiful experience given in the early hours of the morning, or, conversely, shaken by accusations, suggestions, attacks, and conflict manifestly of the Evil One. Faith must be based on an intelligent reliance upon God Himself in His changeless character of faithfulness and love to His own. All workings of the Enemy at night can be made to cease by recognizing their source, and can be definitely refused in the name of the Lord Jesus while revoking all ground unknowingly given in the past for such workings.

Chapter 8

Symptoms of Demonic Attack

*That they may recover themselves out of the snare
of the devil, who are taken captive
by him at his will.*
—2 Timothy 2:26

Before looking at present-day symptoms of demonic attack, let us review examples of demonic activities recorded in the Bible and how they differ from manifestations of the Holy Spirit's working. How evil spirits can manipulate the body through the nervous system we find clearly defined through the Scriptures, but we never find a single instance of the Holy Spirit working in the same way. It is first important to define the meaning of the word *possession*, for it is generally thought to cover only cases of possession in the acute and fully developed degree of certain cases given in the Gospel records. But many degrees of possession are referred to in the Gospels, such as the woman with the "spirit of infirmity" (Luke 13:11); the man who was apparently only deaf and dumb (Mark 7:32); the little girl with the demon that plagued her terribly (Matt. 15:22); the boy who gnashed his teeth and was sometimes thrown on the fire (Matt. 17:15; Mark 9:20–22); and the man with the legion, who was so completely mastered by the powers of evil that he lived secluded, away from other people. (Luke 8:27–30).

Not once in the Acts of the Apostles do we find twitching, writhing, convulsions, or other effects of supernatural power on the human body, recorded as the result of being filled with the Holy Spirit. But we do read that evil spirits can convulse the body, tear it, bruise it (Luke 9:39), cause it to pine away (Mark 9:18), or give it strength (Mark 5:4); they can make a man cry out suddenly with a loud cry (Luke 9:39) or make him dumb, cause him to gnash his teeth or roll on the ground. They can cast someone into the fire to burn him or into water to drown him (Matt. 17:15; Mark 9:20–22).

In this acute form, the symptoms of demon possession and insanity are almost indistinguishable. The difference lies in the fact that in pure demon possession the mind is not impaired, although it may be passive or suspended in action, but in insanity the evil spirit takes advantage of a physical condition. Insane people are more sane than sane people think they are, and there is more truth in what they say than is believed. What they see is not always delusion, but the actual doings of evil spirits. It is necessary, therefore, to distinguish between pure insanity, pure possession, and insanity and possession.

Before declaring a person insane from physical and natural causes, the physician should find out if there is any supernatural cause. Insanity may be caused by natural derangement and by the supernatural interferences of evil powers. True insanity can also be the result of possession, and be (humanly) irrecoverable. In short, under the power of a lying spirit, a person loses control of his body, and is, for the time being, when the intruder manifests himself, irresponsible for his actions.

The spirits in possession of the body vary in character and in manifestation as much as when they are in possession of the mind, or spirit, in spiritual manifestations. Some are malignant and some are milder in their actions, such as the "spirit of infirmity" or powerlessness described in Luke 13:11, or the blind and dumb spirit in Matthew 12:22. These Scriptures show that there were cases of possession that looked like cases for healing, yet the Lord's words and action proved that the woman who was bent for eighteen years did not require healing but deliverance. The bending of the back is one of the symptoms of demon possession, when the body is deeply affected. The distinction between deafness through the interference of evil spirits with the ears, and that which is the result of physical causes, depends upon whether the person has other symptoms of evil spirit possession or whether he is in his normal, "natural" condition.

Another manifestation of the attack of evil spirits may be described as prophetic ecstasy, or "inspiration." This was evident in the girl who had a "spirit of divination" which Paul cast out (Acts 16:16–18). The danger of this kind of spirit is that the manifestations are more like those of the Holy Spirit than are the manifestations in the body. To distinguish between the two in the Corinthian church was the purpose of the apostle in writing the twelfth and fourteenth chapters of 1 Corinthians. "Now concerning spiritual gifts, brethren, I would not have you ignorant" (1 Cor. 12:1), Paul wrote, as he proceeded to show them how to detect the difference between the manifestations of deceiving spirits in demoniacal inspiration or ecstasy, and the true inspiration of the Holy Spirit. The Spirit of God in one believer is in harmony with the manifestation of His power in others, while the demoniacal spirit produces a schism between members of the body of Christ. The Holy Spirit causes interdependence between believers, and they honor His workings in one another. The demoniacal spirit causes lawlessness and confusion. Harmony and confusion are, respectively, the characteristics that reveal whether a supernatural power in the assembly of God's people is from God or Satan.

CHIEF AVENUE OF ATTACK

The chief avenue accessible to deceiving spirits is the mind. This is especially true before the believer comprehends the need of a "renewed mind" (Eph. 4:23) and realizes that his mind can be open to and used by evil spirits—notwithstanding the divine operation of God in the innermost shrine of his being—and before he realizes what he has admitted as ground for evil spirits in the past. For all the thoughts inserted by the god of this world blind the mind (2 Cor. 4:4; Eph. 2:2) and form material that he can work with later on.

These thoughts are those that were lodged in a person's mind unconsciously, perhaps years before: mental conceptions he admitted without examination; floating ideas that drifted into the ground of his mind, unknown to him; a sentence in a paper, a word dropped in his hearing; and the flotsam and jetsam of the mental world; leaving unthought-of effect upon him, coloring Scripture, and later on placing his mind almost at the mercy of any suggestion of evil spirits, under certain conditions.

It is possible for evil spirits to communicate with a believer even though he has not given them a foothold, but evil spirits can never interfere with the faculties of mind or body unless sufficient ground has been obtained by them. Satan had power to communicate with Christ in the wilderness, for the Devil spoke to Him and Christ replied. Yet the Lord Himself said later on (John 14:30) that although the Prince of this world would come to Him, he would find nothing in Him that he could use for his working. The Devil also communicated with Eve when she was in a state of innocence. It is therefore no proof of ground or sin in a believer's mind or life, that Satan is able to communicate with him.

Yet there are various ways in which a foothold may be given to evil spirits. The first is by means of suggestions or thoughts that are admitted to the mind. Every believer immediately rejects thoughts that clearly come from Satan. However, thousands of thoughts come to people apart from their will, for few understand how to control their minds and how to bring "into captivity every thought to the obedience of Christ" (2 Cor. 10:5). To detect the working of evil spirits upon the mind, let the believer note the way in which his thoughts come. If the mind is working easily, quietly, in normal action in the duty of the moment, and sudden "flashes," "suggestions," or apparent "thoughts" arise, not in sequence or in orderly connection with the work he has in hand, then the Enemy may be counterfeiting the operation of the person's own mind and trying to insert his suggestions into it, as if they were the outcome of the person's own thinking. For when he is in the process of thinking, the lying spirits seek to inject some thought or feeling—the first into his mind, and the second into his spirit.

The danger at this point is for the believer to be ensnared by the simultaneous working of his own mind and the presentation to his mind of the evil spirit's pictures or visions—which he thinks come from his own imagination—or of very subtly refined suggestions which have no appearance of being supernatural or even of being distinct from the person at all. Many think everything that is supernatural is strikingly marvelous and awesome, whereas the Enemy's working is very ordinary, so ordinary that he goes unrecognized. In other words, Satan's operations appear so natural that they are not looked upon as supernatural. The Scripture statement that "the whole world lieth in wickedness" (1 John 5:19) is so true, that the Enemy's words and activities are accepted and followed and yielded to as the ordinary things of life and as the ordinary operations of the mental faculties. The kingdom of darkness is near and natural to the whole world under the rule of the Prince of Darkness.

One of the symptoms of demonic attack is the absolute inability, even after willing it, to change the course of one's thinking or subject of thought. The mind appears stiff and laborious in action. It is best to be suspicious of the abnormal in every shape and form. God does not interfere with the natural operations of the faculties. A sudden break in thought or sequence in the action of the mind, in the thinking or memory, as well as acute loss in the use of either, may indicate the interference of evil spirits. The spirits of evil, in controlling some faculty of the mind, can either hold it, or suddenly release it for action. This holding or releasing power explains much that is unaccountable in a person's suddenness of action or change of mind which, like much else, is left in obscurity as unexplainable. When someone says, "I can" one moment, and in the next, "I cannot," people generally put it down to an "erratic temperament" or other causes. The person, however, may be actually unable to act because of the interruption or interference of the Enemy, but he would really have the ability for action if his faculties were free.

Others whose lives are spent in the bondage of a "spirit of infirmity" are only conscious of a sense of inability; they are always too tired, and have no spirit or energy for the ordinary demands of life. Yet they have no disease or reasonable physical ground for their chronic inertness and feebleness. A sudden inability to listen, described as absent-mindedness or preoccupation, when the person is compelled to follow some thought suggested or some picture presented to his mind, or to follow the words of another, can be an indication of the interference of evil spirits—compulsions are especially characteristic of their workings—when the person is in a normal condition of health and the brain is not diseased.

For instance, in spiritual meetings, when people seem hardly able to listen to a vital truth, how many recognize the work of the "prince of the power of the air" (Eph. 2:2) taking away the Word (see Matthew 13:19) by the suggestion of other things not appropriate to the moment and by preventing people's minds from being able to follow the speaker's words and from grasping and comprehending his meaning? Streams of texts, also, which pour through people's minds apart from their own concentration and the volitional action of their minds, may overpower all that the speaker is saying and carry the hearers away into faraway thoughts and daydreams that appear so beautiful and divine yet, after the meeting is over, have no solid result in practical life. Any admittance of these sudden suggestions or passing thoughts means giving a foothold to the Enemy.

The Deceiver has two ways of putting thoughts into the mind: directly, by communication to the mind, and indirectly, by attacks on the spirit that cause undesirable feelings there, such as impatience because of the attacks. These, in turn, produce impatient thoughts in the mind, followed by impatient words.

The believer has a sense of being hindered persistently by some unseen obstacle, for the evil spirit beings suggest a certain action to him, and then when he attempts it, he is hindered. This causes him to have a sense of irritation for which he cannot account. Nothing he does seems to go right, and his life seems made up of endless minor annoyances, too much for him to bear, causing a sense of moroseness and discontent that grows upon him in spite of himself.

Other symptoms of demonic interference with the mind can include: feverish activity that accomplishes nothing; perpetual occupation that gives no moment of rest; difficulty with work in the daytime; dreams at night, with no sense of rest or leisure at any time; and suffering, confusion, difficulty of action, embarrassment, and perplexity. All of these can emanate directly, maliciously, and deliberately from evil spirits, but be unrecognized by a person.

In addition, believers whose circumstances and environment should give them every cause for a glad and quiet mind may be harassed with terrible anxiety and may be rarely free from troubled thoughts. In this situation, the mind overestimates everything because the imagination and mental faculties are in bondage; anthills appear as mountains to them. Everything is exaggerated, so that they shrink from seeing others, as conversation is terribly difficult. They imagine they are only thinking in an ordinary sense. However, it is not true thinking when a thing grips the mind, but when the mind grips the thing. Their thinking goes beyond the line of pure mental action into brooding, troubling thoughts, and anxiety.

Herein lies the real cause of depression as experienced by many believers, apart from purely physical conditions. The victim of depression and melancholia has admitted thoughts suggested by the deceiving spirits until the mind is unable to shake them off, or else the Enemy has obtained such a footing that he holds the mental faculties in a grip of passivity so that they cannot act. The person feels as though his faculties were in a vise, or weighted with some heavy pressure that obscures all light and prevents him from grasping the facts around him or from using his reason at all. The malignant powers of darkness often succeed in keeping people under the most harassing clouds and shadows when they have given the evil spirits an opportunity to get them into their grip.

The powers of darkness rejoice over their own wicked deeds and love to bind their victims and keep them in bondage. This is truly the "oppression" of the Enemy (Ps. 17:9). It is the outcome of the earlier stages of the attacks of deceiving spirits upon the mind, which could have been quenched had they been dealt with at the beginning.

That the Enemy takes advantage of any mental feebleness or overstrain or disease is, of course, to be recognized; but in persons of normal health with no disease of the mind, inherited or induced, much of their depression may be attributed to the inroads of the Enemy, through ground given unconsciously at some previous time.

To review, this entry of thoughts from any quarter results from the deeper cause of passivity of the mind, which, as we have seen earlier, is the chief state that the Adversary seeks to produce before he can succeed in his effort to obtain control of a believer's will. Conversely, the Lord's words in Matthew 13:23, that the "good ground" hearer is "he that heareth the word, and understandeth it," show that the mind is the vehicle through which the truth of God reaches men to win their devotion and to bring their wills back into intelligent and loyal cooperation with God. In a similar way, the mind hinders Satan from carrying out his schemes to win back control of the believer. Therefore, for the success of his plans, the Enemy knows that the mind must be lulled into inaction and disuse by some means or other, either by strategy or attack. The Arch-deceiver is well aware that any teaching of deceiving spirits that is accompanied by supernatural signs, may be received by the believer if his mind is lulled into passivity so that he does not question, or intelligently reason over, the nature of the teachings or their ultimate effect.

ATTACKS ON SOUL, BODY, AND SPIRIT

The widest ramifications of evil spirits and their workings in man can be seen in soul, body, and spirit: some acting upon the mind or intellect, sensibilities, emotions and affections; others acting directly upon the organs or appetites of the body; and others more immediately upon the spirit. They may obtain access gradually and insidiously, as already shown, but there are instances where they make a sudden assault in order to rush the victim into involuntary surrender.

When evil spirits attack the mind, they do so by speaking lies into the mind and thoughts. The speaking of evil spirits may be described somewhat as follows. First, it is not like the vocal speaking of a human being, which must always be stronger than the speaking of spirits because spirits have no force of breath. Therefore, if a man speaks aloud, he can always drown out the speaking of evil spirits. On the same principle, a man can also drown the voice of the Holy Spirit because He is Spirit and His speaking is always in the spirit, or through conscience.

Secondly, it resembles more the thinking of a person, as when one speaks to oneself. When evil spirits are "speaking" to the inner ear, it seems like a ceaseless buzz of inner words, apparently belonging to the person himself. Yet these words are not from his mind, nor the result of mental action, nor from his will, nor do they even express his own personal ideas or desires.

When this buzz of objectionable or annoying or irresponsible words are thus claiming the inner attention of the person, and he has outer claims to deal with, he is liable to speak aloud with a strong voice in order to overpower or dull the inner clamor. Yet he is not conscious of raising his voice, or of why he is doing so. Unknowingly, the person is making an impression on his own mind, through his own ear, by using a loud voice; otherwise, his dulled mind would not be able to take in or retain what he is saying, or get the impression into his mind.

The believer may not be conscious of the inner buzz of the evil spirits' words, and that his voice is raised to express his own thoughts in audible speech, or he may not know why he finds himself obliged to speak to get clear in his own thinking. "Unconsciousness" is a symptom of the depth of the evil spirit's influence, and unconsciousness of facts concerning himself is as detrimental to the person as attempts of strangers to enter a house would be to a householder who is oblivious to all sounds.

Consciousness of all things connected with the inner life and environment is as keenly needed by the believer, and should be cultivated by him, as is consciousness of all exterior matters connected with the duties of life. A person's unconsciousness of how he acts and speaks, thinks or appears, in oblivion to all that is obvious to others, or, on the other hand, an "unconscious" self-consciousness, or ultra-consciousness of the actions of self, may all be results of the work of deceiving spirits.

When a person has been attacked by supernatural voices, some of his symptoms may be: difficulty in listening to others, a contorted expression caused by difficulty in grasping what is said, and a sense of dullness or heaviness in the ear or ears.

In affecting the body, the spirits of evil also interfere with all the functions at various times, and in various degrees. Eating and drinking, the breath and breathing, physical weakness or strength, stiffness of limbs, heaviness, heat and cold, agreeable or disagreeable feelings, sleeplessness, dreams, and restlessness at night, can all be irritated, produced, or exaggerated by the presence and will of evil spirits.

There are other varied symptoms that reveal the disturbance of the entire system of a person who is dominated by evil spirits. The muscles, hands and fingers, or feet act without the control of the mind or will, sometimes in convulsive action, or in twitches and prostration, or else in the paradox of being muscularly weak and strong consecutively, and in rapid succession.

The insidious spirits have prepared for this manipulation or interference with the person by slowly dulling his mind; weakening his reasoning powers, which prevents him from seeing the outcome of a certain step or action; causing him not to use his judgment; and causing him to lose his ability to make decisions and the independent action of his will, so that it "snaps," so to speak, at a critical moment, with fatal results. For without this passivity of mind and will, the emissaries of Satan cannot have the full control of the body that they so keenly desire.

To these effects and influences of evil spirit beings on a person should be added general weakness of the whole man: spiritual, mental, and physical. He becomes erratic in temperament, sporadic in study, wavering in allegiance, and undecided in action. He is easily moved by impulses, such as a sharp movement forward without volition; or repulsion without reason, such as a sharp movement backward apart from volition. His life becomes increasingly full of contradictions. The man seems strong and yet is weak, he is stoical and yet seeks love; he is fitful in his actions, erratic and dogmatic in his beliefs, and utterly illogical in his reasonings. All these symptoms may be visible or invisible, and manifested at different intervals, and in different degrees, concurrently or consecutively.

KEEPING THE DECEPTION GOING

The excuses of the evil spirit to hide the ground it holds now need to be explored. Once ground is taken, and the mind is dulled from its power of critical discrimination, the lying spirit is quick to suggest excuses to the believer in order to hide his presence and the ground he holds. If the mind labors in action, he suggests that "it is natural" or "it is heredity." Where the whole nervous system is involved, "it is fatigue," "it is disease," "it is purely physical," or it is "spiritual." There may be, and there generally is, some basis for the excuse, for the deceivers are keenly clever in working alongside natural conditions, either in circumstances, temperament, or in the disturbance of the bodily functions. For instance, the attack may be in the natural and physical realm, but this is not its source.

The evil spirits like to have, and watch for, some physical or mental ailment to serve as the excuse for their manifestation. They attack a person because they are oppressing, but they make him think and believe it is an indirect attack, for example, through another person. The blame is placed on the person himself or someone else, or on anything but the true cause, so that the intruders may not be discovered and rebuked. It is therefore important that all excuses should be examined, that is, the assumed reasons for unexplainable manifestations. The causes should always be looked into, for by believing a wrong interpretation of the manifestation, more ground is given to the lying spirits. The believer may be refusing ground on one hand and giving new ground on the other, unless he examines all the suggestions that come to his mind concerning his condition.

Deceiving spirits also persistently endeavor to keep the believer occupied with something else to fill up his mind, so that he may not discover his own need of deliverance. People may be almost obsessed with the thought of revival, or the need of others, while they are blind to their own condition. Devotion, singing, preaching, worship—all good things—may so possess the mind as to close it to all personal knowledge of the need of deliverance from the Adversary's deception.

EFFECTS OF DEMONIC ATTACK

After a time the believer may become conscious of his condition, and then he painfully shrinks back from others for fear that these symptoms will be read by them and that this will cause attacks upon him. When they do become too manifest to be hidden or ignored, then he is often said to be suffering from a nervous breakdown, for the symptoms coincide with all the characteristics of neurasthenia and can only be distinguished from it by an examination into past spiritual experiences and the discovery of the working of supernatural powers. Should the apparent neurasthenia really be oppression by evil spirits, no prolonged rest or natural means will set the person free, although such means may give the body a renewing that will enable the victim to face the spiritual truth in due time.

This growing weakness of the body also weakens the spiritual life by preventing its growth into vigorous manhood in Christ, for the inner spiritual man needs the outer man for expression and development. But in oppression through deception, the mind is too passive to act and express the inner life—the expression of the face is passive and dull, the eyes are dreamy and slow. In brief, the outer man becomes a prison, so to speak, of the spirit life at the center within.

Another very manifest effect is that as time goes on, the man lives more in the body than in the soul and spirit. The lawful appetites reassert control, and the life of the spirit is more unrecognized and less followed, while variations and inconsistencies in life, in state, and in actions, all show increasingly the marks of oppression.

A brief consideration of the characteristics of those drawn into abnormal supernatural experiences will bear this out. The invariable effect upon such believers is a weakening of the mental force, the reasoning and judging power; a weakening in moral force and will; often a haunting sense of fear, fear of the future, fear of persons so that they cannot bear to hear them spoken of or to speak to them; and a gradual general weakening of the body. In time there comes an involuntary effect upon the nervous system, often including a twitching action of the nerves, and there is impatience—manifestly nervous and not moral—and restlessness.

In the moral realm there comes an attitude of infallibility, bold assertion, and unteachableness, with the loss of the real power of choice and personal control of mind, speech, manner, and actions. For persons thus oppressed cannot choose or act, because they will not, and they have an acute sense that they "don't know what to do," on account of the evil spirit's hold on them.

The subtlety of the deception has been that, in multitudes of cases, all these symptoms are thought to be physical or morally the outcome of the individual personality. For instance, a person may think that a certain symptom is the result of his temperament, which must be borne with until the release of his body of clay into the grave! Self, he declares, is his trouble, which no acceptance of the fullness of the Spirit, nor spiritual light regarding identification with Christ, has altered. Therefore, wandering of the mind in prayer, restlessness, talkativeness, extreme reserve, and many other hindering troubles in the outer man remain, and are tolerated or grieved over, without hope of change.

But how different the outlook when much that troubles believers is attributed to the true cause. "An enemy hath done this!" In many it is not self after all, but ground unknowingly given to deceiving spirits who could be dislodged by the knowledge of the truth and by refusal of ground.

Chapter 9

The Path to Freedom

And ye shall know the truth,
and the truth shall make you free.
—John 8:32

The very first step to freedom is the knowledge of the truth regarding the source and nature of experiences the believer has had since his entrance into the spiritual life— experiences that may have been perplexing, or else thought with deepest assurance to be of God. There is no deliverance from deception but by the acknowledgment and acceptance of the truth.

When a believer faces the truth in regard to certain spiritual and supernatural experiences, a sharp-edged knife will pierce his self-respect and pride. (See Hebrews 4:12.) This process requires a very deep allegiance to the truth that God desires should reign in the inward parts of His children. It means a believer must accept truth that cuts and humbles as readily as he accepts that which is agreeable. The discovery that he has been deceived is one of the keenest blows to a person who once thought that he was so advanced, so spiritual, and so infallible, in obeying the Spirit of God.

Was the believer not advanced? He was, to an extent, above the "man of soul," but he had not reached the goal as he had thought, for he had only begun the journey in the spiritual plane. He believed a lie about himself and his experience. When the truth breaks upon his mind, its entrance is not agreeable. It is not easy for him to absolutely disbelieve what he once believed so thoroughly.

189

Was he not spiritual? He may have had spiritual experiences, but this does not make a man spiritual. The spiritual man is a person who lives in, and is governed by, and understands, his spirit, and who understands cooperation with the Spirit of God. A great experience accompanying entrance into the realm of the Spirit does not make a believer spiritual.

The deceived believer has laid claim to positions to which he had no right, for with the entrance of truth he discovers that he was neither so advanced, nor so spiritual, nor so infallible as he had thought. He has built his faith about his own spiritual condition on assumption, and left no room for doubt—true doubt, that is—such as doubting a statement that afterwards turns out to be a lie. However, in due season, doubt finds an entry to his mind and brings his house of infallibility to the ground. He knows now that what he thought was an "advanced" experience was only a beginning, and that he is only on the fringe of knowledge. This is the operation of truth. In the place of ignorance, knowledge is given; in the place of deception, truth. Ignorance, falsehood, and passivity: upon these three the Enemy silently builds his castles and unobtrusively guards and uses them. But truth pulls his strongholds to the ground.

ACKNOWLEDGE THE TRUTH

Through the entry of truth, a person must be brought to the place where he acknowledges his condition frankly, as follows:

1. I believe that it is possible for a Christian to be deceived and oppressed by evil spirits.

2. It is possible for me to be deceived.

3. I am deceived by an evil spirit.

4. Why am I deceived?

Then he faces the fact that a foothold or ground does exist, and seeks knowledge regarding what that ground is.

In order to discover the ground, the believer must first, in a general sense, get a good conception of what *ground* is, for he is liable to be deceived in putting down to oppression what belongs to something else, and attributing to something else what belongs to oppression. He may confuse ordinary conflict, that is, the perpetual battle in his spirit against the powers of darkness, with conflict that comes from oppression. And when the deception and oppression are of long standing, the evil spirits may get the believer himself to defend their work in him, and through him fight tenaciously to prevent the cause of his deception from being brought into the light and exposed as their work. They thus get the believer himself, in effect, to take their side and to fight for them to keep their foothold, even after he has discovered his condition and honestly desires deliverance.

OBEY DIVINE LAWS

One of the greatest hindrances to deliverance is an assumption concerning spiritual experiences that believers are loathe to examine and part with. The scriptural ground for obtaining deliverance is the truth concerning Christ's full victory at Calvary, through which every believer can be delivered from the power of both sin and Satan. In actual fact, however, the victory won at Calvary can only be applied when there is conformity to divine laws. As the deceptions of Satan are recognized, and the will of the person is set to reject them, he can, on the basis of the work of Christ at Calvary—as set forth in Romans 6:6–13; Colossians 2:15; 1 John 3:8; and other passages—claim his deliverance from these deceptive and oppressive workings of the Devil.

Just as there are various degrees of deception, so there are degrees of deliverance according to the understanding of the believer and his willingness to face the whole truth about himself and all the ground that he has given to the Enemy. The believer needs to have a steady grasp of his standing in Christ—in identification with Him in His death on the Cross, and in union with Him in spirit in His place on the throne. (See Ephesians 1:19–23; 2:6.) He must "hold fast," with steady faith-grip, to the "Head" (Col. 2:19) as the One who is, by His Spirit, giving him grace (see Hebrews 4:16) and strength to recover the ground in mind and body that he has ignorantly yielded to the Foe.

For the person himself must act to get rid of passivity; he must revoke the consent he has given to evil spirits, and by his own volition he must insist that they retire from the place (see Ephesians 4:27) they have obtained by deceit. Since God will not act for him in regaining the normal condition of his outer man, nor exercise his choice for him, he must stand on the vantage ground of the Calvary victory of Christ and claim his freedom.

STEPS TO FREEDOM

Assuming, then, that the believer has discovered he is a victim of the deceptions of deceiving spirits, what are the steps in the path of freedom? They are, briefly:

- acknowledging the deception
- refusing ground
- steadfastly fighting all that deception is
- being on guard against excuses
- detecting all the effects of deception
- discerning the result of the above actions

The believer must learn to read the signs of deliverance, as well as the symptoms of deception, lest he be deceived again by the Adversary.

Let us now look at these steps in more detail.

Acknowledging the Deception

First, there are four essential stages to acknowledging that deception has occurred in one's life. They are as follows.

Doubt Regarding the Manifestation. We cannot emphasize too strongly the need for not quenching and not ignoring the first doubt, for the so-called doubt is actually the initial penetration of truth to the mind, and therefore the first stage in deliverance. Some have instantly quenched the first doubt because they are afraid to "doubt God," and in doing so have closed their minds to the first ray of light that would have led them into liberty. They have looked upon doubt as temptation, and have resisted it, overlooking the distinction between true and evil, and right and wrong, "doubt."

The root cause of this kind of thinking in the minds of most Christians is that they only associate an evil connotation with such words as *judging*, *criticizing*, and *doubting*, as well as *enmity*, *hatred*, *unbelief*, etc. In reality, these things are evil or good according to their origin in spirit or soul, and in relation to their purpose. For example, enmity against

Satan is God-given (Gen. 3:15), hatred toward sin is good, and unbelief toward spiritual manifestations is commanded until the believer is sure of their source. (See 1 John 4:1.)

To doubt God—which means not to trust Him—is sin; but a doubt concerning supernatural manifestations is simply a call to exercise one's faculties, which all spiritual believers should use to discern good and evil. The deep doubt concerning some supernatural experiences is therefore not a temptation but really the Holy Spirit moving the spiritual faculties to action according to 1 Corinthians 2:15: "He that is spiritual judgeth all things," the "things of God" thus being "spiritually discerned."

Generally, a doubt first pierces the mind from truth pointed out by others, or it arises from some flaw in the experience that arrests the attention of the believer. In the case of some supernatural manifestation that bears the appearance of being divine, there will be some slight contradiction that perplexes the soul. And since no contradictions can possibly occur in any of the workings of the Spirit of God, who is the Spirit of Truth, one single contradiction is sufficient to reveal a lying spirit at work. This principle must not be ignored.

For instance, if a believer declares, under supernatural power—assumed to be divine—concerning one who is ill, that God purposes the restoration of that one, yet the sick one dies, this is a contradiction that should be fully examined, and not put aside as among things "not to be understood." For the supernatural element in the declaration could not be of the Spirit of God, who cannot depart from truth in His revelation of the will of God.

To "try the spirits" (1 John 4:1) in order to discern between the Spirit of Truth and the spirit of error, is a clear command to the children of God. They are to "prove all things; hold fast that which is good" (1 Thess. 5:21), and "reprove, rebuke, exhort with all longsuffering" (2 Tim. 4:2). To question until all things have stood the test of full examination, is the safest course and is far removed from doubting God Himself in His faithfulness and love, the only doubt that is sin.

Admitting the Possibility of Deception. The second stage in "acknowledging the deception" is admitting the possibility of deception, although this may sometimes precede the doubt. The possibility of being deceived or mistaken in any aspect of new experience or action, or even view of truth, is really something that should be acknowledged by every believer. Yet so subtle is the deception of the Enemy, that almost invariably the attitude of believers is that others may be open to deception, and that they are the exception to the rule.

This certainty of personal exception is so deep-seated with the most visibly deceived person that the long battle is simply to get him to consider the possibility that he is deceived in any point at all. The believer seems armed with unshaken assurance that if others are misled, he certainly is not; he sees the "mote" (splinter) in his brother's eye, and is blind—blind to the "beam" in his own. (See Luke 6:41.) But an open attitude to truth says, "Why not I as well as others? Perhaps my assurance of safety is a deception of the Enemy, as much as the deception I see in others?"

Why all believers should admit the possibility of deception by deceiving spirits should now be considered. The primary fact to be recognized by every human being is the complete and utter ruin of the first creation at the Fall, when the first Adam received the poison of the Serpent, which permeated and corrupted his whole being beyond repair. The fact of the utter corruption of the human race as a consequence of this is unmistakably declared in the New Testament:

> *The old man, which is corrupt according to the deceitful lusts.* *(Eph. 4:22)*

> *Having the understanding darkened, being alienated from the life of God.* *(Eph. 4:18)*

> *We all had our conversation in times past in the lusts of our flesh, fulfilling the desires of the flesh and of the mind; and were by nature the children of wrath, even as others.*
> *(Eph. 2:3)*

Thus the apostle Paul described the whole race of man, Gentile and Jew, Pharisee and publican. In all, he said, "the prince of the power of the air" worked as "the spirit that now worketh in the children of disobedience" (Eph. 2:2). These realities, which are declared by the Word of God—the reality of the blinded mind (see 2 Corinthians 4:4), and the ruined condition of every human being—are the only basis upon which the truths we are considering in this book can be understood and proved to be true, in experience and practice.

The second fundamental fact of admitting the possibility of deception—and the logical outcome of the first—is that, unless regeneration by the Holy Spirit and the indwelling of the Spirit means continual sinlessness and the present possession of a resurrection body, every part of a believer not yet renewed and freed from the effects of the Fall by the redemption of Calvary means ground for the possible deception and oppression of deceiving spirits. Since absolute sinlessness and the present possession of the resurrection body are not clearly taught in the Scriptures to be attainable while we are on earth, deception and oppression by evil spirits on the outer man through mind or body is logically and reasonably possible for all, even while the spirit and heart of the person are renewed by the Holy Spirit. If we look at the facts of experience, the proofs are so abundant as to be beyond our power to handle in the limited space of this book, proofs not only from the unregenerate world but from those who are undoubtedly children of God and mature believers.

If we knew ourselves, and our actual condition as sinners, solely as depicted in God's Word, we would be in greater safety from the Enemy. It is the ignorance of our true condition, apart from the new life from God that has been implanted in us, and our blind confidence of being free from deception, without an intelligent basis for our faith, which lays us open to being deceived by Satan.

Discovery of the Deception. The third step in "acknowledging the deception" is the discovery of the deception. Light and truth alone can bring freedom. Once a doubt comes in, and a person opens his mind to the truth that he is as liable to be deceived as anyone else, then light is given to his open mind and attitude. (See Ephesians 5:13–14.) Sometimes the specific deception is seen at once; but more often the discovery is gradual, and patience is needed while the light slowly dawns.

Certain facts in connection with various experiences of the past, which the believer has failed to note, may now emerge into the light, and the half-truths that the Adversary has used to deceive are clearly seen. The twisting of words and the wrenching of sentences out of their context in the Scriptures all come into view as the light is given.

Complete Acknowledgment. Fourthly, acknowledging the deception is now imperative. The truth must not only be faced, but owned, so that things are called by their right names and the Father of Lies is defeated by the weapon of truth.

REFUSING GROUND

This brings us to the second crucial point in the steps to freedom, "refusing ground." Thoughts admitted to the mind; passivity of mind or body; faculties allowed to lie unused; lack of mental control or the use of the will or of decisive power or judgment, etc.: the believer must now deliberately and steadily refuse this ground to the Enemy, especially and specifically the ground on the points in which he has been deceived. For it is of primary importance that the one who is deceived should know the ground that he has given, and refuse it.

Ground refused to the Enemy will result in freedom. The deceived one must pray for light until the causes of the deception are revealed, and he must honestly desire and be willing to receive light on every point. (See Ephesians 5:13–14.) He must be given light from God to detect symptoms and their causes. Yet in the recognition of these he must beware of introspection, that is, a turning in upon himself, which is the opposite of simply refusing ground as it is brought into the light.

Generally, whatever a person shrinks from hearing about, or is troubled about when reference is made to it, may reveal, upon examination, ground given on that point. If the believer is afraid to examine something he shrinks from dealing with, then it is safe to examine that particular thing, for the Enemy most probably has some footing there. What the believer cannot bear to hear about is probably the very thing that he is guilty of doing. Or, he is in some way wrong in his relation to it. Then the ground—and the cause or causes of it—when revealed, must be taken back from the deceiving spirits by the rejection or refusal of these points upon which ground has been given. The believer must persist until the ground given has passed away; for the ground that admits the evil spirit is the ground that keeps him there.

There is also ground given that causes the believer, unknowingly, to take hold of evil spirits, and there are things and ground given that enable them to grip the believer and his faculties. There is also the probability of giving new ground through taking the lying spirits' interpretation of their manifestations, which means accepting lies from them in the present as much as in the past, when ground was first given to them.

STEADFASTLY FIGHTING DECEPTION

The third point in the steps to freedom is "steadfastly fighting all that deception is." What it means to fight through deception may be explained through a specific case. For instance, a believer may discover that he has sunk into passivity, and that an evil spirit has taken advantage of this, so that while his faculties were lying passive, the spirit acted for him or in conjunction with him. When the believer gives up this ground, he finds it most difficult to act for himself again and to regain the use of his faculties. If he has been drifting into passivity in decision making and, refusing this ground to the Enemy, resolves now to decide for himself, and not to act under their control, he finds, at first, that (1) he cannot act and decide for himself; and (2) the evil spirits will not let him act—that is, when the believer refuses them permission to control him, they will not let their captive act without their permission.

The person has therefore to choose between not acting at all, or letting the evil spirit continue to act for him. This he will not do, and so for awhile he is unable to use his own decisive power, and yet he refuses to allow the Enemy to use it. It becomes a fight for the use of his free will and for deliverance from passivity of the will, which destroyed his decisive power and gave evil spirits control over him.

Why do deception and its effects not cease as soon as the man refuses all ground to the deceiving spirits? Because every detail of the ground must be detected; the man must be undeceived on every point, and the evil spirits must be dislodged from every hold. Whatever caused the deception, the opposite must be obtained for freedom: instead of the lies of Satan, the truth of God; instead of passivity, activity; instead of ignorance, knowledge; instead of surrender to the Enemy, resistance; instead of acceptance, refusal.

Actions are the result of thought and belief. Ground is always to be traced back to its radical cause, which is a thought and belief. Wrong thoughts and beliefs, which gave ground to evil spirits, must be detected and given up. The basis of acceptance or refusal must be knowledge, not a passing thought or impression. It is for this reason that understanding is such an important factor in deliverance and the subsequent warfare.

In seeking the ground of any trouble in the spiritual life, believers generally go back only as far as the first manifestation of conscious wrong, instead of seeking the radical cause of the manifestations. Yet, in seeking the root of a tree, men do not content themselves with the discovery of its manifestation above ground. They know that the cause of the growth they see lies deeper down. In the same way, it is very important that believers diagnose the cause of their trouble as going further back than the first conscious manifestation— to some thought or belief that has given the Enemy occasion for deception.

If the believer resists and refuses any specific ground, and cannot get rid of it, he must seek light regarding the cause. He must seek the ground he has given in the past in thought and belief. When this is discovered and refused, the Enemy has to give up the ground. This is why it is necessary to say that each point must be patiently fought through. This means that the refusal of all ground to evil spirits must be maintained, because refusing all ground, and getting rid of all ground, are two different things.

All ground is not necessarily removed at the moment of refusal. The refusing must therefore be reasserted, and the believer refuse persistently, until each point of ground is detected and refused, and the faculties are gradually released to act freely under the will of the person. The faculties that have been let go into passivity should then regain their normal working condition.

For example, the operation of the mind should be kept to true and pure thinking, so that any subject being dealt with is mastered and does not dominate beyond control. It is the same way with the memory, the will, the imagination, and the actions of the body, such as singing, praying, speaking, reading, etc. All must be brought back into normal working order, out of the passive, heavy state into which they have fallen under the subtle workings of the Enemy.

Statements of Refusal

The refusal of the workings of deceiving spirits is necessary along with the refusal of ground that they have obtained. The believer may say as his declaration of decision:

- I refuse the influence of evil spirits.
- I refuse the power of evil spirits.
- I refuse to be led by evil spirits.
- I refuse to be guided by evil spirits.
- I refuse to obey evil spirits.
- I refuse to pray to evil spirits.
- I refuse to ask anything of evil spirits.
- I refuse to surrender to evil spirits.
- I refuse all knowledge from evil spirits.
- I refuse to listen to evil spirits.
- I refuse visions from evil spirits.
- I refuse the touch of evil spirits.
- I refuse messages from evil spirits.
- I refuse all help from evil spirits.

The believer must revoke the consent he unknowingly gave to the workings of the deceivers. They have sought to work through him; therefore, he must now declare: "I, myself, *will* to do my own work. In the past I willed not to do my work. This I now revoke forever."

The "fighting through" period is a very painful time. There are bad moments of acute suffering and intense struggle, arising out of the consciousness of the resistance of the powers of darkness in their contest for what the believer endeavors to reclaim. The moment he begins to advance from weakness into strength, he becomes aware of the strength of the evil spirits resisting him; consequently, he feels worse when fighting through. This is a sign of deliverance, although the believer may not think or feel it to be so.

The last thing given to the spirits of evil is generally the first thing removed, because light is given upon the experience of the moment, and deliverance from the bondage of the moment is the most urgent need. Sometimes it is the advanced stage of terrible bondage that reveals a person's condition to himself, and it is not until he starts, point by point, to fight back to his normal condition that he discovers the depth of the pit he has fallen into, and the slow work of regaining the liberation of his whole being from the power of the deceiving Enemy.

The believer fighting back to freedom must not be deceived about the immediate effects of deliverance, for it may appear, as he advances, that he is slipping back. For instance, when the man is in a passive state under the bondage of the Enemy, he may be absolutely unaware of what he is, what he feels, and how he appears; therefore, he cannot feel and cannot be touched on these points. However, as he fights back to the normal condition, these things become real to him again and he thinks he has regressed; but the fact that he *feels* about these matters proves a degree of deliverance, for his feelings, which had become numb, are once more regaining their normal condition.

Moreover, the believer must not be off guard when he knows a great deal about deliverance, because there are new realms of deception. He must be careful not to confuse ordinary wrestling in spirit with the powers of darkness with manifestations of their workings through deception and oppression.

When the spirits of evil see their hold coming to an end, they never let go until the cause is fully removed, and they continue to attack if the thing through which they have attacked still exists in any degree. When a person is fighting through, the Deceiver has various tactics to hinder his deliverance. Satan will dangle a thing before his mind, which is not the true cause of the deception, in order to get the believer occupied with it. In the meantime, the Enemy is gaining all the time, pouring accusations upon his victim until he is bewildered and confused through charges, accusations, blame, and guilt, which come directly from the Enemy or indirectly through others.

Accusing spirits can tell you that you are wrong when you are not wrong, and vice versa. They can also tell you that you are wrong when you are wrong, and right when you are right; therefore, it is very essential that the believer does not accept blame until he is absolutely sure that it is deserved. Even then, he should not accept blame from Satan's lying spirits, who have not been appointed by God to do the convicting work of the Holy Spirit.

When once the truth has dawned upon the victim, and the powers of darkness no longer hope to gain by deception, their one great attack—which they maintain from the moment the person realizes his deception to his final deliverance—is the perpetual charge, "You are wrong," in order to keep the man in ceaseless condemnation. The poor persecuted believer then goes to God and tries to get victory over "sin," but in vain. The more he prays, the more he appears to sink into a hopeless bog. He sees himself as one mass of sin, without hope of freedom. But it is victory over the powers of darkness he needs, and he will quickly prove this when he recognizes the true cause of his trouble and lays hold of the Calvary victory over Satan.

Our Divinely Provided Weapon

In fighting back to freedom, the believer must wield Scripture as the divinely provided weapon for victory over evil spirits. The verses that have immediate effect, and give evidence of relief, indicate the specific nature of any attack. The believer may reason the cause of the warfare from the effectiveness of the weapon. For instance, if the text wielded is that Satan is the Father of Lies (see John 8:44), and the believer declares that he refuses all his lies, and this brings liberty from the oppression of the Enemy, it indicates that the Enemy is attacking with some of his deceptive workings. Then the believer should not only refuse all his lies, but pray, "Lord, destroy all the Devil's lies to me."

All this simply means that in the path to freedom, the deceived believer must act intelligently. He must know the truth, and he is set free by receiving and acting upon the truth. (See John 8:32.) When he went down into deception, his intelligence was unused, but in recovering freedom he must act with deliberate knowledge. He "goes down" passively, but he must emerge to liberty actively, that is, by the action of his whole being.

The Use of Force

Force must be used against force. There are two aspects of the use of force in the fight against the powers of darkness: using spirit force against spirit force when the believer is undeceived and delivered, and using physical force, brought into action against their power or grip on the body. The Deceiver may suggest that either of these is "self-effort," and deceive the person into taking up a passive attitude, and thus to cease his resistance against him.

When the believer is fighting free from deception, he must bring into action all the forces of his tripartite being, and must know the place of the spirit, the soul, and the body in the conflict. The believer, therefore, must not be afraid to use force—pure force, which simply means active use of spirit, soul, and body in their various actions. Evil spirits, through deception, caused the forces of the tripartite man to be inactive and passive, and now these must be aroused to action against the force holding them. There must be liberation of the physical being—as well as the mind and spirit—from passivity.

But resistance through the action of spirit, soul, or body must not take the place of refusal by the will. A man may fight without any result if he does not first refuse. There is an evil kind of fighting, which is a resistance in body or mind that is due to deception. If it exists it must be refused. To be sure that this evil force is not in operation, the believer can say, "I refuse all evil light now in spirit, soul, or body." The believer may be resisting something in himself that is the fruit of his choice in the past, and which only his refusal, or revoking of his past choice, can touch in the present. Fighting by force, or resistance, must therefore always have behind it the volitional attitude of refusal.

For example, in the refusing stage of regaining the use of the memory, a person should say, "I *will* to remember," and so to speak, by the action of his will, he lays hold of freedom. This is followed by the actual fighting stage where he holds the liberty he has taken by refusal and actively insists that the Enemy give way, until the memory becomes really free from his control.

The deception of the Enemy now slowly weakens as the ground that he held is steadily refused and given up. The Deceiver fought long to obtain the ground, and the believer may have to fight a long time before he is fully set free. Also, the weakening of the foothold is in accordance with the degree to which the ground is removed, and is affected by whether or not the person gives more ground to the Foe in the meantime. This makes the deliverance gradual, it is true, but in most cases the snare may have been gradually woven about him for many years. Film after film may have slowly come upon the mind in preparation for the deception of later years.

BEING ON GUARD AGAINST EXCUSES

The fourth step to freedom is "being on guard against excuses." Following the person's steady attitude of the refusal of ground, light begins to break in with the discovery of the excuses the Enemy is making to hide his influence. For the persistent endeavor is to make the person believe that the manifestations are due to some other cause. The chief excuses for the manifestation of deception center around the suggestions, "it is divine," "natural," "physical," or else that "it is temperament," "circumstances," "others' wrongdoing," etc., in order to hide the ground that is held. But as the excuses are recognized, the believer resists them and calls the excuses what they are: Satan's lies.

After getting rid of the counterfeits of the divine workings, the difficult stage is recognizing and getting free from the counterfeits of the man himself. As the excuses or lies are recognized, the believer becomes more acute in detection and less ready to accept "natural" and "physical" causes as true explanations, without examination and certainty. For example, he inquires why he cannot bear to hear or speak about a person. He asks why an attack on a certain point does not cease. The truth is, a believer cannot bear things because of deception, and he cannot do things because of deception.

DETECTING ALL THE EFFECTS OF DECEPTION

The fifth step is "detecting all the effects of deception." Naming the attack is a great factor in victory. For example, an attack may be made to hinder. The believer must then be on guard against all hindrances, seen and unseen, which the Hinderer is placing in his way. An attack may be made to make him impatient. He must then be on guard concerning all things liable to test his patience. The sooner the attack is recognized and named, the quicker the weapon can be called into use to destroy it.

The attack may be a flood of accusations of wrongdoing, which need to be recognized or tested

208

as to their truth. When the Accuser charges the believer with some specific wrong over a certain thing and the believer surrenders that thing to God, if the accusation does not then pass away, it shows that this is not the true ground for the accusation; it is some other cause hidden from view. The believer should then seek light from God, according to John 3:21, regarding the hidden causes, and refuse the cause of the accusation without knowing what it is, saying, "I refuse the cause of this attack, whatever it is, and I trust the Lord to destroy it." Often, however, when a believer is charged with being wrong concerning a certain thing, and he fights it off again and again in this way, it does not pass away. Then the true cause of the attack is oppression, and not a "thing" at all. The matter to be fought is oppression as a whole. The deceiving spirit will often be found in a direction opposite to the apparent one, for they know they are being exposed and dislodged, and so they vigorously ply an attack upon some other place to divert attention.

DISCERNING THE RESULTS OF THE STEPS TO FREEDOM

The effect of these preceding steps can now be seen. The symptoms slowly pass away, and the believer, returning to normal conditions, finds his faculties usable and his thoughts once more under the control of his volition. It is a spiritual resurrection from a satanic burial.

Now the one who is being freed must be on guard not to think he has obtained final victory, or that the deceiving spirit has been fully refused because the manifestations have ceased. It is necessary to watch and pray as never before. The evil spirit has been exposed, the soul has been undeceived; but the deeper the deception, the longer it takes for the film of Satan upon the mind to be removed, and for the passivity of the various faculties of spirit, soul, or body to be destroyed. To be undeceived does not always mean to be fully delivered. The believer must therefore be wary of the snare of ceasing to fight against deception when ease comes.

It is here that the believer needs to know himself, in order to be able to judge the extent of his liberation. This he does by having a clear criterion of his true normal condition, in order to detect whether he is above it, and is therefore strained beyond his normal poise and measure, or below it, and therefore less capable in all the departments of his being.

For these reasons it is essential and indispensable, for full deliverance from the power of evil spirits, that a believer knows the standard of his normal condition. He must, with this gauge before him, be able to judge his degree of deliverance, physically, intellectually, and spiritually, in order to fight through with steady will and faith until every faculty is free and he stands a liberated man in the liberty with which Christ has made him free.

As he judges himself by this criterion, he may say, "Things are not the same as they were," and he then fights through by prayer to his normal condition. The deceiving spirits will suggest all kinds of excuses to stop a person's advance to freedom. For example, if he is forty years old, they will suggest that his "mind cannot be as vigorous as at twenty," or that "overwork" is the reason that he is below what he should be; but he must not accept reasons that appear to be natural if he has been a subject of oppression. Let the believer know the highest measure of grace to which he has attained in spirit, soul, and body, and resist all attempts of the powers of darkness to keep him below it at any time. If he is vigilant he will know that the lying spirits will endeavor to deceive him about it, and he must resist their lies.

Normal Working Condition

There is a norm of spirit, mind, and body. Some practical ways of keeping the mind in its normal working condition are briefly suggested as follows:

Attitude to the Past. There should be no regrets, or obsessing over things done or not done. This occurs when the ordinary operation of the mind, in thinking over the past, becomes entangled in an evil kind of thinking that is generally described as "brooding." The believer must learn to discern for himself when he is simply thinking, or when he is being drawn into a state of regretting or brooding. For victory in the life, there must be victory in regard to the past, with all its failures. The good of the past causes no trouble to the mind, only the real or supposed evil. This should be dealt with by dealing with God, on the basis of 1 John 1:7, and in this way the believer will be delivered from it.

To regain its normal working condition, the mind must first be brought into action, and then into balanced action. This is very difficult, and at times impossible, while there is evil spirit oppression. The oppression must therefore pass away before balanced working is restored. This principle applies to every faculty.

Attitude to the Future. The same may be said in the action of the mind in regard to the future. It is lawful to think of the past and to think of the future, as long as the evil state of brooding, brought about by sin or Satan, is not yielded to.

Attitude to Evil Spirits. They must not be permitted to interfere. The believer must see to it that no new ground is given to them, either for oppression or interference.

Attitude to the Present Moment. There should be a steady concentration of the mind upon the duties of the moment, keeping it in active readiness for use as occasion requires. This does not mean ceaseless activity, for activity of the mind so that it is never at rest can be a symptom of oppression.

The believer must understand that regaining the ready use of the faculties and maintaining the mind in a healthy condition, after passive surrender to evil spirits, will mean a steady fight with the powers of darkness that will require the use of the weapons of warfare given in the Word of God, which have been tried and proven by experience. We must use weapons, for instance, such as the truth in the verses: "Sufficient unto the day is the evil thereof" (Matt. 6:34), for resisting brooding over the past or torturing pictures of the future; "Resist the devil, and he will flee from you" (James 4:7), when the pressure of the Enemy is severe; and other "fighting texts" that will truly prove to be the "sword of the Spirit" (Eph. 6:17) to thrust at the Enemy in the evil day of his onslaught upon the escaping believer.

The Steady Attitude or Action of the Will. In keeping the mind in normal working condition, free from the interference of the Enemy, the believer should maintain the attitude of a steadily-set will. For example, he should maintain attitudes such as, "I *will* that my mind shall not be passive," "I *will* to have full control of, and to use, my faculties," "I *will* to recognize everything that comes from demon possession," all of which declare the choice of the man, rather than his determination, to do these things. The powers of darkness are not affected by mere determination or resolve, but they are rendered powerless by the act of volition that definitely chooses, in the strength given of God, to stand against them.

The believer now finds the following results through experience. He has: clear vision, in the light of God, of the Enemy's workings, without fear; a clear mind, used intelligently in all its actions; and a calm decision of the will, with a strong, pure spirit in resisting, without hesitation, all he sees to be of the Adversary. Instead of an acceptance of the Enemy's workings there is an established attitude of refusal; instead of a lie in the mind there is truth; instead of ignorance there is knowledge.

The delivered believer now has a deep longing for the deliverance of others he sees to be in the net of the Fowler; acute insight into the Devil's true character in his bitter enmity to Christ and His redeemed; a clear understanding of past perplexities in spiritual experiences; and the ability to detect the Adversary where it was little thought that he had a place. The undeceived one now sees with astonishment the naturalness of the Enemy's supernatural workings. This believer is never off guard now, but is always alert, watching against the powers of darkness while relying upon the strength of God. There is an obvious development of his power of resistance against the wicked spirits that attack him in the heavenly places, instead of the weak and passive attitude he had in the past, which enabled them to hinder or mislead him.

The steps to deliverance that have been given deal with the practical aspect of the believer's actions. On the divine side, the victory has been won, and Satan and his deceiving spirits have been conquered, but the actual liberation of the believer demands his active cooperation with the Holy Spirit and the steady exercise of his volition. He must choose freedom instead of bondage, and the normal use of every faculty of his being, set at liberty from the bondage of the Enemy.

"He that doeth *truth* cometh to the light" (John 3:21, italics added), said the Lord. Evil spirits hate scrutiny, and so they work under cover with deception and lies. The believer must come to the light of God to receive His light upon all spiritual experiences, as well as on all other areas of life, if he is to "cast off the works of darkness" (Rom. 13:12) and put on the armor of God—the armor of light. (See Ephesians 6:11.)

The blood of Jesus Christ, God's Son, cleanses us from all sin if we walk in the light, but the light must shine in for the soul to walk in it. Evil spirits can be cast out in the name of the Lord Jesus, but the foothold they have gained can only be removed by the intelligent choice of the will refusing the ground that has been given to them and appropriating deliverance by death with Christ on Calvary. Let us now review the steps to deliverance from the power of the Enemy that we have discussed in this chapter.

KEYS TO FREEDOM

Here are a few brief suggestions regarding attitude and action for the guidance of any who are seeking freedom from the Enemy's power:

- Keep claiming the power of the blood (Rev. 12:11).
- Pray for light, and face the past.
- Daily resist the Devil persistently in your spirit on the basis of the blood of Christ (James 4:7).
- Never give up hope that you will be set free.
- Avoid all self-introspection.
- Daily live and pray for others, and thus keep your spirit in full aggressive and resisting power.
- Stand daily on Romans 6:11.

Standing on Romans 6:11 means the attitude of the believer in reckoning himself "dead indeed unto sin...through Jesus Christ our Lord." It is a declaration of death to evil spirits as well as to sin—to evil spirits working in, through, for, instead of, or in conjunction with, the person.

To resist the Enemy on the basis of the blood of Christ means wielding by faith the weapon of the finished work of Christ: His death for sin, freeing the trusting believer from the guilt of sin; His death to sin on the Cross and the believer's death with Him, freeing the believer from the power of sin; and His death victory on Calvary, freeing the believer from the power of Satan.

PRINCIPLES FOR DELIVERANCE

The following is an overview of the principles and conditions for deliverance from any degree of deception and oppression by evil spirits:

- knowledge of the possibility of deception
- admission of actual deception and oppression
- attitude of neutrality toward all past spiritual experiences until truth concerning them is ascertained
- refusal of all ground to evil spirits
- the casting out of evil spirits by the authority of the name of Christ (in some cases)
- the believer taking the position of death to sin (Rom. 6:11)
- detection and refusal of all that belongs to deception
- understanding the criterion of the true normal condition, in order to gauge signs of deliverance
- active usage of the faculties so that they reach the normal condition

The steps to deliverance may also be considered in these five points:

- Recognize persistently the true reason for the bondage caused by the work of an evil spirit or spirits.
- Choose to have absolutely nothing to do with the powers of darkness. Frequently declare this.
- Do not talk or trouble about their manifestations. Recognize, refuse, and then ignore them.
- Refuse and reject all their lies and excuses as they are recognized.
- Notice the thoughts, the way in which they come, and when, and immediately declare the attitude of Romans 6:11 against all the interferences of the Enemy.

HINDRANCES TO DELIVERANCE

Some of the most common hindrances to deliverance are:

- not knowing it is possible to be deceived
- thinking that God will not allow a believer to be deceived
- saying, "I am safe under the blood," without intelligent knowledge of the conditions under which we can claim the power of the blood
- saying, "I have no sin," which opens the door to an evil spirit
- saying, "I am doing all that God wants, so all must be right," without seeking to understand what the will of the Lord is (See Ephesians 5: 10–17.)

OVERCOMING PASSIVITY OF MIND

To gain freedom from a passive state of mind:

- Act as far as you can, doing what you can.
- Take the initiative instead of passively depending on others.
- Decide for yourself in everything you can. Do not lean on others.
- Live in the moment, watch and pray step by step.
- Use your mind and think—think over all you do, and say, and are.

Chapter 10

Overcoming Through Will and Spirit

Resist the devil, and he will flee from you.
—James 4:7

Now let us see from the Scriptures the true way in which God works in the life of the believer, in contrast to the way Satan and his wicked spirits work. The principle of *cooperation with God*, and not passive control by Him, must be fully understood, not only as the basis of deliverance from deception, but also as the basis for the warfare that will be discussed in our next chapter.

The Holy Spirit, dwelling in the regenerate human spirit, energizes and works through the faculties of the soul and the members of the body, only in and with the active cooperation of the will of the believer. Paul said, "I also labour...according to his working," and, "His working, which worketh in me mightily" (Col. 1:29). When he said "I labour," this did not mean that his hands and feet and mind worked automatically in response to a divine energizing, as the engine works in response to steam. Behind the "I labour" was the full action of Paul's will. He said, in effect, "I choose to labor," and "as I labor, God's power and energy energizes me" so that it is "I who live and move and work" and "yet not I, but Christ— the 'Spirit of Christ' in me." (See Galatians 2:20; Philippians 1:19.)

This was also so in the life of Jesus, who said, "I came...not to do mine own will, but the will of him that sent me" (John 6:38), and, "The Son can do nothing of himself" (John 5:19). He also said, "My Father worketh hitherto, and I work" (John 5:17) and, "The works that I do shall [you] do also" (John 14:12). Jesus had a separate will; yet He came not to do His own will, but the will of the Father, and He was doing the Father's will when He said to one who sought His healing power, "I *will*; be thou clean" (Matt. 8:3; Mark 1:41; Luke 5:13, italics added).

This is the way it should be in the life of the believer. Once there is the essential union of his will with the will of God, and the energizing power of the Holy Spirit by his own deliberate choice of agreement with that holy will, the believer is to actively use his own will in ruling himself in spirit, soul, and body. God dwells in his spirit, coworking with him through the exercise of his will.

GOD'S PURPOSE IN REDEMPTION

For deliverance from the power of sin and protection from deceiving spirits, it is important to have a clear understanding of God's purpose in redemption. God created man with dominion over himself. This dominion was exercised by an act of his will, in the likeness of his Creator. But man fell and, in his fall, he yielded his will to the rule of Satan, who, from that time, by the agency of his evil spirits, has ruled the world through the enslaved will of fallen man. Christ the Second Adam came and, taking the place of man, chose obedience to the Father's will, and never for one moment diverged from His perfect cooperation with that will. In the wilderness He refused to exercise divine power at the will of Satan, and when suffering in Gethsemane, His will never wavered in the choice of the Father's will. As man, He willed the will of God to the end, becoming "obedient [even] unto death" (Phil. 2:8). In this way, He regained for regenerated man not only reconciliation with God, but liberty from Satan's bondage and the restoration of man's renewed and sanctified will to its place of free action, deliberately and intelligently exercised in harmony with the will of God.

Christ worked out for man upon Calvary's Cross salvation of spirit, soul, and body from the dominion of sin and Satan. However, that full salvation is worked out in the believer through the central action of the will, as he deliberately chooses the will of God for each part of his tripartite nature.

THE REDEEMED WILL

The will of the man, which is united to the will of God, and which, therefore, has the energizing power of God working with it, is to rule the man's "own spirit" (see Prov. 25:28; 1 Cor. 14:32); thoughts or mind (Col. 3:2), including all the powers of the soul; and body (1 Cor. 9:27). When the believer, by the appropriation of God's freeing power from slavery to sin and Satan, regains free action of his will—so that he gladly and spontaneously wills the will of God and, as a renewed man, retakes dominion over spirit, soul, and body—he reigns in life "by...Jesus Christ" (Rom 5:17).

But the natural man does not reach this stage of renewal and liberation of his will without first knowing the regeneration of his own human spirit. God is not in fallen man until the moment of his new birth. (See Ephesians 2:12; John 3:5–8.) A person must be "begotten of God" (1 John 5:18). The very fact that such a begetting is necessary, declares that the divine life did not exist in him previously. After such a begetting, it is also necessary to understand that the regenerated man does not, as a rule, immediately become a spiritual man, that is, a man wholly dominated by, and walking after, the spirit.

At first the regenerated man is but a babe in Christ, manifesting many of the characteristics of the natural man such as jealousy, strife, etc., until he understands the need for a fuller reception of the Holy Spirit to dwell in the regenerated spirit as His sanctuary. The unregenerate man is wholly dominated by soul and body. The regenerate man has his spirit quickened and indwelt by the Holy Spirit. Yet his spirit may be governed by soul and body through bondage. The spiritual man has his spirit liberated from bondage to the soul (see Hebrews 4:12), to be the organ of the Holy Spirit in mind and body.

It is then that, by the Holy Spirit's power, his volition is brought into harmony with God in all His laws and purposes, and the whole outer man is brought into self-control. Thus it is written, "The fruit of the Spirit…is [self-control]" (Gal. 5:22–23). It is not only love, joy, peace, longsuffering, and gentleness that are manifested through the personality—the channel of the soul. In a true dominion over the world of himself, every thought is brought into captivity, in the same obedience to the will of the Father as was manifested in Christ (see 2 Corinthians 10:5); his spirit is also ruled from the chamber of the will, so that he is of a "cool spirit" and can keep back or utter at his will what is in his spirit as well as what is in his mind (see Proverbs 17:27); and his body is so obedient to the helm of the will that it is a disciplined and alert instrument for God to energize and empower. The body is an instrument to be handled intelligently as a vehicle for service, and it is no longer master of the man, or the mere tool of Satan and unruly desires.

All this is made fully clear in the New Testament Epistles. "Our old man was crucified with Him" (see Galatians 2:20) is said of the work of Christ at Calvary. However, the one who wants this potential fact to be made true in his life is called upon to declare his attitude of choice with decisive action, in both negative and positive attitudes. The apostle appealed again and again to the redeemed believer to act decisively with his will, as the following few passages show:

"Negative" Choices:
- "Cast off the works of darkness" (Rom. 13:12).
- "Put off...the old man" (Eph. 4:22).
- "Put off the old man with his deeds" (Col. 3:9).
- "Mortify...your members" (Col. 3:5).
- "Putting off the body of the...flesh" (Col. 2:11).

"Positive" Choices:
- "Put on the armour of light" (Rom. 13:12).
- "Put on the new man" (Eph. 4:24; Col. 3:10).
- "Yield...your members...unto God." (Rom. 6:13).
- "Put ye on the Lord Jesus Christ, and make not provision for the flesh" (Rom. 13:14).
- "Put on...[a heart] of mercies" (Col. 3:12).
- "Put on the whole armour of God" (Eph. 6:11).

All these passages describe a decisive act of the will, not toward exterior things, but toward things in an unseen, immaterial sphere, incidentally showing the effect in the spiritual sphere of a man's volitional action. They also emphasize the effect of the decisive use of the will of man when it acts in harmony with the liberating power of Christ. Christ has done the work on Calvary's Cross, but that work is applied in fact through the action of the believer's own will, acting as if he himself had power to cast off the invisible works of darkness, and finding with this action of his will, the coworking of the Spirit of God, who makes the casting off effectual. In saving the man, God calls him into coaction with Himself, to "work out [his] own salvation" (Phil. 2:12), for it is God who works with and in him, to enable him to will and to do His good pleasure (v. 13).

HOW DOES SATAN LOSE HIS POWER?

In the hour of his regeneration, God gives to a believer the decisive liberty of will to rule over himself, as he walks in fellowship with God. And with this restoration of the will, which is now free to choose God's will, Satan loses his power. Satan is the god of this world, and he rules the world through the wills of men who are enslaved by him. They are enslaved not only directly, but indirectly, because he incites men to enslave one another, and to covet the power of "influence." Men should instead work with God to restore to every person the freedom of his own personal volition, and the power of choice to do right because it is right, which was obtained for him at Calvary.

The liberation of the will from its passive condition and from control by the Prince of this world takes place when the believer sees his right of choice and begins to deliberately place his will on

God's side and to choose the will of God. Until the will is fully liberated for action, it is helpful for the believer to assert his decision frequently by saying, "I choose the will of God, and I refuse the will of Satan." The soul may not even be able to distinguish which is which, but the declaration is having an effect in the unseen world. God works by His Spirit in the person who chooses His will, and He energizes him through his will to continually refuse the claims of sin and Satan. In this way, Satan is rendered more and more powerless; the person is stepping out into the salvation obtained potentially for him at Calvary; and God is once more gaining a loyal subject in a rebellious world.

The action of the believer's will is governed by the understanding of his mind. His mind sees what to do and his will chooses to do it. Then, from his spirit comes the power to fulfill the knowledge of the mind and the choice of the will. For example, a person sees that he should speak; he chooses or wills to speak; and he draws upon the power in his spirit to carry out his decision. This requires knowledge of how to use his spirit, and knowledge of the laws of the spirit, so he can fully cooperate with the Holy Spirit.

HOW TO PERFORM?

But the believer who is cooperating with God in the use of his will must understand that the choice of the will is not sufficient alone. We see this in Paul's words in Romans 7:18. "To will is present with me; but how to perform...I find not." Through the spirit, and by the strengthening of the Holy Spirit in the "inner man" (Eph. 3:16), the liberated will, which desires and is determined to do God's will, is empowered to carry out its choice. "It is God which worketh in you...to will," that is, to enable the believer to decide or choose. Then it is "God which worketh in you...to do of his good pleasure" (Phil. 2:13). In other words, it is God who energizes the believer with power to carry out the choice.

God gives a person the power to act, from his spirit where He dwells. The believer must understand how to use his spirit as clearly as he understands the use of his will, mind, or body. He must know how to discern the sense of his spirit in order to understand the will of God, before he can do it.

That the human spirit is a distinct entity, separate from the soul and body, is very clearly recognized in the Scriptures, as these few passages show:

- "the spirit of man" (1 Cor. 2:11)
- "my spirit prayeth" (1 Cor. 14:14)
- "The Spirit itself beareth witness with our spirit" (Rom. 8:16)
- "my spirit" (1 Cor. 5:4)
- "rest in my spirit" (2 Cor. 2:13)

There is also a separation of "soul and spirit" required and carried out by the Word of God—the sword of the Spirit—made known in Hebrews 4:12. Through the Fall, the spirit that was in union with God, and which once ruled and dominated soul and body, fell from the predominant position into the vessel of the soul and could no longer rule. In the new birth that the Lord told Nicodemus was necessary for every man, the regeneration of the fallen spirit takes place. The Scriptures say, "That which is born of the Spirit is spirit" (John 3:6) and, "A new spirit will I put within you" (Ezek. 36:26). Through comprehending the death of the old creation with Christ as set forth in Romans 6:6, the new spirit is liberated, divided from the soul, and joined to the risen Lord. "Dead to the law...married to another...being dead...that we should serve in newness of spirit" (Rom. 7:4-6).

The believer's life is therefore to be a walk "after the Spirit," minding "the things of the Spirit" (Rom. 8:4-5). The Holy Spirit lifts his spirit to the place of rule over soul and body ("flesh"—both ethically and physically) by joining it to the risen Lord and making it "one spirit" with Him (1 Cor. 6:17). The important point to note is that the believer retains volitional control over his own spirit, and that through ignorance, he can withdraw his spirit from cooperation with the Holy Spirit. In this way, he can "walk" after the soul or after the flesh unknowingly. Having a will that is surrendered to do the will of God is therefore no guarantee that a person is doing that will—he must understand "what the will of the Lord is" (Eph. 5:17) and seek to be filled in his spirit to the utmost of his capacity, in order to do that will.

A believer's knowledge that the Spirit of God has come to indwell the shrine of his spirit, is not enough to guarantee that he will continue to walk in the Spirit and not fulfill the "lust of the flesh" (Gal. 5:16). If he lives by the Spirit, he must learn how to walk by the Spirit. To do this, he must understand how to "[compare] spiritual things with spiritual" (1 Cor. 2:13) in order to correctly interpret the things of the Spirit of God. He must exercise the spirit faculty by which he is able to examine all things, and discern the mind of the Lord.

Such a believer should know how to walk after the spirit, so that he does not quench its action, movements, and warnings, as it is moved or exercised by the Spirit of God. He should cultivate its strength by use, so that he becomes "strong in spirit" (Luke 1:80) and a truly spiritual man of "perfection" (1 Cor. 2:6; Heb. 6:1) in the church of God.

Many believers are not intelligently conscious that they have a spirit, or they imagine that every experience that takes place in the realm of their senses is spiritual. If they seek the baptism of the Holy Spirit and become conscious of His indwelling, they sometimes think that He alone acts in them, and that they are infallibly or specially guided by Him; the result is that they think that everything that takes place in their inner life is necessarily His working.

In these three cases the man's own spirit is not taken into account. In the first instance, the believer's religious life is, if we may say so, "spiritually mental." That is, his mind is illuminated and enjoys spiritual truth, but he does not clearly know what "spirit" means. In the second case, the believer is really "soulish," although he thinks he is spiritual. And in the third case, the believer who thinks that the Holy Spirit's indwelling means that every movement is of Him, becomes especially open to the deception of evil spirits who counterfeit the Holy Spirit, because without discrimination he attributes all inner movements or experiences to Him.

Again, in this final case, the believer's spirit comes into action, and into his awareness, through the reception of the Holy Spirit. However, he then needs to understand that the Holy Spirit does not act through him as if he were a passive channel. The Holy Spirit requires him to know how to co-work with Him in spirit; otherwise, his own spirit—the human spirit—can act apart from the

Holy Spirit, while he may think that God alone is the source of action.

Walking "after the spirit" and "minding the spirit" (see Romans 8:1–5) does not only mean that mind and body are subservient to the spirit, but that the believer's own spirit coworks with the Holy Spirit in daily life and in all the occasions of life. To do this, the believer needs to know the laws of the spirit: not only the conditions necessary for the Holy Spirit's working, but the laws governing his own spirit, so that it may be kept open to the Spirit of God.

When the Holy Spirit takes the spirit of man as His sanctuary, evil spirits attack the spirit to try to prevent it from coworking with God. They first get access to mind or body. Their purpose is to close the outlet of the Spirit of God, who is dwelling at the center. Or, when a believer is mature, and his mind and body are subservient to his spirit, the spiritual forces of Satan can come into direct contact with his spirit. This is followed by the "wrestling" referred to by Paul in Ephesians 6:12.

As we have seen, if a believer becomes open to the spiritual realm through the baptism of the Spirit, and yet is ignorant of the laws of the spirit, especially the tactics of Satan, he is liable to yield to an onslaught of deceiving spirits who force his spirit into strained ecstasy or elation, or press his spirit down, as if into a vise. In the former he is given visions and revelations that appear to be divine, but afterwards are proven to have been of the Enemy because they pass away with no results. In the latter, he sinks into darkness and deadness as if he had lost all knowledge of God.

When the believer understands these direct onslaughts of wicked spirits, he becomes able to discern the condition of his spirit and to retain control over it, refusing all forced elation and strain and resisting all weights and pressure that drive it below its normal balance, in which it is capable of cooperation with the Spirit of God.

The danger of the human spirit acting out of cooperation with the Holy Spirit and becoming driven or influenced by deceiving spirits, is a very serious one. This condition can be increasingly detected by those who walk softly and humbly with God. It can be discerned in a person who is liable to think that his own masterful spirit is an evidence of the power of God because he also sees the Holy Spirit using him in winning souls. Another person may have a flood of indignation inserted into his spirit, which he pours out, thinking it is all of God, while others shrink from it and are conscious of a harsh note that is clearly not of God.

The influence of evil spirits who counterfeit divine workings, or even the workings of a person who is out of cooperation with the Holy Spirit, need to be understood and detected by the believer who seeks to walk with God. He needs to know that because he is spiritual, his spirit is open to both forces of the spirit realm. If he thinks that only the Holy Spirit can influence him in the spiritual sphere, he is sure to be misled. If it were so, he would become infallible. Instead, he needs to watch and pray and seek to have the eyes of his understanding enlightened in order to know the true workings of God.

LAWS OF THE SPIRIT LIFE

Let us now take a look at some of the laws that govern the spirit life. First, the believer must know what is spirit, how to give heed to the demands of the spirit, and how not to quench the spirit. For example, a weight comes upon his spirit, but he goes on with his work, putting up with the pressure. He finds the work hard, but he has no time to investigate the cause, until at last the weight becomes unendurable and he is forced to stop and see what is the matter. He should have given heed to the claims of the spirit at the beginning, and in a brief prayer taken the "weight" to God, refusing all pressure from the Foe.

Secondly, a believer should be able to read his spirit and know at once when it is out of cooperation with the Holy Spirit, quickly refusing all attacks that are drawing his spirit out of the balance of fellowship with God.

Thirdly, a believer should know when his spirit is being touched by the poison of evil spirits. This kind of attack may be detected by the injection, for instance, of sadness, soreness, complaint, grumbling, faultfinding, touchiness, bitterness, feeling hurt, jealousy, etc. All these come directly from the Enemy to the spirit. A Christian should resist all sadness, gloom, and grumbling that are injected into his spirit, because the victory life of a freed spirit means joyfulness. (See Galatians 5:22.)

Many believers think that feeling sad has to do with their dispositions, and they yield to it without thinking of resisting or without reasoning out the cause. If they are asked if a man with a strong disposition to steal should yield to it, they would immediately answer no. Yet they yield without question to other dispositions that are less obviously wrong.

In the stress of conflict, when a believer finds that the Enemy has succeeded in reaching his spirit with any of these "fiery darts" (Eph. 6:16), he should know how to immediately pray against the attack, asking God to destroy the causes of it. It should be noted that when the believer is one who knows the life of the spirit, this kind of attack is not the manifestation of the "works of the flesh" (Gal. 5:19), although the "fiery darts" will quickly penetrate the sphere of the flesh if they are not recognized and dealt with in sharp refusal and resistance.

Fourthly, a believer should know when his spirit is in the right position of dominance over his soul and body, and yet not driven beyond due measure by the requirements of conflict or environment. There are three conditions of the spirit that the believer should be able to discern and deal with:

- when the spirit is depressed, or "down"
- when the spirit is in its right position, in balance and calm control
- when the spirit is drawn out beyond balance— when it is driven or in strain

When a person walks after the spirit, and discerns that it is in any of these conditions, he knows how to take action. For example, he can lift his spirit when it is depressed. Or, when his spirit is drawn out of poise by overeagerness or by the drive of spiritual foes, he can check any overactivity by a quiet act of his volition.

GOD'S WILL AND DECISION-MAKING

In guidance, the believer should understand that when there is no action in his spirit, he should use his mind. If in everything there must be an "Amen" in the spirit, there is no use for the brain at all; but the spirit does not always speak. There are times when it should be left in abeyance. In all guidance, the mind decides the course of action, not only from the feeling in the spirit, but by light in the mind.

Making a decision is an act of the mind and will, based upon the mental process of reasoning, the sense of the spirit, or both. Examples of the sense of the spirit are: movement, impelling; drawing or restraint; no response in the spirit; contraction of spirit; openness of spirit; fullness of spirit; compression of spirit; burden on spirit; wrestling in spirit; resisting in spirit.

THREE WAYS TO KNOW GOD'S WILL

God has three ways of communicating His will to men. He speaks through (1) a vision to the mind, which is very rare, and can be given only to very mature spiritual men, such as Moses; (2) the understanding of the mind; and (3) consciousness to the spirit—by light to the mind—and consciousness in spirit. In true guidance, spirit and mind are of one accord, and the intelligence is not in rebellion against the leading in the spirit, as it is so often in counterfeit guidance by evil spirits, when a person is compelled to act in obedience to what he thinks is supernaturally given by God and which he fears to disobey.

This all refers to guidance from a subjective standpoint. However, it must also be emphasized that true guidance from God is in harmony with the Scriptures. In order for a believer to understand the will of God with his mind, his mind must be saturated with the knowledge of the written Word, and true consciousness in his spirit depends upon its union with Christ through the indwelling Spirit of God. The mind should never be dropped into abeyance.

The human spirit can be influenced by the mind. Therefore, the believer should keep his mind unbiased and in purity. He should also keep his will unbiased. Passivity can be produced by seeking a "leading" in the spirit all day, when there may be no action in the spirit to go by. When there is no movement, or drawing, or leading in the spirit, then the mind should be used in reliance upon the promise of God, that, "the meek will he guide in judgment" (Ps. 25:9).

For example, the apostle Paul used his mind when he had no consciousness in his spirit regarding any special guidance from God. He wrote to the Corinthians that in one matter he had commandment (1 Cor. 7:10), but in another, "I have no commandment of the Lord: yet I give my judgment" (1 Cor. 7:25). In the one case he had guidance through his spirit; in the other he used his mind, and clearly said so. (See verse 40: "after my judgment.")

WALKING ACCORDING TO THE SPIRIT

Through ignorance, a large majority of believers walk in the realm of the soul (in their minds and emotions), while they think they are walking according to the spirit. The satanic forces know this very well and use all their wiles to draw the believer to live in his soul or body, sometimes flashing visions to his mind or giving exquisite sensations of joy, buoyancy of life, etc., to the body. The believer walks after the soul and after the body as he follows these things, yet he believes that he is following the Spirit of God.

233

To depend upon either supernatural things given from outside or spiritual experiences in the sense realm, checks the inward spiritual life through the spirit. When living through the experiences of the senses, instead of in the true sphere of the spirit, the believer is drawn out to live in the outer man of his body. Ceasing to act from his center, he is caught by the outer workings of the supernatural and loses inner cooperation with God.

The Devil's scheme is therefore to make the believer cease walking after the spirit, and to draw him out into the realm of the soul or body. Then the spirit, which is the organ of the Holy Spirit in conflict against a spiritual Foe, drops into inactivity and is ignored because the believer is occupied with the sense experience. The spirit is then practically out of action—for guidance, power in service, or conflict.

Evil spirits then seek to create a counterfeit of the spirit. They do this by getting a foothold in the person in order to produce feelings other than those of the spirit. Then, when these get a hold, they become strong enough to silence or overpower true spiritual feelings, or the true action of the spirit. If the believer is ignorant of the tactics of the Enemy in this way, he lets go of the true action of the spirit—or allows it to sink into disuse—and follows the counterfeit spiritual feelings, thinking all the time that he is walking after the spirit.

When the true action of the spirit ceases, the evil spirits suggest that God now guides through the renewed mind. This is an attempt to hide both their workings and the person's disuse of his spirit. When the person's spirit has ceased to cooperate with the Holy Spirit, and counterfeit spirit feelings take place in the body, counterfeit light to the mind, reasoning, judgment, etc., follows. In this way, the man walks after his mind and body and not after his spirit, with the true illumination of the mind that comes from the full operation of the Holy Spirit.

To further interfere with the true spirit life, the deceiving spirits seek to counterfeit the action of the spirit through feelings of burden and anguish. They do this by first giving a fictitious divine love to the person, which is received by his affections. When the person's affections are grasped fully by the deceivers, the sense of love passes away, and he thinks he has lost God and all communion with God. This is followed by feelings of constraint and restraint that will develop into acute suffering, and which the believer then thinks is in the spirit and of God. Now he goes by these feelings, calling them "anguish in the spirit," "groaning in the spirit," etc., while the deceiving spirits compel him to do their will through the sufferings they have given him in his affections.

LEARN TO DISCERN YOUR FEELINGS

Because of the domination of the physical part of the person, and the emphasis placed upon supernatural experiences in the body, the body is made to do the work of the spirit, and is forced into a prominence that hides the true life of the spirit. It feels the pressure, feels the conflict, and thus becomes the sense instead of the spirit. Believers do not perceive *where* they feel. If they are questioned regarding where they feel, they cannot answer. They should learn to discriminate, and to know how to discern the feelings of the spirit, which are neither emotional (soulish) or physical. (See Mark 8:12; John 13:21; Acts 18:5.)

The spirit may be compared to an electric light. If a person's spirit is in contact with the Spirit of God, it is full of light; apart from Him it is darkness. Indwelt by Him, "the spirit of man is the candle of the LORD" (Prov. 20:27). The spirit may also be compared to elastic; when it is bound, pressed, or weighted, it ceases to act, or to be the source of power and "spring" in the life. If a person feels weighted, he should find out what the weight is. If he were asked, "Is it your body?" he would probably say no, but that he feels "bound inside." Then what is it that is bound or weighted? Is it not the spirit?

The possibilities and potentialities of the human spirit are known only when the spirit is joined to Christ and, united to Him, is made strong to stand against the powers of darkness.

A lack of knowledge of the spirit life has given the deceiving spirits of Satan the opportunity for the deceptions that we have spoken about earlier in this book. Therefore, the great need of the church is to know and understand the laws of the spirit, in order to cowork with the Holy Spirit in fulfilling the purpose of God through His people.

Chapter 11

Victory Over the Powers of Darkness

Put on the whole armour of God, that ye may be able to stand against the wiles of the devil.
—Ephesians 6:11

In earlier chapters, we discussed how believers can find deliverance from deception by evil spirits. Now we turn to the crucial question of how we can be victorious over *all* the powers of darkness. Christians must learn how to have authority and victory over wicked spirits instead of being mastered by them. How can a believer, who has learned the devices of the Enemy and the way of deliverance, and who is now deeply concerned that others should be set free and brought into the place of victory "over all the power of the Enemy" (Luke 10:19), learn to fight the Foe?

First, he must now understand that the degree of Christ's authority with which the Spirit of God will energize him to exercise over the spirits of evil will be according to the degree of victory he has over them in personal conflict. And he must now settle down to face this personal conflict in the sphere of the spiritual life into which he has emerged.

The believer needs to have a thorough knowledge and understanding of the ways and working of evil spirits; of the laws of the spirit; and how to keep in mastery of spirit in all the ups and downs of life. There are degrees of deception and possession and deliverance, degrees of victory over the

Devil, and degrees of temptation and victory over temptation. The power to cooperate with the Holy Spirit in wielding Christ's authority will also be in degrees, and will be gained according to the aggressive spiritual strength obtained by overcoming the Devil in his various workings.

This is true just as victory over sin deepens in strength as a person overcomes temptation to sin (Rom. 6:11–13), and as victory over the world (1 John 5:4–5) is increasingly known by faith in the Son of God. These degrees of overcoming power, with the consequent degree of reward, are clearly seen in the Lord's call to the churches recorded in the book of Revelation. Christ also indicates that there are degrees in our future authority of reigning with Him, in His words in one parable, "Have thou authority over ten cities...over five" (Luke 19:17–19).

The believer who has been delivered from deception by evil spirits must now learn to walk in personal victory over the Devil at every point, if he is to have the fullest victory over the powers of darkness. He needs to know the Lord Christ in all aspects of His name and character, in order to draw upon His power in living union with Him. The believer must also learn to know the Adversary in his various workings, as described in his names and character, so that he may be able to discern the presence of Satan and all his wicked spirits wherever they may be—in attacks upon himself, in others, or in their working as rulers of the darkness in the world.

Personal victory over the Devil as a tempter and over all his temptations, whether direct or indirect, must be learned by the believer through practical experience. He must remember that not all temptations are recognizable as temptations, nor are they always visible, for half their power lies in their being hidden. Believers think that they will be as conscious of the approach of temptation as of a person coming into a room. Therefore, the children of God are only fighting a small proportion of the Devil's workings; they are only fighting what they are now conscious of as supernatural workings of evil.

Because their knowledge of the Devil's character and methods of working is limited and circumscribed, many true children of God only recognize temptation when the nature of the thing presented is visibly evil and according to their own limited knowledge of evil, so they do not recognize the Tempter and his temptations when they come under the guise of natural or physical, or lawful and apparent, "good."

A point that has been discussed before but which is important in this context is that when the Prince of Darkness and his emissaries come as angels of light, they clothe themselves in light that is really darkness. The believer may need to discern evil spirits in the realm of the supposed good. Apparent good may really be evil; the apparent help to which they cling may be really a hindrance. For instance, a difficulty in work may arise when a believer accepts a degree of weakness that is really the result of deception; so while desiring strength, he may fulfill conditions that make him weak. The Devil then tempts him because he is weak, and he succumbs.

Every man needs to continually make a choice between good and evil. The priests of old were especially called to discern and teach the people the difference between "the holy and [the common]," the "unclean and the clean" (Ezek. 44:23). Yet is the church of Christ today able to discern what is good and what is evil? Does she not continually fall into the snare of calling good evil, and evil good? (See Isaiah 5:20.)

Because the thoughts of God's people are governed by ignorance and limited knowledge, they call the works of God, "of the Devil," and the works of the Devil, "of God." They are not being taught the need for learning to discern the difference between the "unclean and the clean," or how to decide for themselves what is of God or what is of the Devil—although they are unknowingly compelled to make that choice every moment of the day. Neither do all believers know that they have a choice between good and good, that is, between the lesser and the greater good, and the Devil often entangles them here.

There are unseen temptations, and temptations in the unseen. There are physical temptations, soulish temptations, spiritual temptations; there are direct and indirect temptations, as with Christ when He was tempted directly in the wilderness or indirectly through Peter. The believer must not only resist the Devil when he tempts visibly or attacks consciously, but by constant prayer he must bring to light the Enemy's hidden and buried temptations, knowing that he is the Tempter and therefore is always planning temptation for the believer.

Those who bring to light these hidden workings by prayer are, by experience, widening their horizon in knowledge of his work as a tempter, and becoming better able to cowork with the Spirit of God in the deliverance of others from the power of the Enemy. For in order to be victorious over the powers of darkness, it is essential to be able to recognize what they are doing. On one occasion, the apostle Paul did not say that it was "circumstances," but "Satan" that "hindered us" (1 Thess. 2:18), because he was able to recognize when it was circumstances, or the Holy Spirit (Acts 16:6), or Satan, which hindered or restrained him in his life and service.

There are also degrees in the results of temptation. After the wilderness temptation, which settled vast and eternal issues, the Devil left Christ. However, he returned to Him again and again with other degrees of temptation (see John 12:27; Matt. 22:15), both direct and indirect.

TEMPTATIONS VERSUS ATTACKS

There is a difference between the temptations and attacks of the Tempter, as may again be seen in the life of Christ. A temptation is a scheme or plot or compulsion on the part of the Tempter to cause another to do evil, whether consciously or unconsciously. Temptation, moreover, means suffering, for it is written, "He himself hath suffered being tempted" (Heb. 2:18).

An attack is an onslaught on the person, either in life, character, or circumstances. For example, the Devil made onslaughts on the Lord through the villagers, when they sought to hurl Him over the brow of the hill (Luke 4:28–29); when His friends brought a charge of insanity against Him (Mark 3:21); and when He was charged with demon possession by His enemies (John 10:20; Matt. 12:24).

Believers must not think they will reach a period when they will not feel the suffering of temptation, as this is a wrong conception that gives ground to the Enemy for tormenting and attacking them without cause. For perpetual victory, therefore, the believer must unceasingly be on guard against the Tempter, praying that his hidden temptations will be revealed. The degree to which a believer understands the Enemy's working will be determined by the degree of victory he experiences, for "in vain the net is spread in the sight of any bird" (Prov. 1:17).

KINDS OF TEMPTATION

In preceding chapters we have given much knowledge that the believer needs if he is to gain victory over every aspect of the Tempter's workings. Yet he especially requires power of discrimination between what is temptation from the Tempter working upon the uncrucified "old man" (Rom. 6:6), tempting through the things of the world (1 John 2:15–16; 5:4–5), and temptation that comes directly from evil spirits. This can be discerned only by basing one's life on Romans 6, and by living its truths out in practical ways.

Temptation from the fallen nature should be dealt with on the foundation of the admonition, "Reckon ye also yourselves to be dead indeed unto sin, but alive unto God through Jesus Christ" (Rom. 6:11), and by practical obedience to the resulting command, "Let not sin therefore reign in your mortal body" (v. 12). In the hour of temptation to sin—to visible, known sin—the believer should stand on Romans 6:6 as his deliberate position of faith, and in obedience to Romans 6:11, declare his undeviating choice and attitude as being dead to sin, united with Christ through His death.

If this choice is the expression of his real will, and the temptation to sin does not cease, he should then deal with the spirits of evil, who may be seeking to awaken sinful desires (see James 1:14) or to counterfeit them. For they can counterfeit the old nature in evil desire, evil thoughts, evil words, and evil presentations; and many honest believers think they are battling with the workings of the old nature, when these things are actually being given by evil spirits. But if the believer is not standing actively on Romans 6, the counterfeits are not necessary, for the old fallen creation is always open to be worked on by the powers of darkness.

VICTORY OVER THE ACCUSER

The difference between the accusation of the Enemy and his temptations, is that the former is a charge of transgression, and the latter is an effort on his part to compel or draw the man into sin. Accusation is an effort to place the believer in the guilty position of having transgressed the law, while temptation is an effort to cause the man to transgress the law. Evil spirits want the man to be wrong, so that they may accuse and punish him for being wrong. Accusation can be a counterfeit of conviction—the true conviction of the Spirit of God. It is important that the believer know, when the charge of transgression is made, whether it is a divine conviction or a satanic accusation.

The Devil may accuse a person when he is truly guilty. He may accuse a person when he is not guilty and cause him to believe that he is guilty. Or he may endeavor to pass on his accusations as a conviction, and cause the man to think that his "sin" comes from the evil nature, when he is not guilty at all. Therefore, evil spirits are able to infuse a sense of guilt.

Sin itself comes from the evil nature within, but it is not forced onto the personality from outside it, apart from the person. How can the believer tell if evil spirits are behind involuntary sin? If he is right with God, standing on Romans 6, and not deliberately yielding to known sin, then any manifestation of sin that unaccountably comes back again may be dealt with as from evil spirits.

The believer must therefore never accept an accusation of having sinned, unless he is fully convinced by intelligent knowledge and clear decision that he has committed sin; for if he accepts the charge when he is innocent, he will suffer as much as if he had really transgressed. He must also be on guard to refuse any compulsory drive to confess sin to others, which may be the Enemy trying to force him to pass on his lying accusations.

Again, the believer should maintain neutrality to accusations until he is sure of their real source. If a person knows he is guilty, he should at once go to God on the basis of 1 John 1:9, and refuse to be lashed by the Devil. For Satan is not the judge of God's children, nor is he commissioned as God's messenger to make the charge of wrongdoing. The Holy Spirit alone is commissioned by God to convict people of sin.

When a believer accepts the accusations of evil spirits, this is what results: (1) The believer thinks and believes he is guilty. (2) Evil spirits cause him to feel guilty. (3) They then cause him to appear guilty. (4) They cause him to be actually guilty through believing their lies; it does not matter whether he is guilty or not in the first instance.

Malicious spirits try to make the believer feel guilty by their nagging accusations, in order to make him act, or appear, guilty before others. At the same time, they suggest to others the very things about which they are accusing him without cause. All such feelings should be investigated by the believer. Feeling wrong is not enough for a person to say he is wrong, or for the Accuser to accuse him of being wrong. If a person says he "feels" wrong, he should ask, "Is the feeling right?" He may feel wrong and be right, or feel right and be wrong. Therefore, he should investigate and examine honestly the question, "Am I wrong?"

There are physical, soulish, and spiritual feelings. Evil spirits can inject feelings into any of these areas. Their aim is to move a person by feelings in order to substitute these for the action of his mind, so that the believer is governed by the deceiving spirits through his feelings. They also aim to substitute feelings for the conscience in its recognition of right and wrong. If believers "feel" they can do a thing, and it is not visibly sinful, they do it, without asking whether it is right or wrong. For victory over the deceitful Enemy, it is essential that the children of God cease to be guided by feelings in their actions.

In other words, if believers feel relief in any course of action, they think that sense of relief is a sign that they have been doing God's will. But in ordinary life, as well as in the spiritual, a person gets rest when his work is done. A sense of relief in any line of action, therefore, is no criterion that the action is in the will of God. It must be judged by itself, and not merely by its effects upon the one who does it. For instance, a believer may say he "felt happy" after doing such and such a thing, and that this was proof that he was doing the will of God. Yet peace and rest and relief alone are no proof at all of being in God's will. Believers also seem to think that if they do some action that the Devil wants them to do, they will feel condemned at once, but they overlook the fact that Satan can give pleasant feelings.

There are innumerable variations of feelings from countless attacks and countless false suggestions caused by evil spirits. These call forth all the spiritual discernment of the believer, as well as his understanding of spiritual things, to recognize them. The Devil as a tempter very quickly becomes an accuser, even if he does not succeed in getting a person to yield to his temptations. As we have seen, deceiving spirits can cause apparent sin to be manifested to the consciousness of a believer, and then lash and accuse him for their own workings. They counterfeit some sin that the believer may call with sadness, "my besetting sin," and as long as it is believed to be sin from the evil nature, no confessing or seeking victory over it will cause it to pass away. Deceiving spirits can also hide behind real sin.

A sense of guiltlessness does not necessarily lead to absolute happiness. Even with the peace of conscious innocence there may be suffering, and the suffering may have its source in some sin that is not known. Walking by known light, and measuring his guiltlessness by his knowledge of known sin, is very dangerous to one who desires a fathomless peace. For this leads only to superficial rest, which may be disturbed at any moment by the attacks of the Accuser, who directs his darts to a joint in the armor of peace that is hidden from the believer's view.

To obtain victory over the Deceiver's accusing spirits, mature believers should, therefore, understand clearly whether any consciousness of sin is the result of real transgression, or is caused by evil spirits. If the believer accepts the consciousness of sin as from himself, when it is not, he at once leaves his position of death to sin and "reckons" himself alive to it. This explains why many who have truly known victory over sin by "reckoning themselves dead to it" (see Romans 6:11) surrender their foundation and lose their position of victory. The Accuser has counterfeited some manifestation of self or sin, and then accused the believer of it, with the taunt that "Romans 6 does not work," and by this device has made him surrender his basis of victory, causing him to fall into confusion and condemnation, as into a pit of miry clay and darkness.

On the other hand, if the believer is tempted in the slightest degree to treat sin lightly, or to attribute it to evil spirits when it is from himself, he is equally on false ground and leaves himself open for the old fallen nature to regain mastery over him with redoubled force. Warfare against Satan must be accompanied by a vigorous, unflinching warfare against sin. Any known sin must not be minimized or tolerated even for a moment. Whether it comes from the believer's fallen nature or from evil spirits forcing it into him, it must be cast off and put away on the basis of Romans 6, verses 6 and 12.

Two misconceptions that give great advantage to the watching Enemy are the ideas in many believers' minds that if a Christian commits sin, either he will at once know it himself, or God will tell him. They therefore expect God to tell them when they are right or wrong, instead of seeking light and knowledge according to John 3:21. Believers who are seeking victory over all the deceptions of the Enemy must take an active part in dealing with sin. They may have thought—based upon a wrong conception of "death"—that God would remove sin out of their lives for them. The result has been that they have failed to actively cowork with Him in dealing with evil within their environment, in others, and in the world.

For a life of perpetual victory over Satan as Accuser, it is very important that the believer understand and detect any inconsistency between the attitude of his will and the actions of his life. He should read himself from his actions as well as from his will and motives. Say, for instance, a person is charged with doing a certain thing, which he immediately denies, because the action does not agree with his will-attitude. He says that it is impossible that he could have acted or spoken in the way stated. The believer has judged himself by his own inner standpoint of will and motives, and not by his actions as well as his will. (See 1 Corinthians 11:31.) Yet this is the responsibility of the believer. On the godward side, the cleansing power of the blood of Christ (1 John 1:7) is needed continuously for those who seek to walk in the light, cleansing themselves from all defilement of flesh and spirit and "perfecting holiness in the fear of God" (2 Cor. 7:1).

The Devil as an accuser also works indirectly through others, inciting them to make accusations that he wants the believer to accept as true, so that the believer will open the door to him to make them true. Or, he accuses the believer to others by giving apparent visions or revelations about him, which causes them to misjudge him. In any case, whatever may come to the believer from man or devil, let him make use of it in prayer, and by prayer turn all accusations into steps to victory.

VICTORY OVER THE FATHER OF LIES

"He was a murderer from the beginning, and abode not in the truth, because there is

no truth in him. When he speaketh a lie, he
speaketh of his own: for he is a liar, and the
father of it."   *(John 8:44)*

This verse does not mean that the Enemy never tells the truth, but that his truth has the objective of getting the believer involved in evil. For example, when the spirit of divination spoke the truth that Paul and Silas were the servants of God, it was to suggest the lie that Paul and Silas derived their power from the same source as the girl who was under the evil spirit's power. (See Acts 16:16–18.)

The Devil and his wicked spirits will speak, or use, ninety-nine percent of the truth in order to float one lie, but Paul was not deceived by the witness of a soothsaying prophetess who acknowledged their divine authority. He discerned the wicked spirit and its purpose, exposed it, and cast it out. In the same way, the believer must be able to triumph over Satan as Liar, and to recognize lies that come from him or his lying spirits in whatever form they are presented to him. He does this by knowing the truth, and using the weapon of truth.

There is no way to gain victory over falsehood except by truth. Satan, the Liar, through his lying spirits, persistently pours lies on the believer all day long: lies into his thoughts about himself, his feelings, his condition, his environment; lies misinterpreting everything in himself and around him; lies about others with whom he is in contact; lies about the past and the future; lies about God; and lies about Satan himself, which magnify his power and authority. To have victory over the Devil as a liar, and over the persistent stream of his lies, the believer must fight with the weapon of God's truth in the written Word, and with the truth about facts regarding himself, others, and circumstances. The believer must be determined always to know the truth, and to speak the truth about everything.

Other sections of this book have shown how to persistently refuse all lies from the Father of Lies and his emissaries. As the believer increasingly triumphs over the Devil as Liar, he grows better able to discern his lies and better equipped to strip away his covering for others.

VICTORY OVER THE "ANGEL OF LIGHT"

Light is the very nature of God Himself. To recognize darkness when it is clothed in light— supernatural light—requires deep knowledge of the true Light, and power to discern the innermost sources of things that appear godlike and beautiful. "For Satan himself is transformed into an angel of light," the Scriptures say, and his "ministers" ("false apostles," "deceitful workers") transform themselves into "ministers of righteousness" (2 Cor. 11:13–15).

Victory over Satan as a false "angel of light" is won in the same way that victory is gained over him as the Father of Lies: by the knowledge of truth, which enables the believer to recognize the lies of Satan when he presents himself under the guise of light. In chapter seven we saw how the Adversary counterfeits the very light of God in order to appear as God. Again, the main attitude the believer must have is a settled position of neutrality to all supernatural workings, until the believer knows what is of God. If an experience is accepted without question, how can its divine origin be guaranteed? The basis of acceptance or rejection must be knowledge. The believer must know the truth, and he cannot know without examination. Neither will he examine unless he maintains the attitude of "believe not every spirit" (1 John 4:1), until he has tested and proved what is of God.

VICTORY OVER THE HINDERER

"We would have come unto you...but Satan hindered us" (1 Thess. 2:18), wrote Paul. The kind of spiritual perception Paul demonstrated also requires knowledge and power to discern Satan's workings and schemings and the obstacles he places in the paths of the children of God. These obstacles look so natural and so like the providence of God, that numbers of Christians meekly bow their heads and allow the Hinderer to prevail. Power to discern comes by knowledge that Satan can hinder, by observing the purpose of the hindrances, and by close observation of the Enemy's methods along this line.

For example, is it God or Satan withholding money from missionaries who are preaching the Gospel of Calvary, and giving abundance to those who preach error and teachings that are the outcome of the spirit of antichrist? Is it God or Satan hindering a believer by "circumstances" or "sickness" from vital service to the church of God? Is it God or Satan urging a family to move their residence to another neighborhood, without reasonable grounds, when it involves the removal of another member from a strategic vantage point of service to God, with no other worker to take his place? Is it God or Satan leading Christians to put first their health, comfort, and social position when making decisions, rather than the needs and requirements of the kingdom of God? Is it God or

Satan who hinders service for God through the objections of family members, or through troubles in business that give no time for such service, or through property losses, etc.? Knowledge of the Hinderer means victory through prayer over his schemes and workings. The believer should therefore know his wiles.

VICTORY OVER THE MURDERER

"He was a murderer from the beginning" (John 8:44), the apostle John wrote about the Enemy. Satan, as the Prince of Death, watches every occasion to take the life of the servants of God, if he in any way can get them to fulfill conditions that enable him to do so. These conditions include a believer's willful insistence on going into danger without being sent by God; and a believer being trapped into danger through visions or supernatural guidance, and being drawn into actions that enable the Enemy to work behind the laws of nature in order to destroy his life.

This is what Satan tried to do with Christ in the wilderness temptation. "Cast thyself down," he said, then quoted Scripture to show that the Lord had scriptural warrant for believing that angel hands would bear Him up and not allow Him to fall (Luke 4:9–11). But the Son of God recognized the Tempter and the Murderer. He knew that His life would end as a man, were He to give occasion to the malignant hate of Satan by going one step out of God's will. He knew that the Deceiver would not propose anything, however apparently innocent or however much it seemed to be for God's glory, unless some great scheme for his own ends was deeply hidden in his proposition.

Christ now holds the "keys of hell and of death" (Rev. 1:18), and "him that had the power of death, that is, the devil" (Heb 2:14), cannot exercise his power without permission. Yet when the children of God, knowingly or unknowingly, fulfill the conditions that give Satan ground to attack their physical lives, the Lord works according to law, and does not save them—unless, by the weapon of prayer, they enable God to intervene and to give them victory over the law of death as well as the law of sin, through "the law of the Spirit of life in Christ Jesus" (Rom. 8:2).

"The last enemy that shall be destroyed is death" (1 Cor. 15:26). Death is therefore an enemy and is to be recognized and resisted as an enemy. The believer may lawfully "desire to depart, and to be with Christ" (Phil. 1:23). But he must never desire death merely as an end to trouble, and he must never allow the lawful desire to be "with Christ" to make him yield to death when he is needed for the service of the church of God. "To abide in the flesh is more needful for you," wrote Paul to the Philippians. "I know that I shall abide" (Phil. 1:24–25).

When a believer wills physical death, this gives the Adversary the power of death over him, and no believer should yield to a desire to die until he knows beyond question that God has released him from further service to His people. That a believer is ready to die is a very small matter; he must be ready to live, until he is sure that his lifework is finished. God does not harvest His corn until it is ripe, and His redeemed children should be "harvested as a shock of corn in its season." (See Job 5:26.)

The Prince of Death, as a murderer, often cuts off God's soldiers from the battlefield by working through the ignorance of His children regarding his power, the conditions by which they give him power, and the victory of prayer by which they resist his power. It is Satan as Murderer who gives visions of glory and a longing for death to workers of value in the church of God, so that they yield to death, even in days of active service, and slowly fade away.

Believers who want to have victory over Satan at every point, must resist his attack on the body as well as on the mind and spirit. They must seek knowledge of God's laws for the body, in order to obey those laws and give no occasion to Satan to slay them. They should know the place of the body in the spiritual life—both its prominence and its obscurity. Paul said, "I keep under my body" (1 Cor. 9:27). They must understand that the more knowledge they have of the devices and power of the Adversary, and of the fullness of the Calvary triumph that is within their reach for complete victory over him, the more he will plan to injure them.

All of the Enemy's schemes against God's children may be summed up in these three points: (1) to cause them to sin, as he tempted Christ in the wilderness; (2) to slander them, as Christ was slandered by family and foes; and (3) to slay them, as Christ was slain at Calvary, when, by the direct permission of God, the hour and power of darkness gathered around Him, and He was crucified and slain by the hands of wicked men.

As the believer gains victories over Satan and his deceiving and lying spirits by recognizing, resisting, and triumphing over them in their varied workings, his strength of spirit to conquer them will grow stronger. He will become more and more equipped to present the truth of the finished work of Calvary as sufficient for victory over sin and Satan, and this will set others free from their power through the power and authority of Christ by the Holy Spirit.

It should, of course, be clearly recognized that victory over Satan in these ways will not be without great onslaughts from him, and sharp conflict, which may well be called "the evil day" (Eph. 6:13). Some points need to be understood in regard to these attacks and conflicts. First, it is always essential to know whether the attack and conflict are the result of ground in oneself or others. For one reason believers get attacks, and do not get through the conflict into victory, is that the cause of the attack and conflict lies in themselves.

The believer must understand that although he has been delivered from the deception he fell into, in the succeeding life of aggressive warfare against the powers of darkness, he may again give fresh ground to the Enemy through lack of knowledge, accepting some lie from lying spirits, or taking their misinterpretations of experiences, conditions, etc. For it must never be forgotten that a wrong interpretation of any experience gives new ground to them—ground being anything in a person whereby evil spirits gain. The believer may attribute the attack to a wrong cause, such as an outside cause; the maliciousness of the Devil; or "local" conflict, meaning the Enemy's workings around him in his environment, or through others.

When attacks come, the believer must know why they have come, and in prayer ask God for spiritual insight, so that he will not give fresh ground to the Enemy. Two or more attacks may be in action simultaneously; therefore, he should at once set himself to understand, watch, and observe all the workings of the Enemy in the new conflict, or anything that will throw light on the situation and show him what to refuse and how to pray.

When there is ground, or when the cause of the conflict or attack is in the believer himself, if he regards the attack as pure conflict, that is, as part of warfare for the church, he will fight with the wrong weapons and will not get through to victory until the true cause is discovered and the ground is given up and refused. When the believer, therefore, finds himself in conflict, he should immediately ask the question, "Is there ground?" in the following three areas of the workings of evil spirits:

1. *In attacks:* Is there ground, or is it purely an attack?

2. *In conflict:* Is there ground, or is it pure conflict?

3. *In communication* (suggestions, thoughts, whisperings of the Enemy): Is there ground, or is it purely from outside, as Satan communicated with Eve?

The believer should then declare the following attitude in the three cases: "I refuse all ground, and the cause or causes of it!"

The last word that is spoken alters, ratifies, or nullifies previous ones. For instance, the believer may refuse in the present moment something he asked for in the past, which may have been the product of the workings of evil spirits. He may say, "Although I asked for, believed in, and accepted such and such a thing in the past, I now refuse it." His present refusal nullifies his previous acceptance.

It is essential for believers to understand the value of the act of refusal, and the expression of it. In short, refusal is the opposite of acceptance. Evil spirits have gained because the believer has given them ground, right-of-way, use of their faculties, etc. They lose when this is all withdrawn from them. What was given to the Enemy by misconception and ignorance, and given with the consent of the will, acts as ground for them to work on and through, until, by the same action of the will, the giving is revoked specifically and generally. In the past, the will was unknowingly put to the use of evil; it must now be put unceasingly to use against it.

Once understood, the principle is very simple: the choice of the will gives, and the choice of the will withdraws, or nullifies, the previous giving. The value and purpose of refusing stands the same toward God and toward Satan. A person gives to God, or refuses to give. He takes from God, or refuses to take. He gives to evil spirits—knowingly or unknowingly—and he refuses to give. He finds he has given to them unwittingly, and he nullifies it by an act of withdrawal and refusal.

How this relates to the aggressive warfare of freshly discovered ground given to deceiving spirits, is that all new ground, which is found to have been given to them and refused, means a renewed liberation of the spirit, along with deepened enmity toward the Foe as his subtle deceptions are increasingly exposed. This is followed by more war upon Satan and his minions. Refusal also means more deliverance from their power, and less of a foothold for their deception, as the believer realizes that symptoms, effects, and manifestations are not abstract things but revelations of active personal agencies against whom he must war persistently.

Moreover, all growth in experiential knowledge means increased protection against the deceiving Enemy. As new ground is revealed, and as fresh truth about the powers of darkness and the way of victory over them is understood, the truth delivers the believer from their deceptions. This protects him from further deception up to the extent of his knowledge, and he finds through experience that as soon as he ceases to actively use the truth, he is open to attack from the watching Foe, who unceasingly plans against him.

For example, if the believer who has been undeceived and delivered, ceases to act on the truths of the existence of evil spirits, their persistent watching to deceive him again, the need for perpetual resistance and warfare against them, the need for keeping his spirit in purity and strength in cooperation with the Spirit of God, and other truths parallel with these—the knowledge of which he has gained through so much suffering—he will sink down again into passivity and possibly into deeper depths of deception. For the Holy Spirit needs the believer's use of truth to work with, in energizing and strengthening him for conflict and victory, and does not guard him from the Enemy apart from his cooperation in watching and prayer.

HOW TO REFUSE

The way to refuse, and what to refuse, is of primary importance in the hour of conflict. As we have seen, the believer needs to maintain an active attitude and, when necessary, the continual and persistent expression of refusal, presupposing the person is standing in faith upon the foundation of his identification in death with Christ at Calvary.

In the hour of conflict, the believer should refuse all possible things in which evil spirits may have gained a new footing, in case new ground was unknowingly given to the powers of darkness through accepting something from them or believing some lie they suggested to the mind. In this way, the conflict will cease as soon as the means by which the Enemy has regained ground is dealt with.

The believer himself will know, from his past experience, most of the ways by which the deceiving spirits have gained advantage over him up to this time, and he will instinctively turn to the points of refusal that have been of the most service to him in his fight to freedom. Refusing in this way takes ground from the powers of darkness in many directions. The wider the scope covered by the act and attitude of refusal, the more thoroughly the believer separates himself, by his choice, from the deceiving spirits, who can only hold their ground by the consent of his will. By refusing all he once accepted from them, he can become relatively clear of ground given to them, as far as his choice and attitude are concerned.

In the hour of conflict, when the forces of darkness are pressing upon the believer, the expression of his active refusal becomes an aggressive warfare upon them, as well as a defensive weapon. It is then as though the will at the center of the soul of man, instead of sinking down in fear and despair when the Enemy assaults the city, springs forth in aggressive resistance against the Foe by declaring its attitude against him. The battle—which hinges upon the choice of the will in the citadel—is maintained through unshaken refusal to yield to any one of the attacking spirits of evil. The whole power of God, by the Holy Spirit, is behind the active resistance of the man in his attitude of refusal to the Enemy.

This refusal of the will on the part of the believer who has been undeceived and delivered, is all the more important to understand in its effectiveness as a barrier against the Foe, because the outer man, through the feelings and nervous system, bears the scars long after his deliverance from the pit of deception into which he has been beguiled. When the wall of the outer man has once been broken into by supernatural forces of evil, it is not quickly rebuilt, so that the forces cease to have any effect upon it in times of severe conflict.

Believers who are emerging from deception should therefore know the power of aggressively turning upon the Enemy, in the moment that he attacks them, with an active expression of their choice and will in regard to him. In this way the aggressive action becomes a defensive action. The believer who is in conflict may say, with effect, "I refuse all the authority of evil spirits over me: their right to me, their claims upon me, their power in me, their influence in or upon me...."

The same weapon of refusing, works in many phases of the conflict. It works, for example, in speaking or writing. If the believer is conscious of difficulties or interferences by the Enemy in what he is doing, he should at once refuse all ideas, thoughts, suggestions, visions (i.e., pictures to the mind), words, and impressions that the evil spirits may be seeking to insert or press upon him, so that he may be able to cooperate with the Holy Spirit and have a clarified mind for carrying out His will.

In other words, the believer, by his refusal and resistance of all supernatural attempts to interfere with his outer man, is to actively resist the powers of darkness while he seeks to cowork with the Holy Spirit within his spirit. At first this means a great deal of conflict. However, as he maintains active resistance, as he increasingly closes his whole being to the spirits of evil, and is on the alert to recognize and refuse their workings, his union with the risen Lord deepens, his spirit grows strong, his vision turns pure, and his mental faculties become clear to realize a perpetual victory over the foes who once had him in their power.

The believer is especially on guard against what may be described as the "double counterfeits" of the deceiving spirits. That is, the counterfeits by the Enemy in connection with attacks upon the believer himself. For example, the Devil attacks him manifestly and visibly, so that he clearly knows that it is an onslaught of evil spirit beings. He prays, resists, and gets through to victory in his will and spirit. Then there comes a great feeling of peace and rest, which may be as much an attack as the initial onslaught, yet it is more subtle and liable to mislead the believer if he is not on guard. The Enemy, by suddenly retreating and ceasing the furious attack, hopes to gain by the second, more subtle attack, the advantage that he failed to obtain in the first.

FIGHT IN COLD BLOOD

It is essential to understand how to fight in cold blood, so to speak. That is, to fight wholly apart from feelings of any kind, for the believer may feel that a situation is victory when it is defeat, and vice versa. All dependence upon feeling and acting from impulse must be put aside in this warfare.

Before the believer received the baptism in the Holy Spirit, he acted from principle in the natural realm, and he must now come back to that same position as a spiritual man. Some can only recognize conflict when they are, so to speak, conscious of it. They fight sporadically, or by accident, when forced to it by necessity, but now the fight must be permanent and part of their very lives. They have a ceaseless recognition of the forces of darkness because they now have knowledge regarding what they are, and they consequently fight from principle. They fight against the unseen foes when there is nothing to be seen of their presence or workings, because they remember that these forces do not always attack when they can. For example, if they were to attack on some occasions, they would lose by it, because it would reveal the character and the source of the thing.

The believer knows that the Devil, as a tempter, is always tempting, and therefore, he resists from principle. In brief, he who desires perpetual victory must understand that it is a question of principle versus feeling and consciousness. He can only have intermittent victory if his warfare is governed by the latter rather than the former. That is why, when the enemy attacks him, he will find a strong, primary weapon of victory in deliberately declaring, as his basic position toward sin and Satan, the Calvary ground of Romans 6:6–11. The believer who reckons himself in the present moment "dead indeed unto sin, but alive unto God," refuses to yield to sin and Satan in any or all of the causes of the attack.

As the believer declares his position in the hour of conflict with the Foe, he will often find himself obliged to wrestle in real combat with the invisible Enemy. Standing on the finished work of Christ in death to sin, the spirit of the believer becomes liberated for action and energized to stand against the hierarchic hosts of Satan: the principalities and powers, the world rulers of the darkness, and the hosts of wicked spirits in the heavenly (or spiritual) sphere.

It is only possible to wrestle against the powers of darkness by the spirit. It is a *spiritual* warfare and can only be understood by the spiritual man—that is, a man who lives by, and is governed by, his spirit. Evil spirits attack, wrestle with, and resist the believer. Therefore, he must fight them, wrestle with them, and resist them.

This wrestling is not with the soul or body but with the spirit, for the lesser cannot wrestle with the higher. Body wrestles with body in the physical realm; soul with soul in the intellectual realm; and spirit with spirit in the spiritual realm. But the powers of darkness attack the three-fold nature of man and, through body or soul, seek to reach the spirit of man. If the fight is a mental one, the will should be quietly and steadily used in decisive action. If it is a fight in the spirit, all the forces of the spirit should be brought to join the mind. If the spirit is pressed down and unable to resist, then there should be a steady mental fight in which the mind, as it were, stretches out its hand to lift up the spirit.

A great spiritual victory means great danger, because when the believer is occupied with his victory, the Devil is scheming how to rob him of it. The hour of victory, therefore, calls for soberness of mind and watching with prayer, for a little over-elation may mean its loss and a long, painful fight back to full victory.

When the spirit triumphs in this wrestling and gains the victory, a stream of triumph and resistance breaks out, as it were, from the spirit against the invisible, but very real, Foe. However, sometimes the Enemy succeeds in blocking the spirit through his attack on body or soul. Again, the spirit needs soul and body for expression. The Enemy attacks to close the spirit up, in order to render the believer unable to act in resistance against him. When this takes place, the believer thinks that he is reserved because he feels shut up, or he feels he has no ability to refuse. In audible prayer his words seem empty; he feels no effect; it seems a mockery. However, in reality it is because the spirit is closing up as the wrestling Enemy grips, holds, and binds it.

The believer must now insist on expressing himself in voice, until the spirit breaks through into liberty. This is "the word of testimony" which is said, in Revelation 12:11, to be part of the overcoming power over the Dragon. The wrestling believer stands on the ground of the blood of the Lamb, which includes all that the finished work of Calvary means in victory over sin and Satan; he gives the word of his testimony in affirming his attitude to sin and Satan and the sure, certain victory through Christ; and he lives in the Calvary spirit, with his life surrendered to do the will of God, even unto death.

PRAYER AND PERSONAL CONFLICT

Closely tied with the wrestling of the spirit is the necessity of prayer. Not so much the prayer of petition to a Father as the prayer of one joined in spirit with the Son of God, with a will fused with His, declaring to the Enemy the authority of Christ over all his power (Eph. 1:20–23).

Sometimes the believer has to wrestle in order to pray; at other times he has to pray in order to wrestle. If he cannot fight he must pray, and if he cannot pray he must fight. For example, if the believer is conscious of a weight on his spirit, he must get rid of the weight by refusing all the causes of the weight, for it is necessary to keep the spirit unburdened to fight and to retain the power of discernment. The delicate spirit sense becomes dull under weights or pressure upon it. That is why the Enemy uses ceaseless tactics to get burdens or pressure on the spirit, which are unrecognized as from the Foe, or else recognized and allowed to remain.

A person may feel bound up, and the cause may be in others. For instance, there may be no open spirit or open mind in another to receive from the spirit and mind of the one who feels bound up; no capacity in the other to receive any message of truth; or some thought in the mind of the other that checks the flow from the spirit.

STAND, WITHSTAND, AND RESIST

As stated earlier, if, in the morning, the believer finds a weight or heaviness on his spirit, and does not deal with it, he is sure to lose his position of victory through the day. In dealing with weight on the spirit the moment it is recognized, the believer must at once act in his spirit, and "stand" (Eph. 6:14), "withstand" (Eph. 6:13), and "resist" (James 4:7) the powers of darkness. Each of these positions means the action of the spirit, for these words do not describe a state, or an attitude (which is mainly an attitude of the will), or an act by the soul or body. To stand is a action of the spirit that repels an aggressive move of the Enemy and his forces. To withstand is to make an aggressive move against them. And to resist is to actively fight with the spirit, as a man resists with his body another who is physically attacking him.

SATAN ALWAYS WORKS BEHIND COVER

Satan's war on the saints can be summed up in the one phrase: "wiles of the Devil." The word *wiles* in the original text (Eph. 6:11) means "methods," and bears in its varied forms the thought of craft or artifice—to "work by method," to overreach, to outwit, to go in pursuit. It also carries the thought of a system, way, or method of doing things.

Satan does not work in the open, he always works behind cover. The methods of the deceiving spirits are adapted to each person, with a skill and cunning gained by years of experience. Generally, the wiles are primarily directed against the mind or thoughts. Apart from yielding to known sin, most of the workings of Satan in a believer's life may be traced back to a wrong thought or belief, admitted into the mind and not recognized as coming from deceiving spirits. For example, if a believer thinks that everything Satan does is obviously bad, Satan has only to clothe himself with "good" to gain full credence with that person. The war, therefore, is a war of deceit and counterfeit, and only those who seek the fullest truth from God about God, Satan, and themselves, can stand against all the wiles of the Deceiver.

The apostle Paul said that the believer is to be able to stand against the wiles of the Devil, and that in order to do this, he is to put on the whole armor (Eph. 6:11). How can a believer stand against a wile if he does not know what the wile is?

There is a difference between temptation and wiles, and between the principles and working of Satan and his emissaries, and their wiles. They themselves are tempters. Temptation is not a wile. A wile is the way they scheme to tempt.

Paul did not say that the believer must stand against temptations or lies, or mention any other specific characteristic of evil spirits. He said the believer must be "able...to stand" (Eph. 6:13) against their wiles; the spiritual man is to be on guard so that he will not be caught by their wiles. If they can be detected, then their objective can be frustrated and destroyed.

The spiritual man needs the fullest concentration and sagacity of mind for quickly reading the sense of his spirit and detecting the active operations of the Foe. He also requires alertness in using the message his spirit conveys to him. A spiritual believer ought to be able to read the sense of his spirit with the same instinctive skillfulness as a person recognizes the physical sense of cold when he feels a draft and immediately uses his mental intelligence in order to actively protect himself from it. In the same way, the spiritual man needs to use his spirit sense in locating and dislodging the Foe by prayer. (See 1 John 5:18.)

Again, an "objective" and a "wile" are quite distinct. A wile is a means used by the Foe to gain an objective. The evil spirits must use wiles to carry out their objective. Their objective is deception, oppression, and possession, but their wiles are counterfeits. They are liars, but how can they succeed in getting their lies into the mind of a person? They do not need wiles to make themselves liars, but they need the wile to get the lie accepted by the believer.

As was mentioned earlier, the wiles of the Devil and his emissaries are countless and are suited to the believer. For example, if a believer is to be moved, through the wile of suffering, from any course of action that is detrimental to the interests of the powers of darkness, they will play upon his sympathies by the suffering they cause to one near and dear to him. Or, if he shrinks from suffering in himself, they will work upon this to make him change his course. To those who are naturally sympathetic, they will use the counterfeit of love; those who can be attracted by intellectual things will be drawn from the spiritual sphere by being driven to over-study, or by being given mental attractions of many kinds. Others, who are oversensitive and conscientious, may be constantly charged with blame for apparently continuous failure. The lying spirits lash the believer for what they themselves do, but if he understands how to refuse all blame from them, he can use their very actions as a weapon against them.

THE ARMOR OF GOD

For this conflict with the powers of darkness, the believer must learn experientially how to take and use the armor for battle described by Paul in Ephesians 6. The objective he described is clearly not victory over sin—this is assumed—but victory over Satan. The call is not to the world, but to the church. This is a call to stand in armor, to stand in the evil day, to stand against the powers of darkness, and to stand after accomplishing the work of overthrowing the Enemy, "having done all" by the strength given by God (Eph. 6:13).

The armor described in Ephesians is provided in detail so the child of God will be "able to stand" (v. 11) against the wiles of the Devil. This clearly shows that a believer can be made able to conquer all the principalities and powers of hell if he fulfills the necessary conditions and uses the armor provided for him. The armor must be real if it is provided for meeting a real foe. The believer is demanded to have real knowledge of the armor; the fact of the provision, the fact of the Foe, and the fact of the fight must be as real to him as any other facts declared in the Scriptures. The armored and non-armored believer may be briefly contrasted as follows:

Armored Christian:
- armored with truth
- righteous in his life
- makes and keeps peace
- has salvation/self-control
- uses faith as a shield
- has Scriptures in his hand
- prays without ceasing

Non-armored Christian:
- open to lies through ignorance
- unrighteous through ignorance
- divisive and quarrelsome

- reclessly unwatchful
- doubtful and unbelieving
- relies on reason instead of God's Word
- relies on work without prayer

The believer who takes up the whole armor of God as a covering and protection against the Foe, must walk in victory over the Enemy. He must have his spirit indwelt by the Holy Spirit, so that he is strengthened with the might of God to stand unshaken and is continuously given a "supply of the Spirit of Jesus" (Phil. 1:19) to keep his spirit sweet and pure. He must have his mind renewed (Rom. 12:2), so that his understanding is filled with the light of truth (Eph. 1:18), displacing Satan's lies and destroying the veil with which Satan once held it—the mind clarified so that he intelligently understands what the will of the Lord is. And his body must be subservient to the Spirit (1 Cor. 9:25) and obedient to the will of God in life and service.

Once the believer is undeceived and spiritually armed in this way, he may move forward in battle against the Enemy. In the next chapter, we will learn how to make war on the powers of darkness.

Chapter 12

War on the Powers of Darkness

To him that overcometh will I grant to sit with me in my throne, even as I also overcame, and am set down with my Father in his throne.
—Revelation 3:21

In the path to freedom, the believer discovers his need for making war against the powers of darkness. For his undeceiving and deliverance reveals to him the depths of the wickedness of Satan and his hosts of wicked spirits. The believer sees that he must make war against their oppression of him, against all their works, and against their deception and oppression of others. He also sees the need for a daily, perpetual fight against all their onslaughts, which come upon him apart from giving them ground. The believer who is delivered is born into the war and is compelled to fight to maintain his freedom. Just as a child is born into the natural world and must breathe to maintain life, there is a birth into the warfare through the sufferings and pains of being undeceived and delivered from the bondage of Satan.

Through his aggressive warfare against the Foe, the believer understands the systematic workings of the forces of Satan. With the knowledge he has gained by reading the symptoms of deception and oppression in his own case, he is now able to read them in others and to see their need for deliverance, and he finds himself compelled to pray for them and to work toward that goal.

There are two principles that govern warfare, whether it is natural or supernatural: offense and defense. The attacking force of believers must be able to defend itself as well as to take the aggressive against the Enemy.

Between the time of being undeceived and the time of being delivered, the believer learns to know his weak points and vulnerable areas. He becomes able to recognize the methodical, planned, and systematic attacks of the forces of the Enemy upon those points. By these attacks, knowledge of the active operations of the lying spirits and of the need for unceasing warfare against them deepens in him. He knows that he must stand against them daily, or again be entrapped by their wiles and fall victim to their wicked devices. For he discovers that even the lesser attacks—which before the time of his deception and oppression would have gone unnoticed—quickly overwhelm him and immediately cause him to lose his equilibrium, or spiritual balance. He knows, therefore, by the lessons of his fight to freedom, that he must from this point forward be on his guard and watch against the attacks of the subtle Foe, whether they come through things around him, or directly or indirectly through others—the indirect onslaughts often being the most violent. Later on, we will discuss how to use the weapon of prayer to fight both offensive and defensive warfare.

During the period of the believer's undeceiving, his eyes also become open to the supernatural operations of the forces of evil. For just as God is known by His workings (John 14:10–11), so the powers of darkness are to be recognized by their activities. Both divine and satanic workings are invisible to the physical eye, but the effects are perceptible to him who has the power to read the signs. The one who has been delivered can see that much that others attribute to God's sovereignty is nothing else but the results of the work of the satanic world rulers.

APATHY IN THE CHURCH

The believer sees that the primary cause of the apathy and deadness of the church is satanic, and that much that has been put down to sin, or the evil nature, is nothing but the work of evil spirits. Therefore, he must war against false teaching, which settles down to accept satanic workings in the world as the "operations of God." As his eyes are opened, his old thoughts about things connected with God and Satan fall to the ground as untested theories, and he receives two blessings through his enlightenment: a purified theology and a true demonology.

INTENSELY PRACTICAL CHRISTIANITY

The undeceived and delivered believer also becomes intensely practical. He discovers that God is practical. Since the Devil is also practical, the believer must be practical to join with the One against the other. The believer sees that one of the ways in which the Son of God destroys the work of the Devil is through the instrumentality of prayer. It cannot be emphasized enough that he must now live a life of prayer, since prayer is the mightiest weapon against the Foe.

Through his undeceiving, the believer has been made conscious of the actual force that the powers of darkness bring to bear upon and against his tripartite being. He therefore learns that all the strength of his redeemed, renewed, and liberated powers—mental, spiritual, and physical—must be set against them in order to stay free. Because of the experience he has gone through, he has become more and more conscious of his own spirit, and the need for using it in strength, purity, and power against them. He has also discovered that in the perpetual war that the deceiving spirits wage against him, neither time, place, nor season are exempt from their attacks. In this way, wherever he is, whatever he does, and whatever state he is in, he must wage equally persistent war upon them.

YOU CAN RESIST EVIL

If the believer finds himself in keen suffering and anguish, he knows that it is "the hour, and the power of darkness" (Luke 22:53). Through the suffering that the evil spirits cause, he learns that they are unmerciful and evil—intensely evil, nothing but evil, aiming at nothing but evil—and with all the power they are able to wield, are endeavoring to draw him into evil, doggedly, silently, persistently, wickedly. They are always at work, driven by undying hatred and malice against the human race. Enemies they are, and will be. They have always been and always will be evil and only evil. In this way, the believer learns and knows that he must resist them, and that the fight to keep his spirit strong, pure, and buoyant for victory over them needs all the force of his being, in the power of God, if he is to be victorious.

In his discovery of the wickedness and hatred of the supernatural powers of evil against him, the believer learns that he is not fighting against the intelligence of one supernatural being, but against principalities and powers with vast resources at their command, and that if he stands victorious against their wiles he has conquered not only one evil spirit, but all hell. (See Ephesians 6:12.) He finds that the powers of darkness will not allow one single believer to be victorious over them until they, as a whole, have failed to conquer him. This explains their onslaught on the one who elects to be victorious over them all, in vital union with the Victor Lord who put them to open shame through His death on the Cross of Calvary.

The believer is called to triumph over all the powers of darkness. However, to reach the goal, it is crucial that he put on the whole armor of God and lay hold of divine strength, truth, righteousness, peace, faith, the mighty sword of the Scriptures, watchfulness, and prayer. It is important to remember that this armor, and the weapons belonging to it, will enable him to "stand against [all] the wiles of [Satan]" (Eph. 6:11). If he stands, all heaven sees it; if he is defeated, all hell knows it. If he triumphs, the hosts of darkness are not only conquered, but discouraged, and rendered less effective in their schemes.

The believer who would overcome such a disciplined and stubborn Foe will never dare put his armor aside or give himself to careless work, for he finds that his foe is as tenacious and desirous to conquer as he is. But he who fully knows the Foe and the warfare and its eternal issues, finds his joy in the joy of warring against an Enemy who is devastating the earth, and finds the joy of victory to be a foretaste of the future triumph with the Lord Christ over all His foes. (See Hebrews 10:13; 1 Corinthians 15:25–26.)

275

It is essential to study the powers of darkness from the point of view of their depraved nature. To be conquered, or to lose a point, is torment to them, for the fallen nature of both men and angels rebels against admitting it is vanquished. In the days of Christ, to be driven out of their hiding places, commanded to go, and therefore deprived of rest, was considered by demons to be "torment" before their time. (See Matthew 8:29.) They are being tormented in the same way by any truth made known about them today. The truth concerning them and their workings, with its consequent liberation of men from their power, is disturbing their rest at the present time. What happened when Christ was on earth will happen again when the casting out of evil spirits becomes a recognized part of all Christian and ministerial activity. The Gospels record how Satan and his minions objected to Christ's presence on earth, for He moved about as the Victor, and they were shown to be the vanquished ones.

The believer who has thus learned, through fire, the real schemes and workings of the satanic forces, and realizes that he must make war upon them for his own defense, as well as for the liberation of others, now discovers that Christ has given authority over "all the power of the enemy" (Luke 10:19) to all who will lay hold of it as part of the finished redemption of Calvary. He gives the believer power, through union with Him, to wield His name and to have authority to cast out demons in His name.

This was one effect of the enduement of power upon the believers of the early church. "In my name shall they cast out devils," Christ said of His followers (Mark 16:17). On the eve of His Cross, He said, "Hitherto have ye asked nothing in my name" (John 16:24). But after Pentecost, they wielded His name and found the Spirit of God witness to its authority. "Such as I have give I thee: In the name of Jesus...rise," said Peter (Acts 3:6). "I command thee in the name of Jesus Christ to come out," said Paul to the evil spirit (Acts 16:18). "The spirits are subject unto you" (Luke 10:20) must be true of all who are, in actual experience, "one spirit" (1 Cor. 6:17) with the Lord.

The authority of Christ is therefore open to the faith of all His children who are united to Him in spirit, even though they may not be wholly free, through ignorance, from the power of deceiving spirits in their outer man. This makes sense, because the authority of Christ as Conqueror over the evil hosts of Satan is not inherent in the believer. It is laid hold of by him through the power of the Holy Spirit, and He bears witness to it only in response to faith.

However, if a believer, by faith, commands evil spirits to depart, they will make the most of any occasion he may give them, after he has dared to assert the authority of their Victor's name. For instance, if a believer knows the truth, and will not refuse the ground that he has given to the Enemy, and clings to known sin, his innermost life will become seriously affected. God will use a person as long as he is honestly true to known light, even through glaring inconsistencies—unknown to himself—may stumble others.

Again, there are degrees in the manifestation of Christ's authority over evil spirits through the believer, according to the degree of that believer's personal victory. Two believers may have faith to wield the authority of Christ; however, they may have different results because the difference in their knowledge of the workings of the powers of darkness means a difference in their ability to discern, and consequently to diagnose, the case before them.

<h2 align="center">TRUTH AS A WEAPON OF AUTHORITY</h2>

Knowledge and discernment enable the believer to see where the Spirit of God wants him to lay hold of the authority of Christ, and when to do so. For instance, authority to cast out evil spirits is of no use in meeting their lies. Truth then becomes the weapon of authority—the truth of God, spoken with the authority of knowledge that it is the truth that will set the soul free. (See John 8:32.)

The degree of authority over evil spirits, then, depends not only upon personal victory, but also upon knowledge. The believer who desires to know how to lay hold of the fullest authority over evil spirits, for the sake of the deliverance of others, must set himself to understand their workings as well as to be victorious in all and over all he passes through. Let him note how much is said in the Scriptures about knowledge and understanding.

The apostle wrote to the Colossians about being filled with "the knowledge of [God's] will in all wisdom and spiritual understanding" (Col. 1:9). The Lord said, "This is life eternal, that they might know thee" (John 17:3), and, "If we walk in the light...we have fellowship" (1 John 1:7). To walk in the light is to know God, and in knowing God, we know the powers of darkness in relative degree. For light makes manifest the works of darkness. (See Ephesians 5:11–13.) Those who are mature in the spiritual life, "by reason of use have their senses exercised to discern both good and evil" (Heb. 5:14).

The believer must be willing to pay the price of gaining the knowledge necessary for discernment. For can he take an attitude of resistance to a thing he believes is of God, or is good, or toward which he is neutral? He must know whether or not a thing is of God. Therefore, the degree of knowledge he has about the workings of the spirits of evil, determines the degree of his discernment, resistance, and authority over them in wielding the name of Christ—whether exercised in casting them out (commanding them to leave a person), or dispersing them by the light of truth. The believer must know their wiles, schemes, methods, and accusations. He must know about weights on the spirit and their causes, and when hindrances and obstacles are brought about by the Enemy, so that he may be able to discern all these things and resist them.

Knowledge also affects faith. The believer must know that it is God's will that evil spirits should be, not only potentially, but actually, subject to him as one joined in vital union to the Holy One of God, who was Victor over them all when He walked on earth and gave His messengers authority over them through using His name. (See Luke 10:17–24.)

Some of the expressions used in Scripture describing the attitude of the church and of individual members of Christ toward the powers of darkness, clearly show God's will and purpose for His people. Paul said that God would "bruise" Satan under the feet of His children (Rom. 16:20).

The principalities and powers were to be "wrestled against" (see Ephesians 6:12)—surely not so they would triumph over the Christian; to be "resisted" by a steadfast attitude of faith (see 1 Peter 5:8–9)—surely not by ignoring their presence and workings; and "withstood" (see Ephesians 6:13) in their onslaughts—surely not by ignorance of such attacks. Their "devices" were to be recognized in order to be guarded against (2 Cor. 2:10–11). They were to be "cast out" with the word of command by the authority of the name of Jesus (Mark 16:17), as those who are compelled to go when a believer identifies himself with their Conqueror, and acts in reliance upon the authority of His name.

Knowledge also affects the use of the will in resistance to the Enemy. How can the believer take an attitude of resistance to evil spirits in a meeting, unless he has knowledge concerning whether the power in that meeting is divine or satanic? The senses also, when acute, are factors in knowledge. If they are dulled by deception, the knowledge necessary to actually read and discern the workings of the powers of darkness is hindered.

KNOWLEDGE GOVERNS PRAYER

When Abraham reverently questioned the Lord about Sodom, he was seeking knowledge regarding the conditions upon which God could spare the doomed city. (See Genesis 18.) He wanted to know God's conditions before he was able to pray for Sodom. It is essential that the believer understands the workings of the powers of darkness in order to pray effectively against them.

Without this knowledge, they may be actively at work all around him, but he will be unable to stop them by prayer because he is unconscious of their presence or what they are doing. That this is true can be seen by the way the Devil is working among God's people regardless of the fact that there is much prayer. Believers are not able to defeat him by prayer because they are unable to recognize his works.

Believers must remember that prayer is the primary and mightiest weapon in aggressive warfare upon the powers of darkness and their works, in the deliverance of men from their power, and against them as a hierarchy of powers opposed to Christ and His church. For the believer should pray against them, not only for himself, but for the whole church (Eph. 6:18) and the whole world, which in due time will be absolutely freed from their presence and power.

A systematic warfare of prayer is possible against the kingdom of darkness. If the believer did this, it would mean cooperation with the Spirit of God in the liberation of the church, and would hasten the ultimate binding of the great Serpent and the casting of him down into the pit. (See Revelation 20:1-3.) A material chain could not bind a supernatural being. It may be that the great strong angel in Revelation 20 typifies the mystical "Christ" consisting of the Head and its members— the "Man-Child" caught up to the throne—when the members will have been liberated from the power of the Enemy and then commissioned to lay hold of him to cast him into the abyss and shut him up for the thousand years.

We do not fully know how much prayer has to do with setting in motion the hosts of light against the hosts of evil. There are many passages in the Scriptures that show that the unfallen angels have a ministration of war for the saints on earth, which the latter have but faintly realized. In the Old Testament, the heavenly company surrounds Elisha as in battle array (see 2 Kings 6:15–17), and in the New Testament, Michael and his angels are seen warring against the Dragon and his angels (see Revelation 12), with the church on earth sharing in this war. The forces of the angelic hosts and the church on earth are manifestly joined against the satanic hosts: the church fighting by the "word of testimony" and faith in the precious blood, not only as single individuals, but as a united company. "They overcame him..." (v. 11), recognizing their union against a common foe.

The angels' ministration of war against the powers of darkness on behalf of the saints on earth is strikingly revealed in Daniel 10:10–13. The archangel Michael resists the satanic "prince of Persia" and "prince of Grecia," which were interfering with God's messenger to Daniel. In the same way, Michael and his angels fight against Satan and his angels, as depicted in Revelation 12:7–8. The Lord also referred to the "legions of angels" (Matt. 26:53) that He could call to His aid to protect and deliver Him in the "hour, and the power of darkness" (Luke 22:53), but He elected to fight the battle through alone, accepting no heavenly help but that of the angel sent to strengthen Him in Gethsemane (Luke 22:43).

WEAPONS OF WARFARE THROUGH PRAYER

There are many aspects of the war through prayer against the powers of darkness, which space does not allow us to deal with fully. For example, lessons such as Moses lifting up his hands on the hilltop, which was an outward expression of a spiritual deed. The result of his action was clearly seen when the forces of Israel triumphed. The cause of the victory was invisible. Something in the spiritual realm was accomplished by the outward, visible attitude of the man upon the hill, which was manifest to him and the men with him when he let down his weary hands. (See Exodus 17:9–13.) That no intermission in the act of faith was vital, is to be seen in that the moment his hands went down, the Enemy triumphed, and as they went up, Israel prevailed.

The powers of evil that attacked Israel through Amalek are the same forces against the church of Christ today. There are times in a prolonged fight with the hosts of Satan when it is clear to the spiritual vision that the Enemy gains ground as the word of testimony fails, and that the forces of God conquer as the Lord's praying ones maintain the cry of victory. There are hours, too, when the battalion of wicked spirits stands back, and the Prince of Darkness himself stands against the believer, as in Zechariah 3:2. Then the words, "The LORD rebuke thee, O Satan," never fail.

There are many weapons available to the armor-clad believer as he stands in Christ, withstanding the hosts of wicked spirits in high places, especially when he needs patient, persistent, prolonged periods of prayer in order to focus upon some stronghold of the Enemy, or when he is wrestling in spirit in a great crisis of battle against the forces of darkness who are holding some position they have taken. Besides the principle of the lifted hands of Moses, and rebuking Satan in the name of the Lord, the believer may hold out the curse of God upon the Prince of Darkness and all his hosts—the curse upon the great spirit-being, clothed in the guise of a serpent, which the Lord God pronounced upon him in the Eden tragedy of the Fall. This curse has never been revoked, and Satan knows that it lies before him in its final climax in the lake of fire. The reminder of this curse is often an effective weapon against the Foe.

The believer who has been patiently and persistently laboring for others in prayer and conflict with the Enemy must hold himself ready for action, for God may use the one who has prayed to be the instrument for the deliverance of the one prayed for. It is essential to have action as well as prayer. Many think it is quite enough to pray, because God is omnipotent; but God needs praying believers who are also ready to act. Cornelius prayed and then acted by sending for Peter. (See Acts 10:7–8.) Ananias had very likely prayed about Paul before he was sent to speak to him. (See Acts 9:11.) Moses prayed for the deliverance of Israel, but he himself was called to be a great factor in the answer to his prayers. (See Exodus 3:10.)

There is also a time for answered prayer (Luke 2:26), and a time for hinderers to answered prayer (Dan. 10:12–13). Those who pray for the deliverance of others must have patience to plod in prayer for many days. People sometimes have a wrong idea about prayer. They expect a flow of prayer if it is truly in the spirit. When believers find no easy flow, they cease to persevere in prayer, whereas prayer, when opposed to the Enemy, often means hewing out words in a real fight against the hinderers to prayer.

Believers must not expect those who are deeply deceived to be delivered in a few weeks, for it may take months and even years of prayer. Contact with those who are being prayed for may hasten their deliverance, because God can work more quickly when He can use others to help immature Christians when they do not understand. We indirectly answer our own prayers when we go to the ones we are praying for and give them the light they need. Patience and perseverance are needed, because, as we have seen, people needing deliverance may hinder the process through ignorance when they side with evil spirits in believing their suggestions and excuses, even while they sincerely desire to be liberated from their power.

The one who prays may be called upon to act by the transmission of truth through preaching. If so, he will need to understand the place of prayer in his preaching: he needs the prayers of others in order to speak effectively (Eph. 6:19), and he himself must carry out the warfare experientially when he is transmitting truth that affects the kingdom of Satan. If by prayer he deals with the powers of darkness before preaching, the flow through his spirit may be unhindered; however, if evil spirits are hindering his message, he may have to fight his words out with difficulty because his spirit is at the same time resisting obstacles in the spiritual realm. This may cause his voice to sound harsh because of the resistance, the voice breaking through into clear tones when the resistance gives way. Whenever the spirit is thus engaged in conflict, the outer man is affected and less calm in action or speech.

While the believer is actually preaching, deceiving spirits can endeavor to interfere with his delivery by a stream of comments to his mind, charging him with their own workings. For example, they may whisper to him every cause but the true one for the condition of the meeting, pouring out accusations while he is speaking, challenging the words coming out of his mouth. If he is speaking of the holiness of life necessary for the children of God, he is told how far he comes short of what he is preaching to others. These accusations can be so persistent that the speaker may suddenly insert into his message depreciative words about himself, and through these words, suggested by evil spirits but believed by the speaker to be his own, the spirits pour a stream into the atmosphere of the meeting that brings a dark cloud upon the people.

Prayer fulfills a law that enables God to work, and makes it possible for Him to accomplish His purposes. If such a law does not exist, and God has no need for the prayers of His children, then asking is a waste of time. But, in fact, prayer is the greatest conceivable weapon of destruction at the disposal of the believer to destroy obstacles to God's working, either from sin or the works of the Devil.

Pray Specifically

Prayer is destructive as well as constructive. For this it must be radical, piercing to the very source of things, destroying the causes of hindrances to the operations of God. Prayer needs to be specific and radical, and it must include *personal prayer,* covering personal needs; *family prayer,* covering family needs; *local prayer,* covering community needs; and *universal prayer,* covering the needs of the whole church of Christ and the entire world. (See 1 Timothy 2:1–3; Ephesians 6:18.)

Prayer should not only be exhaustive, but persistent. The believer needs strength to pray, vision to pray, and knowledge of what to pray. For prayer needs to be understood intelligently, and there is a work of prayer demanding as much training and equipment as is needed for preaching.

Types of Prayer

The trained prayer warrior knows something of all the various aspects of prayer: the prayer of asking (John 14:13); the prayer of interceding (Rom. 8:26); the prayer of "saying" (Matt. 21:21; Mark 11:23–24); and the "burden" prayer, which may be a burden in the spirit or on the mind. (See Colossians 2:1; 4:12.) The prayer warrior knows that burdens of prayer may be conscious, but that he must neither expect a conscious burden for every prayer, nor wait until he feels moved to pray. He knows that to see a need for prayer is sufficient call for prayer. To wait for a "feeling," so that he can pray when he has vision to pray, is sin. He understands, too, in the sphere of the universal, the oneness of the whole body of Christ, and he knows that in that sphere of union he can say "Amen" to the prayers of the whole church, as long as they are of the Holy Spirit, in the will of God.

DEALING WITH DEMON POSSESSION

It is important for the prayer warrior to recognize that an evil spirit's actions are in, but not of, a person who is demon possessed. In this way, he will not be diverted from dealing directly with the Enemy by blaming the one in whom they have obtained a foothold for their manifestations.

The believer who seeks to help another who is under the possession or oppression of evil spirits, must be prepared for the deceiving spirits to distort the truth that their captive desires and needs for his deliverance. He must also expect that the spirits will misrepresent him to the person he is trying to help to freedom. Sometimes the truth that is meant to and does deliver the deceived one, in spite of all that appears to the contrary, is used by the lying spirits as a whip to beat him. The poor captive has the actual sense of being lashed with rods as real as if the stripes fell on his body. It seems to him as if the words of truth that the other person is speaking to him, and that he himself desires to have spoken to him, are as rods beating him.

However, if the person refuses to be moved by the pain of the lashing, lays hold of the truth being told him, and at once turns it into prayer and a fight against the Enemy, he grasps the weapon of victory. For example, if a person is told, "The Enemy is now deceiving you," and he at once replies, "It is against my will. May God reveal all deceptions from Satan to me!" he at once lays hold of a weapon for victory.

All truth imparted to a deceived person should inspire antagonism to the lying spirits of Satan, instead of causing the person to despair or to resist the truth or to give labored explanations to prove other causes for a particular manifestation. The person who desires freedom should thankfully receive all light that will expose the Enemy, saying, "How can I get the benefit of this as a weapon against the Foe?"

But in the stress, and oftentimes confusion, of the deliverance period, the deceived person unknowingly fights against his deliverance by covering and siding with the evil spirits who have deceived him. The will may be set and declared for deliverance, yet when the truth is given, evil spirits may manifest their presence by arousing feelings of rebellion against the very truth, or messenger of truth, which the person in his will has chosen to receive.

In brief, the evil spirits bring into play all the resources they have at their disposal. They pour a flood of confusing thoughts into the mind with suggestions utterly foreign to the desires of the person. Sometimes they give raging feelings in the body, as if it were being wrenched with pain; the spine and nerves appear to be racked with irritation; and the head looks as if it would burst with pressure. Yet none of this arises from any physical cause.

For the time being, the messenger with truth for the deliverance of this captive appears to have done far more harm than good to the victim of Satan. However, if the truth has been given, and the prayer warrior stands unmoved by the outward storm, quietly resisting by prayer the evil spirits arousing it, sooner or later the captive emerges into freedom, and a greater degree of deliverance, if not full victory.

CONDITIONS FOR CASTING OUT DEMONS

Prayer against evil spirits in others may have to be accompanied by an inaudible command to leave the person, or else a direct and audible command to cast out the demon, or demons. There are several conditions for doing this, which need careful and prayerful consideration before such a course is taken.

1. The possessed person may first need truth regarding his condition, and the ground in which

the evil spirit has found lodgment. This requires knowledge and discernment on the part of the worker, and sometimes very exhaustive dealing with the possessed one.

2. The ground that has been discovered must be given up definitely and specifically by the victim, or the casting out may fail.

3. There is a primary need for definite prayer to God to reveal His will concerning the whole matter, and how the Spirit of God wants it to be dealt with.

4. The authority of Christ needs to be specifically taken by the one called upon to deal with the person.

5. Wrestling prayer that reaches fasting may be needed if the case is a very difficult one.

FASTING FOR DELIVERANCE

The fasting that is of spiritual effect in such a case means that the one who is dealing with the possessed person is brought into such a hand-to-hand conflict of spirit with the evil spirit, or spirits, in possession, that the sense of any bodily need ceases until the victory is won. The Lord's wilderness conflict throws light upon this, for it appears that it was not until after Satan had left Him and the tension of the conflict was over, that His physical needs asserted themselves, and He "hungered" (Matt. 4:2). True fasting, therefore, appears to be not so much the result of a believer's choice and determination to fast from food, as the result of some spirit-burden or conflict that constrains him to fast because of the dominance of the spirit over his body and no sense of physical need at all. But when the conflict is over and the spirit is disengaged, the requirements of the body make themselves felt once more.

There is also a permanent attitude toward the body that may be described under the word *fasting*, and which is a necessary condition for continuous victory over evil spirits. It is imperative, especially for the casting out of evil spirits, that the believer has complete mastery over his body, is able to discriminate between its legitimate demands and the spirits of evil seeking to gain a foothold behind its lawful needs, and can detect all the wiles seeking to rob him of victory over them.

When casting out evil spirits, the believer's voice may be strong or weak, as it is governed by the circumstances of the occasion. If it is weak, the weakness may be caused by fear, ignorance, or an immaturely developed spirit. Or, it may be the result of the strength of the opposing spirit. The Holy Spirit, who energizes the believer for the act of "casting out," is of necessity hindered in His operations by these factors. An undeveloped spirit is especially a limitation. This shows the nonuse of the spirit in general conflict, for the spirit grows strong as it maintains resistance and conflict with the powers of darkness, and by obtaining complete mastery over soul and body, as did John the Baptist in the wilderness. (See Matthew 3:4.) For "every man that striveth for the mastery" (1 Cor. 9:25) over himself gains a capacity of spirit for the Holy Spirit's energizing that can be obtained in no other way.

The special inflow of the Holy Spirit, which equips believers for cooperating with Him in wielding the authority of Christ over evil spirits, is discussed in the last chapter. Briefly, the Holy

Spirit, in the spirit of the believer, is the power behind the act of casting out, and the servant of God should watch carefully not to move into any aggressive step apart from Him. Paul endured for many days the attack of the evil spirit upon him through the girl who was possessed with a spirit of divination. But there was a moment when, "being grieved," the apostle turned upon it, and speaking directly to the spirit and not to the girl, commanded it to come out of her. (See Acts 16:18.) The believer who can discern the sense of the spirit knows the right moment, and, coworking with the Spirit of God moving in his spirit, finds the power of the name of Jesus over the demons of Satan as effective today as in the time of the apostles and the early Fathers of the church.

POWER IN THE NAME OF JESUS

The chief factor in casting out, or commanding evil spirits to come out of a person, is faith in the power of the name of Jesus. This faith is based on the knowledge that evil spirits must obey the authority of Christ, exercised by Him through those who are united to Him. Any doubt on this point will render the commanding fruitless. The casting out is always done by speaking directly to the spirit in possession, and in the name of Christ, saying: "I command thee in the name of Jesus Christ to come out" (Acts 16:18). An important point to remember is that believers who are called upon to deal with evil spirits in others, should deliberately declare their stand upon the Calvary basis of Roman 6:6–11 before they do so. This is the only safe way of dealing with the basic ground of the old creation, which unknowingly may give place to the Enemy.

Much of the knowledge needed for the "discerning of spirits" can be obtained by a careful reading of preceding chapters, but there is a gift of "discerning of spirits" that is referred to in 1 Corinthians 12:10 as a manifestation of the Holy Spirit in the members of the body of Christ. Like all the gifts of the Spirit, it requires the full cooperation of the believer for use, and becomes clearer and stronger as it is used. For this reason, it may appear so ordinary in its exercise, and so much like the use of a spirit sense faculty belonging to the person, that it escapes the attention of others. That is, it may not appear supernatural, nor operate in a miraculous way. Also, like all the other gifts, it is not for show but for spiritual profit (v. 7). It is only recognizable when it is in operation, and even then, it may need a spiritual man to discern its presence and manifestation.

The power of "discerning of spirits" proceeds from the spirit of the believer, as the place from where the Holy Spirit manifests His presence and power. It develops in manifestation through the mind, as the believer grows in his knowledge and experience of spiritual things, and learns to watch and observe the ways of God and the workings of the evil supernatural powers. Discernment is a gift of the Spirit, but it is manifested as a fruit of watchfulness, and watchfulness is the fruit of keen alertness on the part of the believer. A person requires great patience, great skill, and great perseverance to become proficient in discrimination and discernment.

The faith necessary for laying hold of and exercising the authority of Christ over evil spirits cannot be "made." If there is any effort in its exercise, the believer should know that there is something wrong that needs examination, and seek to understand the hindrances to the working of true faith. When a prayer warrior finds it difficult to believe, he should find out the cause, whether it is from the opposition of the powers of darkness, or the nonworking of the Holy Spirit with him in respect to the matter at hand. (See Mark 16:20.)

There is also what may be described as an "evil" faith, a compulsion to believe that comes from evil spirits. The fact that the Devil fights against a believer's exercise of faith, is no proof that it is true faith, and vice versa. It is true that the Devil tries to quench true faith, and the believer may need to fight to keep it alive; but he must examine and know the nature of the faith that is in him. Is it of God in the spirit, or is it from the mind or will, and based on a personal desire? In brief, is its origin from the believer, or from God?

WE MUST BE WILLING TO LEARN

If it is possible for the believer to conduct a systematic warfare of prayer against the forces of darkness, through which God could hasten the deliverance of the church of Christ in preparation for the Lord's appearing and its future destiny, such a warfare by prayer needs to be learned as much as any other subject of knowledge in the world of men. If we compare the war by prayer to a war in the natural sphere, those who would lead must be willing to be trained, and to take the same learner's attitude as a recruit in the natural sphere. Such believers do not only need to understand the intelligent use of the weapon of prayer, but they need to obtain knowledge of the organized hosts of darkness, and of how to exercise their spiritual vision so that, "by reason of use" (Heb. 5:14), it becomes acute in discerning the operations of the Enemy in the spiritual sphere. The believer must learn to observe. In this way, he will discover the methods of the forces of darkness in their war against the people of God.

The church of God now needs leaders trained in the knowledge of the world campaigns of the Enemy—believers able to foresee his wiles and to guide the rank and file of the church into aggressive war against him. The church needs leaders skilled in the knowledge of the armor and the weapons of warfare provided in the Word of God in order to detect any weak places in their use, especially in prayer as an intelligent, systematic, aggressive countercampaign against the strategic methods of the hierarchy of Satan.

The believer who makes war upon Satan must learn both the defensive and the aggressive sides of prayer warfare. For to take the aggressive against such a wily foe, without fully understanding how to maintain the defensive position, will mean that the Enemy soon ends the believer's aggressive warfare by attacks upon the undefended places in his life or environment. These attacks will quickly compel the person to draw back in defense of his own position. For instance, a believer may make war upon the Foe and press out into the open with a bold testimony of the way the weapon of prayer drew some stronghold to the ground. However, before long the testimony may be challenged by some onslaught upon his inner circle, or upon himself, and the eager warrior may find he has failed to guard his own domain by prayer.

The importance of the defensive aspect of the warfare against the powers of darkness, and of the power of the believer to stand immovable, is again shown in Ephesians 6. Seven verses are used to describe the armor and the defensive position, and only one verse describes the aggressive war by prayer. The fully armed prayer warrior must be alert in the defensive position, ready to stand against all the wiles of the Devil or the hosts of wicked spirits, whether they come as "powers" (v. 12), or with darkness, or in a rush of numbers upon him. He must know how to withstand in the "evil day" (v. 13) of satanic onslaughts, and, "having done all," he must know how to stand in the hour of victory by discerning all their new attacks upon him as they change their tactics to defeat him during the moment of triumph.

To maintain his defensive position, the believer needs to know what evil spirits can cause to be done to him and about him. He must especially be on guard so that he will not yield to their workings, thinking he is submitting to God. He must know that lying spirits can burden other Christians about him, give visions to them, misinterpret things about him, cause these "burdened ones" to write about him to others, and suggest thoughts to others to his detriment.

In brief, evil spirits can use every possible device to move him from his position of victory over them in his own personal life and environment. The greater his position of triumph ("having done all," Eph. 6:13), the keener the wily Foe's new schemes will be to dislodge the victorious one from his armor-encased position. If by any of these means they can get him to turn from aggressive warfare upon them, or be disturbed by the apparent misjudgments of others, or be beguiled into looking upon these things as a "cross" he must bear, he will have failed to discern the tactics of the wily Foe.

But when the believer knows what evil spirits can do to him, he can distinguish their workings through others, and, standing steadily in his defensive position, can protect himself by aggressive warfare upon them as they work in these special ways. He does not settle down to accept all these things as the will of God, but sets himself to extinguish them by a systematic and persistent countercampaign of prayer.

In the war upon the powers of darkness, prayer can be persistently and specifically directed against the works of the Devil as the believer moves about in his ordinary activities and sees their doings. It can be brief and ejaculatory, but it is effectual. It need only be "Lord, destroy that work of the Devil!" or "May God open the eyes of that man to the deceptions of Satan around him!"

The believer may also engage in prayer for others, directed specifically against evil spirits influencing them. Yet this first requires knowledge, in order to discern the symptoms of their presence, and to gain the ability to distinguish between the person himself and the evil spirits. Any uncertainty here will weaken the force of prayer. If the prayer warrior has a doubt about the source of certain characteristics in another, which cause a person to act as if he were two persons, one contradictory to the other, and one clearly not his true character, he can pray that any evil spirit present may be exposed, so that the person himself will recognize it, or so the prayer warrior may be sure of the source in order to direct prayer to the right cause.

One special mark of an evil spirit's presence in, with, operating upon, or through, another, is an unreasonable and unreasoning antagonism to all truth in connection with the powers of darkness, especially about evil spirits. For, a person who is untouched by them can calmly open his mind to knowledge about them, as easily as about the things of God. There is also resistance in the mind or spirit of such believers to other aspects of truth—whether it is scriptural truth as applied to themselves personally, or truth concerning facts in their spiritual experience, or truth about themselves or their actions, which the lying spirits do not wish them to know.

Conversely, a special mark of the presence of the Holy Spirit operating upon, or through, another, is an openness to truth. It is a desire and even a keen hunger for truth, regardless of the consequences or the feelings of pain it causes. Believers of all degrees of spiritual life place themselves on the side of the God of Truth when they specifically declare, "I open myself to all truth," and by so doing they enable the Spirit of Truth to do His work.

All this only touches the fringe of the war by prayer that could be waged upon the forces of darkness for the deliverance of God's people, which is the true objective of revival.

Chapter 13

The Holy Spirit, Revival, and Ultimate Triumph

And they overcame him by the blood of the Lamb,
and by the word of their testimony.
—Revelation 12:11

We have seen that the period in the believer's life in which he receives the baptism of the Holy Spirit is a special time of danger from the evil supernatural world, but that the baptism of the Spirit is the essence of revival. The dawn of revival is therefore a major opportunity for deceiving spirits to find a foothold in the believer by deception through counterfeits.

The hour of revival is a time of spiritual crisis and possible catastrophe. It is a crisis in the history of every individual, as well as in the history of a country, a church, or a district. It is a crisis for the unregenerate man in which he settles his eternal destiny, as he accepts or rejects conversion to God. It is a crisis for those who receive the fullness of the Holy Spirit and for those who reject Him. For the believer who yields and receives the Holy Spirit, it is the day of the visitation of the Most High. However, for others it means the decision of whether they will become spiritual men or remain carnal (1 Cor. 3:1), whether they will elect to remain in defeat in their personal lives, or determine to press on as overcomers.

Few go through the crisis without being deceived by the Enemy to a greater or lesser degree, and only those who cling to the use of their reasoning faculties at this time can hope to be saved from the catastrophe of becoming a victim to the subtle workings of evil supernatural powers. If the believer does become deceived by evil spirits when he is baptized with the Spirit, almost immediately following the highest point of his experience he begins to descend into a pit that ultimately means depth of darkness, bondage, and misery, until he is undeceived and returns to the normal path. Those who do not discover the deceptions sink into deeper deception and become practically useless to God and to the church.

REVIVAL: THE HOUR OF BOTH GOD AND THE DEVIL

Revival is the hour and power of God and of the Devil, for the descent of the divine power brings the accompanying onslaught of evil supernatural powers. It means movement in the spiritual realm. Revival itself is the hour of God, when heaven is opened and the power of God works among men. However, when the divine power appears to pass away, and evil supernatural powers manifest their workings in a man, a church, or a country, then men marvel that the Devil's work should be where God had been so manifest. They do not realize that the Devil was planting his seeds and doing his work from the beginning of revival. Revival ebb began with its flow, but this went unnoticed.

In the hour and power of God in revival, the Tempter appears to be absent, but he is present as the Counterfeiter. People say there is no Devil, and yet this is his greatest harvest time. He is netting his victims, mixing his workings with the workings of God, and beguiling the saints more effectively than he was ever able to do with his temptations to sin. As a counterfeiter and deceiver, the ever-watchful Foe uses his old methods of deception and guile on new converts. These, having victory over known sin, think the Tempter has left them, not knowing his new ways. His absence is only apparent, and not real. Satan was never more active among the sons of God.

The Devil's great purpose is to stop the revival power of God. Every revival that has been given by God to awaken His people has ceased after a time—more or less short—because of the church's ignorance of the laws of the spirit for co-working with God, and because of the insidious creeping forth of the powers of darkness which are unrecognized and which are yielded to by the people of God through ignorance.

Those who are born of the Spirit at such a period of the manifested power of the Holy Spirit, emerge into a spiritual world. In this new world they come into contact with spirit-beings of evil, of whose existence they have no knowledge through experience. They become conscious of spiritual forces and things that they think must be of God and, as we have seen, they do not know that workings produced by wicked spirits can be mixed with the things of God. This is the reason that revival, which quickens the church, and for a period manifests to the world the regenerating, uplifting power of God, produces as an aftermath a number of genuine Spirit-born believers who are said to have religious mania, or who are called fanatics. This is why revival is sooner or later halted and discredited. This is why the testimony to the world is destroyed. And this is why the stable, earnest section of the church is dismayed and made fearful of its effects.

To put it bluntly, revival is the occasion for evil spirits to deceive and oppress mature believers, and revival ceases because of this deception. The most spiritual believers, who are baptized in the Holy Spirit and are most suited to be used by God in the service of revival, may become deceived and oppressed by evil spirits through accepting the counterfeits of Satan. Believers who are not so abandoned to the Spirit escape acute oppression, but in their contact with hitherto unknown workings from the spiritual realm, are equally open to deception that is manifested in a less recognizable way.

THE FANATICAL SPIRIT

What is called the "fanatical" spirit, which in some degree follows revival, is purely the work of evil spirits. At the dawn of revival, the ignorant are teachable, but through their apparently spiritual experiences they later on become unteachable. Pre-revival simplicity gives way to a satanic attitude of infallibility, or an unteachable spirit. Dogged, stubborn obstinacy in a believer after revival does not come from the person himself. It comes from evil spirits deceiving his mind, holding his spirit in their grip, and making him unbending and unreasonable.

The scheme of the powers of darkness at the beginning of revival is to drive, or push to the extreme, what is true. Their push is very slight and imperceptible at the beginning, as they suggest thoughts or impel actions only slightly contrary to reason. However, as the push is yielded to, and the use of the reason is silenced, those who are thus deceived, in due course become fanatical. The judgment of the believers who are impelled to unreasonable actions may be against, and may even be resisting, the things they are supernaturally urged to do, yet they are unable to stand against the supernatural power driving them, which they think and believe is from God.

All this, together with the history of revivals of the past, and much else that has already been dealt with in preceding pages, show that revival without war on Satan and his wicked spirits must always appear to end in partial failure, through the mixed results that come from the workings of God and the counterfeits of Satan. The church, therefore, desperately needs believers who are equipped with knowledge and discernment in order to meet the satanic counterfeits that invariably follow the advent of revival. They must know all the symptoms of satanic deception and possession, and be able to resist the powers of darkness and teach the children of God the way of victory over them. They must know aggressive warfare upon the powers of darkness. For war upon the attacking spirits of evil is indispensable for maintaining the health, sanity, and spiritual power of those who are revived.

CAN WE HAVE A PURE REVIVAL?

A pure revival—free from the usual aftermath—is possible, but only if the church understands these truths about the powers of darkness, as well as how to cooperate with the Holy Spirit. Apart from this knowledge of the workings of Satan and his wicked spirits, which will enable the believer to recognize their presence under any guise, no one can safely accept all the supernatural manifestations accompanying revival, or believe that all seeming "Pentecostal power" is of God. A pure revival is divine power in full operation, minus sin and Satan. It is not cold belief, but life, and it has to do with the spirit, not the intellect.

Apart from the knowledge of the workings of the Enemy, those who pray for revival will not clearly understand what they pray for, nor how to act when their prayers are answered, for they will not be prepared to meet satanic opposition to their prayers, nor the dangers that come with prayer for revival.

WHY NO WORLDWIDE REVIVAL?

Why is there not yet worldwide revival in answer to worldwide prayer? For the same reason that revival subsides when it has begun, and that prayer meetings for revival end in catastrophe or powerlessness. The block to prayer preceding revival and to revival itself, is caused by evil spirits deceiving or hindering the praying ones.

The hindrance to revival at the present time lies not only in this opposition, but in the present condition of the most mature believers of the church, through whom alone God can work in revival power. These are believers who know the baptism of the Holy Spirit and were liberated in spirit in the revivals of the last decade, but who are now driven back into themselves by the pressure of the Enemy, or who are in captivity to the Foe through his counterfeits. If these quenched or deceived believers were again liberated, those who are now useless would be priceless for teaching and strengthening others when revival is once more given.

The Holy Spirit is still in those who were baptized with the Spirit during the last revivals. The mistake at the time of the revival in Wales in 1904 was to become occupied with the effects of revival, and not to watch and pray to guard the cause of revival. The Spirit-baptized believers, who are presently locked up in spirit or sidetracked through satanic deceptions, are still those who would be the instruments through whom God could work, if only they were set free. They are useless now, but will be priceless in maturity and experience and knowledge for the guiding and guarding of a revived church, when they are once more liberated for true coworking with the Holy Spirit of God.

HOW SHOULD WE PRAY FOR REVIVAL?

Therefore, the Lord's prayer warriors should now pray

1. against evil spirits currently blocking and hindering revival
2. for the cleansing and deliverance of those who became deceived or oppressed during revival
3. that when revival is once more given it may be kept pure
4. for the preparation of instruments for revival, trained and taught by God to guard against further inroads of the powers of darkness

In brief, let all who pray for revival, pray that light will reach those who have been ensnared into bondage to the deceiving powers of darkness—pray that they may be set free and once more become usable in the service of revival. Then the forces of evil will be beaten back from the ground they have regained, which still belongs to God.

The baptism of the Holy Spirit is the essence of revival, for revival comes from a knowledge of the Holy Spirit and of the way of coworking with Him that enables Him to work in revival power. The primary condition for revival is therefore that believers should individually know the baptism of the Holy Spirit. This term is used as a convenient expression for describing a definite inflow of the Holy Spirit that thousands of believers throughout the church of Christ have received as a definite experience. Such an infilling of the Spirit was the cause not only of the Welsh Revival in 1904–05, but of all other revivals in the history of the world. The fact that following revival Satan counterfeits the work of God under the guise of the divine Spirit, must not be used by evil spirits to hold back the children of God from seeking the true flood tide of the Spirit, in order to bring about pure revival and the emancipation of the church of Christ from the bonds of sin and Satan.

WHAT IS THE BAPTISM OF THE SPIRIT?

It is of primary importance to understand what is a true baptism of the Spirit, the conditions for its reception, and the effects of obtaining it. Previous chapters have thrown much light upon what it is not, and the dangers to be avoided in seeking it. It is not an influence coming upon the body, nor, according to the records in the Acts of the Apostles, does it result in physical manifestations such as convulsions, twitching, and writhing, nor does it rob a man of the full intelligent action of his mind, or ever make him irresponsible for his speech and actions.

In brief, the place where the Spirit of God dwells in man, provides us with the key to all the true manifestations connected with the baptism of the Spirit, as well as the conditions for receiving it, and its results in personal experience and service. That place is in the human spirit. Once the believer understands that his spirit is the instrument through which the Holy Spirit carries out all His operations in and through him, he will be able to discern the true meaning of being filled with the Holy Spirit and how to detect the counterfeit workings of Satan in the realm of the senses.

The baptism of the Holy Spirit may be described as an inflow, sudden or gradual, of the Spirit of God into a person's spirit, which liberates it from the vessel of the soul, and raises it into a place of dominance over soul and body. The freed spirit then becomes an open vessel for the Spirit of God to pour through it an outflow of divine power. The mind receives, at the same time, a clarifying enlivening, and "the eyes of [the] understanding" are filled with light (Eph. 1:18). The body comes entirely under the person's control, as the result of the dominance of the spirit, and often receives a quickening in strength for endurance in the service of warfare he finds he has emerged into.

The fact that the Spirit of God operates through the instrument of a man's spirit, as revealed in the epistles of Paul, needs to be kept in mind when reading the records of the working of the Holy Spirit in the Acts of the Apostles. On the day of Pentecost, the 120 disciples—men and women—were filled in the spirit as the Spirit of God filled the house where they were (Acts 2:2). Their tongues were liberated so that, as intelligent personalities, they could speak of the mighty works of God as the Spirit gave "utterance," that is, gave them power to speak (v. 4). The record gives no hint that they became robots, or that the Spirit spoke through them, or instead of them. From their spirits, which were under the clothing and inspiration of the Spirit of God, they themselves were given intelligent insight into, and utterance about, the wonderful things of God (v. 11), as they were moved in spirit by Him.

This inflow of the divine Spirit into their spirits not only left their mental powers in full action, but clarified them and increased their sharpness of discernment and power of thought. This can be seen in the actions and words of Peter, who spoke with such convincing power that through his words—inspired by the Spirit, but spoken by him in intelligent clearness of mind—three thousand were convicted and saved. The true influence of God the Holy Spirit was manifested through Peter, not in controlling those who heard him, but through a deep conviction in their consciences that turned them to God. They were not conquered by terror of God, but by a godly awe, which led them to godly sorrow and repentance (v. 37).

The "pouring out" of the Spirit (Acts 2:17–18) is therefore upon the *spirit,* clothing it with divine light and power, and raising it into union of spirit with the glorified Lord in heaven, and, at the same time, baptizing the believer into one spirit with every other member of the body of Christ, joined to the Head in heaven. All who are thus liberated and clothed in spirit are "made to drink into one Spirit" (1 Cor. 12:13)—the Holy Spirit—who, through the capacity of the spirit of each member of the body, is then able to distribute to each the gifts of the Spirit, "dividing to every man severally as he will" (see 1 Corinthians 12:4–11) for effective witness on behalf of the risen Head.

SEATED IN HEAVENLY PLACES IN CHRIST

Another aspect of the true baptism of the Spirit that has an important bearing upon the experiences of believers today, is to be found in the words of Peter on the day of Pentecost, which show that the revelation of Christ given by the Holy Spirit at such a time was of Christ as the glorified Man in heaven (Acts 2:33–34), and not in any vision or manifestation of Him as a person within. The same attitude to Christ, as seated on the right hand of God, is uniformly seen in all the later records of the work of the Spirit in the Acts of the Apostles. The martyr Stephen saw the "Son of man standing on the right hand of God" (Acts 7:56), and Paul on the road to Damascus was arrested by a light from heaven (Acts 9:3; 22:6; 26:13), out of which clothing of light the ascended Lord spoke to him, saying, "I am Jesus" (Acts 9:5; 22:8; 26:15).

The Holy Spirit fills the spirit of the believer and communicates to him the very Spirit of Jesus, joining him in one spirit to the Spirit of the glorified Lord, imparting to him the life and nature of Christ for the building up of a new creation in His likeness. (See Romans 8:29; Hebrews 2:2–13.) Through this, instead of being turned inward to a self-centered understanding of Christ, he is lifted, so to speak, by the inflow of the Spirit of God into his spirit. He is lifted out of the narrow limits of himself and into a spiritual sphere, where he finds himself one spirit with others who are joined to the living Head, forming one spiritual body for the inflow and outflow of the Spirit of the Lord.

This aspect of the true meaning of the baptism of the Spirit and its spiritual effect has an important bearing upon revival, and why revival does not come. Revival is an outflow of the Spirit of God through the organ of the human spirit, liberated for His use. When the inflow of the Spirit into the spirits of many believers takes place, and finds outlet through all, the unity that was so marked in the early church can be seen, and the united power becomes strong enough to overflow through all these liberated ones to others.

But the believer may turn inward through the pressure of opposition, the powers of darkness, or to worship and pray in a self-centered way. Or he may become occupied to any degree with an inward experience. When this happens, the outflow of the Holy Spirit is hindered; the unity with other liberated believers is stopped by an invisible barrier; and the released spirit, which was kept dominant over soul and body as long as the person turned outward as a vessel for the inflow and outflow of the Holy Spirit, sinks down into the soul, a spirit in prison, so to speak, once more. Revival is then checked at its very birth, because believers who seek and obtain a baptism of the Spirit do not clearly understand the conditions upon which the inflow was given, nor how to cooperate with the Holy Spirit in the purpose of His coming, which is to make them channels for the outflow of rivers of living water. (See John 7:38.)

The inflow of the Spirit of God to a believer's spirit means love, joy, liberty, buoyancy, light, and power. It means a revelation of Christ as the risen and ascended Lord, which brings joy unspeakable and full of glory, and an intimate sense of His nearness in fellowship and communion that makes the "I in you" a living power. (See John 14:20.)

It is at this time that ignorance is dangerous. If the believer does not understand that all this is an effect that is inward as a result of union with Christ in heaven, and an effect that will continue only as long as he remains in the right attitude toward the glorified Christ in heaven, he will turn into and sink down into the soul, that is, into himself. Then the deceiving spirits will counterfeit, in the sphere of the senses, the true experiences that he had in his spirit through the incoming of the Holy Spirit.

When the true inflow of the Holy Spirit to the spirit took place, there was unity with others in the same spirit, joy, liberty of speech, power to witness to Christ, effective and permanent results in the lives of others, and a heavenly fire from God in a burning, consuming, white-heat intensity of spirit (Rom. 12:11) in service to God. But when the sense counterfeit takes place, supernatural experiences frequently occur at the same time that a wrong spirit is discernible, such as harshness, bitterness, pride, presumption, disunion, etc., showing that the experiences are not from the spirit, or that the spirit is out of coworking with the Holy Spirit and that the Holy Spirit is no longer able to bring forth the pure fruit of the Spirit through the believer's spirit and life. This may only be temporary, until the believer becomes conscious that something is wrong and takes steps to regain his right condition of spirit, and the Holy Spirit again manifests His presence and power. (See Ephesians 4:3, 13.)

HINDRANCES TO THE HOLY SPIRIT'S WORK

Also, the counterfeit of the true inflow of the Holy Spirit is marked by an inability to recognize and unite with the Spirit of God in others, contrary to the pattern of the oneness of the body shown in 1 Corinthians 12, where the same Spirit in one member is in harmony with the Spirit in the other; and it can also be seen in the spirit of separation and division that results from not seeing eye to eye in non-essential matters. For union of spirit, where the Holy Spirit is ruling and working, is possible apart from unity of faith, which can only be according to degree of knowledge.

Believers who know that a baptism of the Spirit is possible and obtainable by them, may not receive that baptism because of many misconceptions about experiences. The reception of the Holy Spirit and the measure of the giving, or clothing, of the Spirit, vary in manifestation and result according to the preparation and knowledge of the believer. Many do not receive the baptism of the Spirit (1) because they have misconceptions that hinder them from cooperation with the Spirit of God in His workings, (2) because of these varying facts in connection with it, and (3) because of the consequent apparent contradictions of teaching about it.

From the example of the way the Lord deals with His disciples, which is borne out in the experience of many today, it is clear that there is a reception of the Holy Spirit comparable to the experience of Pentecost. This initial stage of the manifestation of the Holy Spirit is an enduement of power by an inflow of the Spirit of God into the human spirit that liberates the man for utterance and bearing witness.

STEPS TO RECEIVING THE HOLY SPIRIT

Reception of the baptism of the Holy Spirit in its initial form requires certain conditions that the believer should be able to quickly and simply fulfill:

- putting away every known sin in the life
- definite trust in the power of the blood of Christ to cleanse from all unrighteousness (1 John 1:9)
- obedience to all known light through the Word of God
- full surrender to God, belonging to Him entirely with nothing withheld
- an act of faith in which the believer, fulfilling these conditions, takes the gift of the Holy Spirit as simply as he received the gift of eternal life through Christ

Believers should understand that these simple conditions can be carried out by an action of the will alone, with no conscious feeling of any kind. Once the transaction is made, it should be held to persistently and steadily with a fixed will, without question or deviation. In some cases, the entry of the Holy Spirit into the renewed spirit in the manifestation of the fruit of the Spirit (Gal. 5:22) very quickly follows the fulfillment of the conditions. But the believer should be on guard not to turn to any experience as the basis of continued faith, or it will quickly pass away. The transaction with God upon His Word stands good, whether or not it is manifested in a consciousness of the Holy Spirit's presence. Once made, the transaction should be held to, experience or no experience, by the surrendered believer.

It is from this stage that the Spirit of God now works to discipline and lead the believer on into a knowledge of the greater inflow of His power, which is the enduement for service, and for aggressive warfare against the principalities and powers of Satan. Some say they have prayed for hours for this needed equipment, to no avail. Others have spent weeks or months in waiting upon God for some experience they think accompanies this baptism, with very grave results. A counterfeit power has broken forth upon them, with manifestations afterwards acknowledged to have come from the deceiving spirits of Satan.

CONDITIONS FOR ENDUEMENT

In light of this, here are the conditions for knowing the enduement for service, and the effects which follow.

In the first place, there must be a definite assurance that such an enduement of power is possible, and a deep conviction and sense of need. This may come about by a believer's discovery that he has no effectiveness in his life and service, although he may have known the Holy Spirit in His indwelling power for years. His sense of need may be especially acute in his lack of ability to speak and lack of power to witness for God, and in the almost complete absence of aggressive power against the forces of darkness, a power that was so remarkable in the early church.

Sometimes those who are being moved by the Spirit to a sense of need—which precedes the greater inflow of His power—are diverted or hindered from pressing on to obtaining the equipment desired, because others who are not at the same stage of the spiritual life say that this enduement is not obtainable. A believer in such a case should put aside the voices of men, and, dealing with God directly, should put to the proof for himself whether or not God will meet his awakened need. This means a definite transaction with God, that He will give to the petitioner what He means by a "baptism of the Holy Spirit," and grant in His own way to His redeemed one the liberty of speaking and power for effective service that he should have in order to fulfill his part as a member of the body of Christ. This should be a transaction with God in a deliberate act of the will, which must not be departed from, whatever the after-experience may be. This means taking the enduement of the Spirit by faith on the basis of the Word of God. "Christ hath redeemed us...being made a curse for us...that we might receive the promise of the Spirit through faith" (Gal. 3:13–14).

As we have seen, there is no command given to the church after Pentecost to wait for a personal enduement for service. The Spirit of the Lord fell upon those in the house of Cornelius without any waiting, and He will still do so upon any believer when he is in the right attitude, and when he is fulfilling the conditions for the Spirit of God to flood his spirit with His power.

The waiting on the part of the believer is really a patient waiting for the Spirit of God to do the work in him that is required, after he has definitely dealt with God for such an enduement of His Spirit. This is a waiting that is consistent with the faithful discharge of the duties of ordinary life, and through which he learns careful obedience to all of the known will of God, that is necessary when he is given more definite service later on. During this period, the believer's faith in God must continue to be active, trusting the Spirit of God to prepare him for the enduement required for his sphere of service.

The danger now is that the believer will use excuses to cover up a lack of power, or shrink from the examination of points in his life that the Spirit of God is dealing with, or even quench the Spirit by refusing to yield up to God what He claims, or flinch from some sacrifice, upon which hinges the liberation of his spirit for the inflow of the greater measure of power.

The conditions necessary for the initial reception of the Spirit involve only a narrow sphere. Just the center of the person is dealt with, in will and heart—the former in surrender to God and the latter cleansed from the love of sin. But in the enduement of power, the scope of God's dealings widen. The believer's spirit has to be separated from the entanglements of the soul, and the lawful things belonging to the natural man have to be surrendered, so that he may become a spiritual man, governed only by his spirit. He must have every trace of an unbending spirit removed, so that his spirit may cooperate with the Holy Spirit with pliability. He must lose every degree of an unforgiving spirit, in order to allow no foothold for evil spirits when, by the moving of the Holy Spirit, he may be charged to rebuke sin, or suffer rejection for Christ's sake. He must be freed from a narrow, grasping spirit if he is to be a wide channel for the outflow of the gracious, life-giving Spirit of God.

Moreover, the believer who seeks an enduement of power must be willing to let the Spirit of God thoroughly deal with his life, and remove from it every obstacle to his immediate readiness to fulfill all the will of God. His motives must be searched. He must be taught the principles of righteousness. For, the enduement of the Spirit that he seeks to know, means aggressive warfare against sin and the powers of evil, and how can the Holy Spirit convict people of sin by the preaching of righteousness if the man He equips as a messenger of God is ignorant of the law of righteousness? The believer must learn the attitude of God to sin in his own life before he can be God's witness against sin in others.

If a believer has made the transaction with God for the baptism of the Spirit and has taken it by faith, and for a prolonged period there is no evidence in experience, he should renew his prayer to God for the removal of all obstacles as quickly as possible and be on the alert to cooperate with God in every trace of light that is given him. Misconceptions regarding the way the Spirit will work may prevent the believer from recognizing the evidence that his prayer has been answered. He may be expecting an experience similar to some other believer, or have some thought in his mind governed by his wishes or prayers that blinds him to seeing the Holy Spirit working in an opposite manner.

It is here that the evil spirits take advantage. If the believer is counting on some special mark as evidence of the baptism, the deceiving spirits use every possible means to give the seeker the counterfeit. The true inflow of the Spirit of God into the believer's spirit bears its own evidence in the release of the spirit into light, liberty, and power, resulting in liberty of speech for bearing witness, and the conviction of others by the Holy Spirit, which is the ultimate purpose of His coming.

Believers who are being disciplined and trained by the Holy Spirit for the enduement of power should continue in present service for

Christ with the keenest faithfulness to all known spiritual light, using to the fullest measure the grace they have already received. For it is in the path of faithful service that the assurance of the enduement of power may be given. It is God's law that His children use all He has given them before He gives more. (See Matthew 25:14–28.) The believer must demonstrate his obedience to God to the utmost extent of his present knowledge, learning to listen to the sense of his spirit and using his mind and judgment in reliance upon the illuminating of the Spirit of God as he seeks to know the mind of God in His Word.

To summarize, revival is an outflow of the Spirit of God through the vessel of the human spirit, and the baptism of the Spirit is the inflow of the Spirit of God into a person's spirit whereby it is released from all obstacles and bonds that oppress or hold it down, and which close or reduce its capacity as an outlet for the Holy Spirit. These obstacles may return through the deceptive workings of the Adversary, and the believer may become locked up in spirit again, or rendered practically useless to God and His people.

REMOVING OBSTACLES

There are two objectives to the truths that have been set forth in the preceding pages. The first is the removal of these obstacles, so that the revival power that is lying locked up in many may break forth once more, and the church of Christ may press on into maturity and power, victorious over the powers of darkness hindering her progress. These powers of darkness have achieved their purpose of halting revival through the ignorance of

God's people. However, they can be defeated and driven back from the ground they have gained, through knowledge of their workings and through aggressive prayer against them. The truths about them, when put into operation, will not only set individual believers free, but will also disperse the spiritual block in the atmosphere of a church, a town, or a country.

If it has been proven that one evil spirit can be rendered powerless by prayer, then all the hosts of Satan in their onslaught on the church can be conquered, if the children of God would use the weapons of victory. If all hell has been conquered by Christ, the forces of Satan can be turned back and the church of Christ can be delivered from their power. An understanding of the broad principles showing the basic differences between the way God works and the deceptive imitations of Satan, will enable spiritual believers to discern for themselves all the counterfeits they meet with today.

ARE WE WILLING TO FACE THE TRUTH?

The hindrance to aggressive warfare against the Foe lies in the unwillingness of the church to face the truth, not in the lack of weapons for victory. Believers are happy because they are ignorant of their state. The good they have blinds them to the greater good and the greater need of the church. Therefore, to arouse them from their self-satisfied condition, God has permitted Satan to sift His people, for Satan cannot go one shade beyond the permission of God.

Believers will be taught the truth about themselves only by experience; therefore, God permits experience. The church of Christ must be matured and prepared for the Lord's appearing; therefore, God permits the onslaught of the Foe. For only through the fire of refining will the people of God be urged forward to the battle and victory that will drive the forces of Satan from their place in the heavenlies, making way for the church to ascend to her place of triumph with the Lord.

Wrong conceptions of divine things can only be destroyed by experience. Many of the children of God are deceived while they think they are protected by God. They comply with the conditions for God to work apart from intelligent understanding of why He does so, but they do not realize that it is just as possible to ignorantly comply with the conditions for evil spirits to work, through ignorance of the laws governing both divine and satanic workings.

In the midst of the supernatural manifestations of the present time—which the church of Christ is being forced to notice because of the undermining of both God's work and devoted individual believers—many children of God go forward in a blind confidence that God will protect them. Yet they are not protected, because they do not understand the conditions for such protection. Sometimes their confidence prevents them from recognizing a wrong condition in themselves. For example, they may have a secret self-confidence that they are capable of judging what they see and hear, which is not based on true reliance upon God through a deep consciousness of their ignorance. They may have a secret spirit of curiosity, of desiring to see what is extraordinary. They may have a secret desire to go to gatherings in which supernatural manifestations may take place, without first seeking, with unbiased mind, a clear knowledge of the will of the Lord. Or, they may have a real purpose of obtaining more blessing from God, which obscures a pride or ambition to be among the first in the kingdom of God.

Any of these hidden causes can frustrate God's protection. However, when a believer has a true, pure, single-eyed reliance upon God to protect him from the wiles of Satan, a keen watchful prayerfulness, and a ready mind that is open to truth as God gives it, combined with an unbiased faithfulness to the will of God—even though, for purposes greater than his personal good, the far-seeing wisdom of God may allow him to discover by painful experience the deceptive workings of the Counterfeiter—such a one will be able to say, "out of them all the Lord delivered me" (2 Tim. 3:11).

WHEN HE APPEARS

The second and greatest result of the operation of the truths concerning the deceptive workings of Satan and the way of victory, relates to the closing days of the age and the millennial appearing of the ascended Lord. What does that millennial appearing of the glorified Christ mean to Satan and his hierarchy of powers? It means the triumph of his former victims and their ascension to the throne of Christ, where, in reigning with their Lord, they will "judge angels" (1 Cor. 6:2-3). It means to the fallen archangel, the deepest cup of humiliation he has yet to drink. Redeemed man, who was for a little while made "lower than the angels" (Heb. 2:5-7) and was cast down near the level of the beast by the Fall, will be lifted up again, and made to sit among princes; lifted up above the high position that Satan once occupied as a great archangel of God; lifted up to one nature and one life and position with the Son of God, as an heir of God and joint-heir with Christ (see Romans 8:17; Hebrews 2:11–12); lifted up with the redeeming Lord, far above all principality and power and every name that is named in heaven or on earth, or below the earth (see Ephesians 1:21); lifted up to the very side of the triumphant Lord, to the place of judgment of the Foe. For Satan, there awaits the abyss—the bottomless pit—the lake of fire. For his victims, the sharing of the throne of the Son of God, above the angels and archangels of God.

Is it any marvel, then, that at the close of the age the whole hierarchy of evil powers would endeavor to submerge the future judges of the fallen hosts of Satan? Is it any marvel that God permits the onslaught? For it has been His way throughout the ages to use this planet as the battleground and training school of His people. The Son of God Himself had to become obedient unto death, even the death of the Cross, before He was given the name that is above every name (Phil. 2:9), that name which now speaks of the conquest of Calvary to every fallen angel and every evil spirit among the dregs of the spirit world.

And every member of Christ, who will reign with Him and will share in His judgment of the fallen angels, must first—individually, while on earth—learn not only to walk in victory over sin, but to trample underfoot the viper brood of hell in the name of the Conqueror. All members of the body of Christ must overcome as He overcame (see Revelation 3:21), if they are to share His throne and conquest. He led the way. They must follow. He passed through the hour and power of darkness on Calvary, and passed through it to the place of victory. United to Him in spirit, they pass through the same dark atmosphere, filled with the hosts of evil, to their place of triumph in Him.

That closing onslaught from the hosts of darkness is upon the church. Not one living member of the risen Head can escape attack if he is a true "joint" in the body of Christ (Eph. 4:16). Some will know it before others, according to their place in the body. "If the whole body were an eye, where were the hearing?" (1 Cor. 12:17). They who are of the "feet" will know it last, but they will know it, for they must also ascend, though the foot is the part of the ascending body that is nearest earth and may be the last part to move heavenward.

Some of the elect of the body—even many— may fall victims to the deceptive wiles of Satan. They may seem submerged for a time, and, in their own eyes, may seem rendered useless to their Lord. But if they can only see how all the deceits of Satan can be turned into steps of victory and equipment for the deliverance of others from his power, they can arise again, and become, as it were, "eyes" to the body of Christ (see Numbers 10:31), in its advance through the hosts of darkness contesting the way. They can arise again when they discover that what was meant by Satan to overwhelm them can be changed by the light of truth into a glorious liberation from the Enemy's power, and thus make them witnesses of "the manifold wisdom of God," not only to men, but to the "principalities and powers in heavenly places" (Eph. 3:10).

THE OUTCOME OF THE LAST REVIVAL

The hierarchy of the satanic powers may hope to delay their judgment for a season, but the purposes of God must ultimately come to pass. He will draw His church through, to join the risen Head in due season, even though the hour and power of darkness now surrounds her. The final result of the call to war against the powers of darkness is revival! But the outcome of that revival, which will come as the result of victory over Satan, is ascension triumph, the appearing of the Christ, and the casting of Satan and his evil powers into the abyss.

Even so, come, Lord Jesus.
—Revelation 22:20